On Elton John

On Elton John

An Opinionated Guide

MATTHEW RESTALL

OXFORD
UNIVERSITY PRESS

Oxford University Press is a department of the University of Oxford.
It furthers the University's objective of excellence in research, scholarship,
and education by publishing worldwide. Oxford is a registered trade mark of
Oxford University Press in the UK and certain other countries.

Published in the United States of America by Oxford University Press
198 Madison Avenue, New York, NY 10016, United States of America.

© Oxford University Press 2025

All rights reserved. No part of this publication may be reproduced, stored in a retrieval system, transmitted, used for text and data mining, or used for training artificial intelligence, in any form or by any means, without the prior permission in writing of Oxford University Press, or as expressly permitted by law, by license or under terms agreed with the appropriate reprographics rights organization. Inquiries concerning reproduction outside the scope of the above should be sent to the Rights Department, Oxford University Press, at the address above.

You must not circulate this work in any other form
and you must impose this same condition on any acquirer

Library of Congress Cataloging-in-Publication Data
Names: Restall, Matthew, 1964– author.
Title: On Elton John : an opinionated guide / Matthew Restall.
Description: [1.] | New York : Oxford University Press, 2025. |
Includes bibliographical references and index. |
Identifiers: LCCN 2024059870 (print) | LCCN 2024059871 (ebook) |
ISBN 9780197684825 (hardback) | ISBN 9780197684856 | ISBN 9780197684832 (epub)
Subjects: LCSH: John, Elton. | Composers—Biography. | Singers—Biography. |
Popular music—History and critcism. | Rock music—History and critcism. |
LCGFT: Biographies.
Classification: LCC ML410.J64 R473 2025 (print) | LCC ML410.J64 (ebook) |
DDC 782.42166092 [B]—dc23/eng/20241213
LC record available at https://lccn.loc.gov/2024059870
LC ebook record available at https://lccn.loc.gov/2024059871

DOI: 10.1093/oso/9780197684825.001.0001

Printed by Sheridan Books, Inc., United States of America

for Amara
(they're all your songs)

"I want to quit while I'm at the top and then I'll fade into obscurity."

Elton John, 1971

"Don't rely on me—I'm liable to make things up."

Bernie Taupin, 2023

Contents

Chapter-Opening Songs	ix
List of Illustrations	xi
Preface	xv

1. Half and Half — 1
   Elton and Bernie

2. Once Upon a Time — 19
   Elton and Bowie, Part 1

3. Starmen — 34
   Elton and Bowie, Part 2

4. Pride — 49
   Elton and David

5. For All Seasons — 66
   Elton and Rod

6. Fantasies of Difference — 88
   Elton and Aretha

7. Perfect Mistakes — 102
   Elton and Bennie

8. Queens — 112
   Elton and Diana

9. Poppermost — 123
   Elton and Dua

10. No Jexit — 141
    Elton and Jesus

Source Notes	153
Discography	163
Bibliography	175

Filmography 179
Other Media 181
Index 183

Chapter-Opening Songs*

1 "I'm Still Standing" (3:02, 1983)
2 "Someone Saved My Life Tonight" (6:45, 1975)
3 "Rocket Man" (4:42, 1972)
4 "Philadelphia Freedom" (5:38, 1975)
5 "Electricity" (3:30, 2005)
6 "Border Song" (3:22, 1970)
7 "Bennie and the Jets" (5:23, 1973)
8 "Candle in the Wind" (3:50, 1973; 4:10, 1987; 4:11, 1997)
9 "Cold Heart" (3:22, 2021)
10 "This Train Don't Stop There Anymore" (4:37, 2001)

* Available on Apple Music as a playlist under "On Elton John (book playlist)."

Illustrations

P.1: Open Wide. An iconic shot of a legendary moment: clichés justified by Terry O'Neill's photographs of Elton John's sellout week at Dodger Stadium in Los Angeles, August 1975. (Photo credit: Terry O'Neill / Iconic.)   xvii

1.1: Still Falling. A still from the Russell Mulcahy–directed video for "I'm Still Standing," shot in Cannes in 1983. Elton John's best-known music video, it was partially (and lovingly) reproduced in the 2019 movie *Rocketman*.   2

1.2: Tiny and Bernie. The mock-up by designer David Larkham for the *Madman across the Water* LP inner lyric book, showing four of its pages, with Maxine Feibelman's photograph on the "Tiny Dancer" page, and Bernie Taupin's on the page for the closing song, "Goodbye." The two married in England four months before the album was recorded. From the 50th Anniversary (2022) release booklet, p. 47.   11

2.1: Double Trouble. One of many Elton covers of the US's *16 Magazine*; this December 1975 issue came less than a year before his 1976 *Rolling Stone* cover story resulted in his permanent banishment from *16*. Was Elton really a star born "out of tragic teen years"? In 2024, copies like this sold on eBay for roughly ten times the original (inflation-adjusted) cover price.   27

2.2: What's His Name? The cover of 1973's *Don't Shoot Me I'm Only the Piano Player*, with one "movie" poster showing John playing the album and another poster of the Marx Brothers' 1940 movie *Go West*. The reference to an exchange with Groucho Marx at a party was explained numerous times, with various versions of the story evolving over the years.   31

3.1: Space Cowboy. Record label MCA's promotional print ad for "Rocket Man," accompanying its "launch" as a single in April 1972. Elton John's outfit suggests that the stars in his future are not in outer space.   35

3.2: A Star Full of Stars. Elton John wore outfits decorated with stars as early as 1970 and continued to do so through 1975, when he received his own star on Hollywood Boulevard's Walk of Fame (photo credit: Wikimedia Commons).   44

3.3: A Star Still Full of Stars. John wore star-decorated outfits throughout the 1970s and 1980s. By the time of this 1986 example, ornate head gear and costumes had long been an Elton tradition (photo

xii ILLUSTRATIONS

       credit: Pictorial Press Ltd / Alamy Stock Photo). In all cases, the stars
evoke celebrity stardom more readily than they do outer space.   45

4.1: Acoustic Set. Elton John and Billie Jean King, holding tennis rackets like guitars, in a classic Terry O'Neill photograph from the time of "Philadelphia Freedom." (Photo credit: Terry O'Neill / Iconic.)   51

4.2: Frank and Elton. The cover of the October 7, 1976, issue of *Rolling Stone*, in which Elton confessed to being "bisexual"—to the extended detriment of his career in the US.   58

4.3: Nutty Butty. The January 16, 1978, *People* cover that showed an attempt of sorts to walk back the confession of sexual orientation that Elton had made in *Rolling Stone* eighteen months earlier.   59

5.1: Tutu Too. On various occasions, in theaters in multiple countries—as here, in the Victoria Palace, on the third anniversary of the play's London run—Elton John has donned a tutu and joined the *Billy Elliot the Musical* cast on stage for the curtain call. (Photo credit: PA Images / Alamy Stock Photo.)   68

5.2: What Soap? The famous photograph of Rod Stewart and Elton John in the baths of the Watford Football Club, taken November 7, 1973, for the UK's *Daily Mirror*. Their passion for football helped bond the friendship between the two English rock stars. It was also part of their early branding and marketing. The photograph's enduring appeal also lies in its ambiguity as both innocent and homoerotic. (Photo credit: Trinity Mirror / Mirrorpix / Alamy Stock Photo.)   72

5.3: No Skyline Pigeon. One of Elton John's famous feathered costumes, this one for his 1977 appearance on *The Muppet Show* television series. He sang "Crocodile Rock."   86

6.1: Cocktail Pianists. Elton John and Stevie Wonder, on the *Starship* touring airplane, in 1973. (Photo credit: Bob Gruen.)   97

6.2: A Different Storm. The cover of Elton and Aretha's 1989 single, "Through the Storm," which was a minor UK hit (#41), but a US hit (#16, Billboard Hot 100) that also succeeded on both the Adult Contemporary chart (#3) and the Hot R&B/Hip-Hop Songs chart (#17).   99

7.1: Bendy. An example of the mistaken (and potentially gender-altering) spelling of "Bennie" on some 7" single releases of the song.   105

8.1: Jukebox John. Elton John and Princess Margaret, with her husband Lord Snowdon—who was, as this photograph captures, far less interested than the princess was in the palace's pop star. (Photo taken backstage at the Royal Festival Hall in 1972. Credit: Michael Putland.)   116

8.2:	Very Versace. This 2022 Sierra Leone postage stamp is an example of the widespread use of images from this photo shoot of Elton John and Princess Diana, both Versace-clad, at a 1993 awards ceremony. It also reflects their persisting global celebrity. Their friendship, dating from 1981, was facilitated by John's prior relationship with his royal neighbors in Windsor. (Photo credit: Peregrine / Alamy Stock Photo.)	119
9.1:	Warm Heart. One of the several versions of the cover art to Elton John and Dua Lipa's "Cold Heart." Australia's Pnau produced the single and album version, also being given co-writing credit.	125
9.2:	Want Wax? Elton John at home with his record collection in Windsor, in the mid-1970s. (Photo credit: Terry O'Neill / Iconic.)	127
9.3:	Beauty and the Beat. Britney Spears and Elton John as children on the cover of 2022's "Hold Me Closer" single.	130
10.1:	Leaving Already? Sir Elton at Glastonbury, Britain's biggest annual music festival, on June 15, 2023, the final performance in his home country of his five-year Farewell tour. (Photo credit: Matt Crossick / Empics / Alamy Live News.)	150

Preface

Sir Elton John is a living superlative. As the solo musical artist who has sold more singles and albums worldwide than any other artist in the history of recorded music, racking up an ever-growing list of awards, achievements, and broken records (pun intended), his biography is packed with "mosts."[†] His acquired middle name could be Most (it's actually Hercules).

And how has he so often beaten his idols and rivals to the most post? The sheer quality of his songwriting is the obvious answer. The dozens of books and hundreds of articles about him are littered with exultations regarding the "genius" and "magic" behind his ability to turn piano chords into melodies—inventive, captivating, and so essential that it is impossible to imagine the present world without them. Those hundreds of songs have sold hundreds of millions of albums, and millions of fans have seen and heard them performed at the 4,600 concerts he has given so far. But, in addition to musical quality and quantity, Elton's timing and longevity have also certainly helped him. He began recording in the late 1960s, just as the popular music industry began to explode; and he then rode the successive format waves of vinyl LPs, cassette tapes, and compact discs. Now approaching eighty, and in his sixth decade in the music business, he just finished enacting his prolonged retirement (his "Jexit," as the British press have dubbed it, with just a hint of sarcasm), while simultaneously working as hard as ever to burnish his status as an icon not just of popular music, but of popular culture.

Elton has recorded thirty-five studio albums, not counting ten soundtrack albums, and if we also add live albums and compilations, the total approaches ninety. And he is still going. By the time you read this, I wouldn't be at all surprised if the number had reached one hundred—a moment that John himself will relish and celebrate with that characteristic combination of crowing and modesty that he somehow manages to pull off. (He titled his

---

[†] The statistics on worldwide singles and albums sales are not surprisingly contested, with the top contenders for male solo artist usually Elton John, Michael Jackson, and Elvis Presley; all three have "certified" or industry-verified global lifetime sales in the 215–285 million range, with claims for John's sales of over 300 or 350 million bested by unverified (and unverifiable) claims of 400 or 500 million by partisans of Presley and Jackson. Stream-counting increasingly complicates such statistics.

fourteenth studio album *21 at 33*, released the year he turned thirty-three, by counting live albums, compilations, a soundtrack, and by double counting double albums, the hubris of which was softened by his numerological nerdiness and endearing exuberance.) Forty of his albums have made the Top 40. A John single was in the US Billboard Hot 100 every year from 1971 through 2000—a unique achievement. One of those is the world's best-selling single of all time.

His list of awards is more or less the list of all awards that a musician can possibly win, but only he has won them all—including five Grammys, five Brit Awards, thirteen Ivor Novello Awards, medals and inductions and honors galore, and a knighthood in 1998. In January 2024, John became the nineteenth member of the EGOT elite—artists who have won an Emmy, Grammy, Oscar, and Tony. Having received six Grammys during his career, two Oscars—for *The Lion King*'s "Can You Feel the Love Tonight" and for *Rocketman*'s "(I'm Gonna) Love Me Again"—as well as a Tony for the *Aida* Original Score, he completed the EGOT set with an Emmy for *Elton John Live: Farewell from Dodger Stadium*. That film documented the final US concert of his five-year Farewell Yellow Brick Road retirement tour.

"I am incredibly humbled to be joining the unbelievably talented group of EGOT winners tonight," John declared at the Emmy ceremony. "Thank you to everyone who has supported me throughout my career." A blandly diplomatic script, to be sure, but one that nonetheless reflects a constant and sincere John refrain: his gratitude for "the unwavering support of my fans all around the world." Sir Elton positively swims and splashes in his success, and yet the humble, hesitant Reginald Dwight that still lives inside him can't quite believe it all—and he is ever so grateful.

John chose Los Angeles' Dodger Stadium as the venue to end the US leg of his tour because his run of concerts there in August 1975 are his most famous; they cemented his status as the world's #1 rock star and, in retrospect, represented the peak moment of his imperial phase—his half-decade of record-breaking ticket and album sales (see Figure P.1). In 1975, one in fifty records sold worldwide, in all genres of music, had Elton John's name on the cover. He had yet to complete the first of his six decades in the business, yet he was already "not only a musical legend; he was an industry unto himself." Pick whoever you think was the biggest rock star at the time—the Rolling Stones, Eagles, ex-Beatles, Bruce Springsteen, David Bowie; he was bigger than them all. To repeat an oft-quoted line: "In an era in which rock stars were larger than movie stars, Elton John was the biggest star in the world."

Figure P.1 Open Wide. An iconic shot of a legendary moment: clichés justified by Terry O'Neill's photographs of Elton John's sellout week at Dodger Stadium in Los Angeles, August 1975. (Photo credit: Terry O'Neill / Iconic.)

The heartland of that unprecedented stardom was the US, as John told the audience at that final 2022 Dodger Stadium show: "I became successful first in America," he said, "so I want to thank you for that. You made me. Without America, I wouldn't be here."

That is an appealing narrative of arrival, one that Elton favors and crafts well: I came from humble origins; I met my songwriting partner Bernie, of equally humble origins; music-loving fans gave us a career; above all, America made us, with Dodger Stadium a milestone moment; I am back there now to retire, to complete that circle. But reality is a tad more complex than that clean arc. The curve has been closer in shape to a roller coaster, with more than one flying-off-the-rails moment. Elton has seldom been classified by critics as cool, and even today the reality that he was once the world's biggest rock star is often ignored or denied. The fact that he outsold the Stones and Bowie combined in the 1970s is still held against him. *Uncut*'s 2023 ranking of the *500 Greatest Albums of the 1970s*, for example, packs the Top 10 with two Stones and four Bowie albums, and every one of Bowie's 1970s records are in the Top 100; John is a distant also-ran with just two, *Goodbye Yellow Brick Road* at #147 and *Tumbleweed Connection* at #444.

Regardless of how we view a career—record and ticket sales, album quality and critical reception, press coverage and its tone—there is no escaping the fact that the journey has been far from an uneventful stroll down that yellow brick road. And, indeed, John himself recognizes that; he knows that the brick-road metaphor, long and winding, works well because the road from there to here was never a straight shot.

My contention is that the ups and downs are elemental to understanding Elton's success. Certainly, the factors already implied—the sheer quantity and quality of songs, the decades of hard graft, right timing, and a long life—take us a long way toward that understanding. But the speed bumps, potholes, and unintended detours on the brick road have required a relentlessness, a death-defying persistence, that have made John the ultimate survivor. "I'm Still Standing" becomes more apt as his anthem every year.

What makes him interesting, then, is not just that he is still standing, but the nature of the hurdles and hindrances that have threatened to knock him down and out: his struggle to turn himself from an ugly duckling into a spectacular swan, only to find that the cool/uncool divide policed by critics placed him on the opposite side from the likes of his "frenemy" David Bowie; his harrowing and protracted struggle with his sexuality and the homophobia of his era; his epic fall into the fires of addiction and his phoenix-like recovery; his personal and musical mistakes. His unequaled, astounding success has not come despite all that. It has come because of it.

As this is my second book about Elton John, those who knew I was writing it invariably asked if I was some kind of Elton fanatic or superfan. A few friends of mine were aware of Will Brooker's immersive Bowie-fan project, in which the cultural studies scholar from suburban London (where we are all from— Bowie and Brooker, Elton and me) adopted Bowie's personas in sequence, spent time in the places Bowie did, and so on. Was I, they wondered, similarly becoming bonkers for Elton? It's a fair question, so let me answer it at length, especially as I suspect your fan experience is comparable to mine.

I have been an Elton fan of sorts since I discovered pop music at the age of eight, when I was sent off to boarding school in England (at the time my family were living in Spain, then still under a fascist dictatorship, and I had not heard much English-language pop on the radio). Based on my parents' record collection, I had thought that the musical world beyond classical and jazz comprised the Beatles, Simon and Garfunkel, Joan Baez, and fewer than a dozen similar artists. I was stunned to discover that there were in fact scores, possibly hundreds, of pop and rock artists. My entry point was the BBC singles chart, to which I immediately became addicted.

I arrived in school in 1972; that year, Elton John had three UK hits. "Rocket Man" went to #2 in the spring, "Honky Cat" peaked at #31 in the summer (when "Rocket Man" was still ubiquitous on the radio), and "Crocodile Rock" reached #5 that autumn. There was no let-up: in January 1973, still my first boarding school year, "Daniel" was released, and it soon went to #4. Later that year came the juggernaut of *Goodbye Yellow Brick Road*, while the endless string of new hits dragged 1970's "Your Song" back into regular airplay. I had a transistor radio not much larger than a modern smartphone, with a single earbud. Most of my listening was done at night, under the covers. The only pop station was BBC Radio 1, but sometimes I could pick up pirate stations—Radio Luxembourg or Radio Caroline—and the Elton hits permeated their chart shows too.

So, the songs of Elton John's imperial phase became hardwired into my young brain. *Don't Shoot Me I'm Only the Piano Player* (the first of John's two 1973 albums) was one of the first albums I acquired on pre-recorded cassette. I followed every album and single through my decade of schooling, acquiring them all on vinyl or cassette—the latter more often by taping than by buying them. But I did not consider myself a superfan in any sense. Elton was one of many artists that I enjoyed, and as the 1970s wore on, he was increasingly lost in the crowd of my devotion. I became fanatical about popular music of all kinds, acquiring albums by the hundreds, devouring new sounds as the 1970s turned into the 1980s. I was merely a casual John fan by the 1980s, not seeing him play live until the 1990s, when a new Elton returned to form. Then, starting with 2001's *Songs from the West Coast*, John hit a comeback run that really grabbed my attention. I started filling in the gaps of his back catalogue, revisiting old favorites.

Then I discovered the 33⅓ series of books, each one about a music album, and I had a notion to propose writing one myself (as a university professor, writing books is part of my professional life). I pondered many artists and albums, hitting inspiration when I came across my original prerecorded cassette of *Blue Moves*—a John album I had not much liked upon its release in 1976, but which I later came to appreciate. The album's reception by music critics mirrored my own. There was, I felt, an interesting story there, which I ended up telling in my *Blue Moves* book (published in 2020). And that book prompted Norman Hirschy at Oxford University Press to suggest I write this book for the press's Opinionated Guides series.[‡]

On Elton John is therefore designed to complement *Blue Moves* as two slightly different ways of writing about Elton John as a creator of music and as a cultural icon. Neither book is a conventional biography, being loosely chronological in structure, turning to Elton's personal life only where it impacts his music, and focusing on thematic arguments. The many dozens of John books include recent autobiographies both by him (titled *Me*) and his lyricist Bernie Taupin (*Scattershot*). Another straightforward biography would thus be hard to justify unless it offered "new" facts or viewpoints through original interviews. I make no such pretense.

Instead, I have selected details from the myriad available sources and organized them in service of a series of contentions and opinions, structured around ten songs that introduce ten chapters. In each chapter John is paired with someone else (real or fictional). The book's core features are thus twofold. First, each chapter explores a topical theme and presents an argument—a persuasive assertion about how we might better understand John and the era of his career. Second, the use of an Elton song and a paired figure lends each chapter a structure that allows me to engage John's catalogue, while efficiently linking it both to my argument and to the larger pop cultural context.

The paired figures begin with Taupin himself, prompting an opinion on the significance of their songwriting style, and a perspective on issues of authorship and authenticity; they end with Jesus, a rather facetious contrivance to permit a pondering on John's particular kind of (im)mortality. In between there is David Bowie—twice, on their comparative origin mythology and on the contrasting "Starman"/"Rocket Man" metaphor. A pairing with Rod Stewart helps further illuminate issues of artist branding and popular music genres, as does one with Aretha Franklin, with the addition of considerations of racial categories. Elton is paired through marriage to David Furnish; their pairing here prompts a discussion of sexuality and identity (in which Bowie briefly returns again). The imaginary Bennie (she of the Jets) introduces the mistake/perfect paradox, while the very real Dua Lipa kicks off an exploration of John's collection history—and a proposal that his whole career can be better understood through the lens of collecting. Added to these various

---

[‡] I am most grateful to Norm for the opportunity and for his support throughout the process, as I am to the press professionals who worked on the book, and to the external readers whose comments were insightful and invaluable. My academic and music support networks are too vast to detail, but specific contributions were made here by Travis Meyer, Bianca Nottoli, and Sophie Restall. Above all, I am immensely indebted to Amara Solari and to Hope Silverman for the particularly important roles they played in making the book possible; thank you so much.

ways of examining Elton's evolving public persona is a pairing with Princess Diana, who helps us to perceive his transformation into the semi-royal elder grandee of pop music.

John's tortured and then triumphant struggle with his public sexual identity, paralleled with his musical identity and genre associations, tracks the shift during his lifetime in societal homophobia, sexism, and attitudes toward musical genre. Issues of fame and of race are tied up in there too. In other words, his career and its six-decade social context illuminate each other.

I am an historian, not a musicologist. This is therefore not the place to find technical explanations of John's compositional genius. Nor is my profession that of literary and cultural critic. You may thus find the book's paucity of theoretical rigor and analytical jargon to be lamentable or laudable (depending on who you are). That said, I do, however, take Elton seriously as a subject of scholarly study. My larger contention is that John's career offers us a novel way to see and understand the last half century of popular music and culture history—the period that I call here the *Top of the Pops* era[§]—a perspective that is as valid and revealing as that of any other artist of the last eighty years. It is to that end that David Bowie appears as the paired figure in two of the book's chapters. As just mentioned, by whatever criteria that John was deemed uncool, Bowie has been revered as cool. For every dismissal of John as trivial and beneath serious analysis, Bowie has been elevated and apotheosized as the ultimate object of critical appraisal. I maintain that by deploying Bowie—for example—as a way to think about Elton, by exploring the striking but overlooked similarities as well as the illuminating contrasts, we gain insights into both John and the cultural world through which he has navigated for six decades. (It is also an interesting and original way to view Bowie.)

I do not go so far as to claim that Sir Elton has changed the world. But I opine that the dramatic shifts in popular culture since the 1960s are reflected in, and illuminated by, the long and winding yellow brick road of his career.

Am I a superfan, then? Maybe (I'm still missing a couple of Elton albums, even if I now have half a dozen copies in three formats of *Blue Moves* and *Madman across the Water*). But I'll be forlorn when, one day, there are no new episodes of Rocket Hour and the email blasts from the Rocket Club no longer contain new video messages from Uncle Elton. So, a deeply engaged old fan? No doubt.

[§] The British TV show *Top of the Pops* ran on the BBC from 1964 to 2006, a period that encompasses the Album Era, mid-1960s through the 1970s; the CD/MTV era, early 1980s to 2000; the Rock Era, mid-1960s to 1990s; and the era of postmodernism, 1970s and 1980s.

1

Half and Half

Elton and Bernie

"I'm Still Standing" (3:02, 1983)

"They're all classics," said Annie Lennox, asked to name her favorite Elton John song for the 2017 Elton episode of the British television show *The Nation's Favorite Song*. Other musicians were able to commit; Lulu chose "I'm Still Standing." Before the results of the audience vote were announced, Elton John was asked for his prediction. "Ten years ago, I'd have said, maybe, 'Your Song.' I'm not so sure anymore. Can I make a bet?" "Ok," responded the host, comedian David Walliams, adding with a deadpan serious expression, "What do you think it is?" John's guess: "Candle in the Wind."

In fact, "Candle in the Wind" came in second. "Your Song" won. It had won similar competitions before, such as a seven-week phone-line vote prior to a 2002 concert special in New York City. Elton seemed disappointed, even a tad annoyed. "I guess I peaked early," he groused. His reaction is understandable. "Your Song" was the first hit of his career, released in 1970. But his subsequent 140 singles have sold over 100 million copies. A third of those sales were for the 1997 Princess-Diana-tribute remake of "Candle in the Wind" (more on the world's biggest-selling single ever in a later chapter). His guess that night in 2017, when Elton was clearly hoping the British public would recognize that he hadn't "peaked early," suggests that "Candle" would have made him happier. Or perhaps he'd have settled for one of the two most recent songs in the audience's top ten: at #5, "Can You Feel the Love Tonight" (from *The Lion King* soundtrack), and at #4, Lulu's favorite, "I'm Still Standing."

"I'm Still Standing" certainly works well as an Elton signature tune, despite the fact that—or perhaps because—it is something of an outlier. He has tended either to tease his piano keys into a ballad or pound them into a

Figure 1.1 Still Falling. A still from the Russell Mulcahy–directed video for "I'm Still Standing," shot in Cannes in 1983. Elton John's best-known music video, it was partially (and lovingly) reproduced in the 2019 movie *Rocketman*.

rock song, with the combination of the two, the rock ballad, often attributed to him as the inventor. But "I'm Still Standing" is none of those. It is pure pop, with a dance beat. In fact, at 177 beats per minute, it has the fastest tempo of any single in the John catalogue (3 bpm ahead of "Honky Cat").

The song is also closely associated with its video—the best-known music video by an artist not generally associated with such a medium (see Figure 1.1). Indeed, up to this point Elton had refused to appear in videos for any of his singles. But he was not only willing to dance—and badly—in this one, but to romp around and ham it up along the beachfront promenade of Cannes. The idea was reputedly his, featuring an endless array of brightly dressed body-suited dancers and his own Bentley (shipped over from England). But it also undeniably bore the mark of director Russell Mulcahy, who had extensive experience making videos for British artists and would go on to a successful movie-directing career. The timing of the video, released with the single in 1983, just as the two-year-old MTV network was entering its 1980s heyday, was perfect.

The video's over-the-top production also matched the attitude projected by the song. Years later, John remarked that he thought the song "worked as a message to my new American record company, who were, quite frankly, turning out to be a terrible pain in the arse." In the UK, John's records had since 1976 been released on separate labels, one being his own, Rocket Records. But in the US, he had signed in 1980 with brand new label Geffen, and the first two albums released on the imprint—1981's *The Fox* and 1982's *Jump Up!*—fell far from the commercial and critical heights of John's 1970s imperial phase. David Geffen was disappointed with what his label had been delivered, but John blamed the label and their treatment of 1970s superstars like Donna Summer, Neil Diamond, Joni Mitchell, and him. "I didn't like the look of any of it and thought 'I'm Still Standing' sounded like a warning shot across their bows. It was a big swaggering, confident, fuck-you of a song."

The song was well reviewed and sold very well, helping to make its parent album, *Too Low for Zero*, a hit as well, his biggest since the mid-1970s; a "fuck you of a song," indeed. But neither the single nor the album kick-started a sustained second imperial phase. In fact, "I'm Still Standing" was, in terms of worldwide sales, the biggest John song between 1976's "Sorry Seems to Be the Hardest Word" and the hit singles of the 1994 *Lion King* juggernaut. And that fact lent its title and lyrics the meaning usually assigned to it: a simple, defiant statement by Elton that he is "still standing." Not only still on his feet, but as the chorus goes, "better than I ever did, lookin' like a true survivor, feelin' like a little kid."

That resonated in 1983, as John's record-setting imperial phase of the 1970s was widely perceived to have come crashing to an end in 1977, with the release of an apparent misstep of an album the previous autumn. The "failure" of that double album, *Blue Moves* (it "only" reached #3 after the previous seven albums had been US #1's), precipitated a retirement, followed by a series of half-hearted comebacks and one disappointing album after another. The true story was far more complex than that (as I explained in my *Blue Moves* book), but that was the general perception. And this was also true: the classic Elton John Band lineup had not recorded an album since 1975's *Captain Fantastic and the Brown Dirt Cowboy*; but in 1982 they signed on to play the *Jump Up!* world tour, taking a fortnight's break in September to record *Too Low for Zero* at George Martin's studio on the Caribbean island of Montserrat. "It was like a well-oiled machine coming back to life," Elton later remembered of the reunion of guitarist Davey Johnstone, bassist Dee Murray, and drummer Nigel Olsson.

The result was indeed a strong and coherent set of songs, the best John album of the 1980s. But it was only 1983, and the decade would produce five more studio albums—as well as years of brutal press coverage in the UK stemming from Elton's addictive behavior, an ill-conceived marriage, those weak albums, and the sheer vindictiveness of Britain's gutter journalists. So, with each passing year that John kept going, and then with his rehabilitation in the 1990s—sobering up, marrying the right person, founding the Elton John AIDS Foundation, and other developments to which we shall return—the refrain "I'm Still Standing" seemed increasingly apposite. In 2001, the song's title was the tag line for a "got milk?" advertising campaign, featuring Elton standing in energetic pose at a milk-colored piano, his "strong bones" attributed to the dairy product. By the time of the *Rocketman* biopic in 2019, the song could be deployed, anachronistically but irresistibly, as a post-rehab exaltation of triumph and survival.

There is a wonderful twist to the tale, however. The title and lyrics are not about Elton John at all. They were written by Bernie Taupin, and they refer to his recovery from the end of a love affair. The final line of the chorus suggests as much: "pickin' up the pieces of my life without you on my mind." The return of the dream team of musicians in 1982 was accompanied by the return of Taupin too, as John's exclusive lyricist. Taupin had only written some of the lyrics on John's albums since 1976's *Blue Moves*, which had been the last time he'd written the words to a whole Elton album. But from the start of John's solo career and through to *Blue Moves*, Taupin was the lyricist on almost every song. And he has played that role on almost every studio album since then. So, who is in fact still standing? And is Elton John really a solo artist?

He is and he isn't. That is, I don't believe John can be fully understood if we see him strictly in solo artist terms. Certainly, it is his name alone on the spines of his records. And on almost every track, he alone composed the music on a piano, then played and sang the songs. But the lyrics to most of those songs—and to almost all the songs now accepted as the classics of his catalogue—were written by Bernie Taupin. "I know you and you know me, it's always half and half"—wrote Taupin, and sang John, on "Writing," their 1975 composition about this very process. More than that, the creative lives of these professional partners have always been deeply intertwined, inspiring and influencing each other from the very start and for the last five decades. As a result, what we hear on Elton John records is Bernie's emotional life, as told by Elton. That fact is foundational, coloring how we see subsequent elements of the Elton John story.

There are many famous songwriting duos of the *Top of the Pops* era, but they have tended to be either romantic partners (Goffin and King, Ashford and Simpson) or band partners (Lennon and McCartney, Jagger and Richards, Rogers and Edwards). Furthermore, such pairs typically contributed to music *and* lyrics; and those pairs who divided the two tasks tended not to be the performers (Bacharach on music, David on lyrics). John and Taupin are thus a unique case within the pattern, with their strict division of labor, and with John as the sole performing face, the public articulator, of Taupin's words. "Very few partnerships establish the single authorial voice," DJ-journalist Paul Gambaccini once noted. "When you listen to Elton John sing 'Someone Saved My Life Tonight,'" he added, "it never occurs to you that somebody else wrote the words, because it sounds so first person."

And there's a further twist: not only were they never romantic partners, but Taupin's romantic life—and the subject of a fair number of his lyrics, including many of the best known—contrasted strongly with John's. This was especially true during John's 1970s heyday as a rock star and his 1980s comeback as a pop star, when Taupin cycled through a series of straight marriages, channeling their romantic beginnings ("Tiny Dancer"), their agonizing endings ("Sorry Seems to Be the Hardest Word"), and the eventual bounce-back ("I'm Still Standing") into words that were immortalized by John—who was struggling along the very different romantic journey resulting from being gay and famous in a homophobic era. Ironically, it was John's convincing transformation of Taupin's lyrics into song that helped maintain the veneer of his straightness, even when—or particularly when—that veneer became wafer-thin.

Indeed, at times, Taupin's words, written in one context, served perfectly to express the emotions of his writing partner in another context. The 2019 fantasy biopic *Rocketman* repeatedly (but, I think, inadvertently) captured the contradictory complexity of this partnership. The most vivid example was the scene in which young Reg Dwight's mother and stepfather sang, in his 1950s childhood home, the words to "I Want Love": the lyrics were in fact penned by Taupin almost fifty years later, in the wake of his third divorce. The film did not claim to be historically accurate, thus avoiding accusations of anachronism, just as John and Taupin were always transparent about their writing method—thereby largely (but not entirely) avoiding accusations of inauthenticity, despite their rise to fame in the years when singer-songwriter "authenticity" was heavily policed by critics.

We can explore these themes further by looking briefly at three threads, here expressed as a trio of queries. How do other songwriting partnerships shed light on the John/Taupin union? What aspect of Bernie's personal life has most dramatically manifested itself in their songs? Has Elton ever contributed lyrics, and if so, how does that complicate or illuminate the partnership?

"I do love Chris. I'd agree with him that our relationship is a love story," recently confessed Glenn Tilbrook of Squeeze, the English new wave/pop rock band that has been going on and off since 1974. But then he added that he and his bandmate and songwriting partner through all those decades "exist in degrees of light and dark. What we have isn't a friendship, it's a partnership. There's some sort of love in there somewhere, but it's a love with next to no contact." That partner, Chris Difford, clarified this paradox—sort of—with this: "Glenn and I have a complicated relationship—I think that's why our songs are so brilliant."

The Tilbrook/Difford partnership began half a century ago through a mechanism similar to the one that brought Taupin to Dwight, one that seems reflective of popular music culture in the first half of the *Top of the Pops* era: one of them answered an advertisement. Difford had placed an ad, in search of band members, in the window of a South London newsagent. Tilbrook was the only person to respond. Difford had lyrics, ones so witty and poignant that Tilbrook was thereby freed from the burden of his own lyrics, which "weren't so good" (his phrase). Tilbrook's contribution was then to provide the melodies, as he proved to be "very clever at writing amazing songs" (Difford again).

The parallel London advertisement that a few years earlier had brought Taupin to Dwight has become part of Elton mythology. On June 17, 1967, Liberty Records had placed an ad in the *New Musical Express*, seeking talent of various kinds, including lyricists. Sitting at the kitchen table in his childhood home in Lincolnshire, Bernie wrote a response. According to legend, he had second thoughts and binned the letter, only for his mother to fish it out and mail it, making Liberty's subsequent invitation to appear in their

London office a surprise. According to Taupin, there is much "mythology attached to its mailing" of a letter whose pitch was "fantastic codswallop." Either way, both Taupin and Dwight (on the brink of becoming John) answered the same ad, thereby putting them together like yin and yang.

"It was really 'you and me against the world,'" Taupin recalled. "We were so incredibly close." That closeness was immediate and astonishing for its endurance. "He has a sixth sense about what I want, and I have a sixth sense about him," John said fifty years later. "We're always on the same page." "What Elton and I create," Taupin has said, is "based on mutual observation, a panorama of varying subject matter, and a completely synchronous union of our combined history." There was not, and never has been, any of the tension that not only tested the Tilbrook/Difford partnership but fueled its creativity (Difford in 2019: "We're not quite as bad as The Everly Brothers for fighting, but we're also not exactly like Lennon & McCartney. We're somewhere in the middle"). The Squeeze creative pair write together but cannot otherwise be together. In contrast, Bernie not only moved into Reg's house; he took the bottom bunk in his childhood bedroom. They each took a bed and one side of the room for their budding collections of records, books, and magazines. And in that small house in the sleepy northwest London suburb of Pinner—Reg's mother's and stepfather Fred's home, not even the whole house but just the upstairs floor—Bernie wrote lyrics, and gave them to Reg, who then composed the melodies on the upright piano down the hall.

That proximity, once established, proved crucial. When Elton went to the US on his first small tour, the trip of summer 1970 that laid the foundation for his career, Bernie went with him. That is worth emphasizing because Bernie didn't *need* to be there; the songs were already written. And unlike the songwriters who were also band members, exampled above, Bernie was not a musician. Also, the cohabitation of the young songwriters ended soon after that breakthrough tour (apart from other developments, it was on that trip that Bernie met his first wife), and soon they were an ocean and a continent apart; starting in 1973, Taupin was based in Los Angeles, while John remained based in London. Yet they remained inseparable, going into the studio together, on tour together, and on vacation together—and in John's imperial phase of 1971–1976, those three activities took up almost all their time (no wonder that first Taupin marriage faltered).

When they took a break in the late 1970s, Elton suffered. And, by his own admission, it didn't make Bernie any happier, or less miserable, either.

The impact of Bernie's absence on the music is more complicated. Taupin skipped the entire Toronto recording sessions for 1976's *Blue Moves*, but he had already given John lyrics to dozens of songs, and that album is masterful (albeit misunderstood). And whatever was disappointing about albums to which Gary Osborne contributed lyrics, such as 1978's *A Single Man*, the problems did not lie in the words; they lay in Bernie's absence (although, again, I would argue that it was Elton, not the resulting album, that most suffered). Not that Elton went off the rails without Bernie and stayed on them with him around. On the contrary, the relationship has worked for so long because it has existed as a rock-solid reality despite the ups and downs of their respective personal lives, perhaps even making those extreme moments—Taupin's marriages and divorces, John's addictions—possible as sources of inspiration. Each man could encounter great happiness or deep despair, but the other would always be there to channel those emotions into words and music.

The efficacy of that dynamic is far from given. Take, as another example, the songwriting team of Dave Gahan and Martin Gore, who helped found Depeche Mode in Basildon, Essex, in 1980, and are today its sole members. When Vince Clarke left in 1981, Alan Wilder was recruited through an anonymous ad placed in *Melody Maker* (that plot device again), and he served as a kind of musical director, shaping the band's sound, until quitting in 1995; Andy Fletcher, who was in the band from 1980 until his death in 2022, was credited with holding the band together (he made no contributions to songwriting). Gore, therefore, was the primary songwriter, with Gahan making musical contributions and being the main vocalist. That partnership grew productively during the 1980s. But, at the same time, Gahan married his girlfriend from Basildon, where, despite the band's increasing success (and his fame and wealth), he settled down. Gore, in contrast, moved to London, where he explored his fascination with S&M culture. As a result, Gahan found himself having to sing—and obliged to explain in interviews—increasingly "odd, dark, depressing songs he couldn't fathom and that didn't exactly move him."

One could argue that this tension resulted in albums that endure as pinnacle synthpop achievements (1990's *Violator* is an enduring masterpiece, for example). I suspect that the songwriting partnership would not have survived such lifestyle contrasts for long, and that it was saved by the shift in that dynamic in the 1990s—as Gahan slid into heroin addiction, followed by rehab and recovery, while Gore married and had children, creating a partial reversal of their 1980s pattern. In the new century, a new partnership emerged, with its own tense dynamic: Gore and Gahan started writing in parallel as well as, loosely, together. In a 2017 interview with a Dutch magazine, Gahan revealed another dimension to that shared yet difficult partnership: "For two autistic people who make music, communication is not easy." Yet those "tensions, and the way in which they were ultimately resolved, resulted in a better record."

Such stories help us to see how well, and miraculously so, the John/Taupin creative union has worked. From the early days, three aspects of Taupin's mental and emotional life were manifested on the page in ways that inspired, rather than alienated or confused, John. One was Bernie's passion for Americana, especially the kinds of romantic narratives about an idealized America that he had voraciously consumed as a boy; he later explained that he had spent his entire adult life in the US because "an Americanism" had always been "in my soul," its culture having "inhabited my imagination since I straddled a broom and galloped across my old front lawn." Elton was more obsessed with Americana's musical traditions than with its traditional tropes and tales, but he certainly understood where Bernie was coming from. Another, closely related aspect was their fascination with their new identities as budding rock stars, even with the performance of stardom that was required of them in the US in 1970 and 1971 in order to actually become stars. And the third aspect of Taupin's interior world was his love life.

All three of these are evident on the 1971 album that fell relatively flat at the time, but which was later recognized as one of their greatest triumphs: *Madman across the Water*. As Taupin later noted, the previous album, *Tumbleweed Connection*, was "completely American," but it was the product of English boys imagining a kind of historical fantasy of America, "written before we'd set foot in the US." In contrast, "*Madman* was completely soaked in first impressions" of their 1970 stateside tour. "The album is like an American road trip," said Taupin. "It's the most American record we've ever made." No longer drawing upon the songs they had written in John's childhood home, the pair had to compose with a new urgency—most of *Madman* was recorded in four days in August 1971, having been written almost as fast. "Some of Bernie's lyrics were like a diary of the last year," Elton recalled. The songs are long, the production languid, a culmination of the sound that had evolved across John's 1970–1971 trio of *Elton John/Tumbleweed/Madman*. The observations are sometimes murky (if the title track was not about Richard Nixon, what was it about?), sometimes too much of a projection (they weren't yet fed up with the hard labor of rock star touring, surely), sometimes more comic-book tourism than on-the-ground understanding (although John really delivers *Indian Sunset* with conviction—as he did decades later in some of his *Farewell Yellow Brick Road* sets).

But above all, it is the partnership that works. Here, as on so many later albums, Taupin articulated in words what he thought about what he saw, and John articulated in chords and melodies how he felt about both Taupin's observations and his own. The creative pairing of Taupin's fingers on the pen and John's fingers on the piano has a timeless efficacy. Even as the album ages in other ways, that dynamic remains compelling. (And it had impact then that is felt today in various ways; Kate Bush, for example, still enthuses over *Madman* as the "absolutely fantastic" album that made John her childhood hero and set her on the path to inventive piano-based songwriting.)

Even the album's song that is now famous, "Tiny Dancer," adds to its touring-America coherence ("count the headlights on the highway"), despite the fact that its subject is the teenage girl that Taupin met on the trip. There was no mystery there: her photograph, captioned "With love to Maxine," was included with the song's lyrics (see Figure 1.2). Still, "Tiny Dancer" made little impact at the time (it peaked at #41 in the US and wasn't even released as a single in the UK). Nor did it for decades afterward. As a review of the album's 50th anniversary re-release remarked, "there are people in their twenties now who sing along to 'Tiny Dancer' with no idea that it was relatively unknown, even within the Elton canon, until the turn of the century." The turning point was its use in Cameron Crowe's 2000 film *Almost Famous*, a romanticized ode to the rock music scene of the 1970s that made "Tiny Dancer" seem like the emblematic love song that it had never been. It then took on a life of its own, from a 2009 DJ Ironik and Chipmunk remix that was a UK #3, to various cover versions, to "Hold Me Closer," the 2022 reworking of the song into a global dance/pop smash hit with Britney Spears.

Madman is now the "Tiny Dancer" album. As music writer Chris Roberts recently put it, "that slow-burn sleeper, near-freakish success" of the opening track means the album "is perceived through a different prism than it was then." But when it was brand new, in November 1971, "Tiny Dancer" eased listeners into the John/Taupin experience of America; even the now-anthemic "hold me closer" chorus doesn't first come until two and a half minutes into the song.

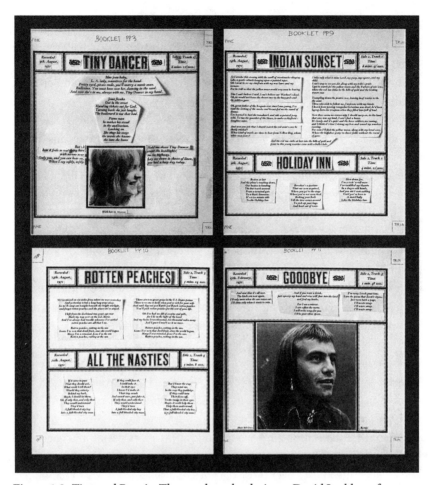

Figure 1.2 Tiny and Bernie. The mock-up by designer David Larkham for the *Madman across the Water* LP inner lyric book, showing four of its pages, with Maxine Feibelman's photograph on the "Tiny Dancer" page, and Bernie Taupin's on the page for the closing song, "Goodbye." The two married in England four months before the album was recorded. From the 50th Anniversary (2022) release booklet, p. 47.

Also brand new was Taupin's marriage to the tiny dancer herself, Maxine Feibelman. The wedding took place in April that year, in Market Rasen in Lincolnshire, covered by a local newspaper unused to seeing "familiar figures of the world of pop, giving the scene an appearance of showbiz unreality." The best man was "Elton John, Bernie's pop-star partner…outshining all the Rasen best men who ever were." Taupin, "remembered not so long ago as a rather shy and unassertive Market Rasen schoolboy, returned to the town again on Saturday as a songwriting hero of the pop world who was marrying a sweet girl from Los Angeles—who arrived at the Holy Rood Roman Catholic Church in a lilac-colored Aston Martin." The car matched Bernie in a "white velvet suit, a lilac shirt and earrings."

That giddy newness, and things happening quickly—too quickly—was an experience to which John could relate. Suddenly, he was famous, his music everywhere, his face in the papers; no longer living at home, he had a new house and a new manager, John Reid, who had also become his illicit live-in boyfriend. They couldn't marry, or even be out in public, but in their own way they had both married music men.

It couldn't last, of course, and it didn't. Elton's romance with his manager would end badly (even though Reid remained manager for a while). And Taupin's marriage to Feibelman was on the rocks within a couple of years. And he'd start to hedge on the connection between Maxine and "Tiny Dancer," which became an attempt "to capture the spirit of that time, encapsulated by the women we met . . . these free spirits, sexy, all hip-huggers and lacy blouses, very ethereal the way they moved." Or was it inspired by cover designer David Larkham's wife Janice? Or—another Taupin claim—by "fragments of a handful of LA females: a Whisky a Go Go waitress, a girl who worked in a Beverly Hills shoe store, and a hitchhiker in cutoffs on Pacific Coast Highway"?

Other Taupin relationships would follow, plus a series of marriages—to Toni Russo in 1979, to Stephanie Haymes in 1993, and to Heather Kidd in 2004. He penned lyrics over those decades that reflected those romantic ups and downs, a pattern that eased off as his fourth marriage settled into being his final one. But it did not disappear. As late as 2006, he wrote about a young woman with whom he had briefly been involved decades earlier, and who had later overdosed; the fleeting nature of sex and romance seeds the song, but it is developed into a heartbreak that is less romantic than it is a reaction to the woman's needless and premature death ("Blues Never Fade Away").

And yet, most of Taupin's lyrics are *not* about his loves and losses. He has made the point himself, insisting that "only a handful of songs" on the ten albums of *Empty Sky* through *Rock of the Westies* "could be deemed love songs in the traditional sense." He "made up for it" with the lyrics of "bitter disappointment" on *Blue Moves* and regular slices of "romantic balladry and up-tempo love anthems" in the 1980s and beyond—and yet his essential point, that those have never been his predominant lyrical concern, still holds. As with the songs on *Madman*, Taupin's main focus has always been on observing people and telling stories, some true, some imagined, most a mix of the two. From the very start, "I knew I wanted to write stories." Even his love affair with an imaginary America was rooted in the stories told in country music, in boyhood-treasured albums like Marty Robbins's *Gunfighter Ballads and Trail Songs* and the Louvin Brothers' *Tragic Songs of Life*. He insists he is not a poet ("It's an insult to real poets") but a teller of tales ("I create a song like writing a story").*

Take, for example, two Taupin/John tracks that readily come to mind in the "love song" category, and indeed were among the seventeen tracks on Elton's 1995 *Love Songs* compilation album: "Your Song" and "Candle in the Wind." The first was written in John's mother's house, the product of a teenage boy's imagination, and the latter was about Marilyn Monroe. Stories, not love poetry. In fact, almost none of the tracks on *Love Songs* is about a Taupin romance. The Apple Music playlist of the same title is similar, and while it places "Tiny Dancer" as the second song, it is sandwiched between—you guessed it—"Your Song" and "Candle in the Wind."

So, the Elton love songs that aren't really love songs add to the impression—boosted by the slow-burn success of "Tiny Dancer"—of Taupin/John as composers of romance. That impression is fueled by the emotional impact of that minority of Taupin/John songs that stem from Taupin's love life, his marriages and divorces; and which, in their musical composition and vocal delivery, add the additional layer of John's own experience of love and loss. And that, of course, is where the partnership has been truly interesting.

There were thirty-three years between "Tiny Dancer" and Taupin tying the knot with the woman to whom he is still married, the year before John entered into a civil partnership with the man to whom he is still married. That's a long time for two men to find love and lust, disappointment and heartbreak. Within those decades, "Tiny Dancer" was followed by "Harmony"—the only real love song on *Goodbye Yellow Brick Road*, the only other ode to Maxine. But there were also the poignant, captivating, sometimes harrowing end-of-love songs on *Blue Moves*, such as "Tonight." And then we are back to "I'm Still Standing," written in the wake of Taupin's second divorce—and inspired both by that experience and that of "my failed

---

* Taupin is too modest: his published poems are evidence of his status as a "real poet." See, for example, his first solo record, *Bernie Taupin* (released on Elektra in 1971), although I recommend *reading* the enclosed poems rather than listening to Taupin's deadpan delivery of them over the minimal backing music by Caleb Quaye and Davey Johnstone.

love" with another woman, Loree Rodkin, about whom a previous lover, Don Henley, wrote "Wasted Time" and part of "Hotel California." Taupin says all three remain good friends today, adding that at least Rodkin got "three good songs" out of it. The point, of course, is that *we* got three good songs out of it.

Half a decade later came "Sacrifice," which Taupin called a "bookend" that paired with "Your Song": the earlier song was "was about absolute naiveté in love while 'Sacrifice' is the complete opposite, the story of someone who's seen and done it all, as far as love's concerned, and come out the other end scarred but realistic." On another occasion, Taupin paired "declarations of love like 'I Guess That's Why They Call It the Blues'" with "aching admissions of adultery like 'Sacrifice.'" How do you go from one to the other? "Living life like I was living it," confessed Taupin; but of course, his songwriting partner was also living life as *he* was living it. Bookended pairs like "Tiny Dancer"/"Tonight" and "Your Song"/"Sacrifice" (or "Blues"/"Sacrifice") may be a minority of Taupin/John songs, but they stand out in the catalogue either as hits and/or as the compositions that hit hardest.

"Sacrifice" was to *Sleeping with the Past* what "Tonight" was to *Blue Moves*: just one song on an album that expressed Taupin's end-of-love angst across various tracks. In addition to "Sacrifice," the lyrics to "Whispers," "Blue Avenue," and "Stone's Throw from Hurtin'" were a "veritable cypher of cryptic confessions" over a relationship that was going under, "spelling out how rapidly the ship had been sinking." But, as on *Blue Moves*, John interpreted them musically in various ways, sometimes leaning into the melancholy, sometimes offsetting it with a jovial melody or an up-tempo composition. John was nearing the end of a difficult decade, in terms of his personal life; we now know that he was on the verge of a successful stint in rehab, followed by unprecedented romantic stability, but *he* didn't know that. We therefore get something of his processing of those same emotions, an often messy mix of empathy and indifference, acceptance and denial.

In the decade following "Sacrifice," another Taupin marriage came and went, inspiring "I Want Love," written by him after his third divorce as an expression of hope, but a determined hope uttered between gritted teeth. Taupin has told of the "emotional tailspin of disillusion and depression" into which the divorce threw him, and that seeking to "extract a cathartic remedy out of pain"—a technique from which we long benefited, through the John/Taupin catalogue—he wrote "I Want Love." It worked superbly. The words "encapsulated my feelings completely in a way like no other song I've written," and the resulting song is among the best in the catalogue.

John later described the song, with a touch of dismissive reductionism (unintended, I suspect), as one "Bernie wrote about himself: a middle-aged man with a few divorces, wondering if he's ever going to fall in love again." But as happy as John had become by this point (2001), the track works so well (and should have beaten John Mayer's "Your Body Is a Wonderland" for the Grammy for which it was nominated) because John is in there too, remembering exactly what that felt like. Indeed, John is present in all of these, in ways that are not always predictable; just as he brilliantly captured the mood of "I Want Love" with brooding piano chords and an aching vocal delivery, he turned "I'm Still Standing" into a joyful expression of survival.

Then there are the rare moments when John has contributed lyrics to a song—typically just a line or two—standing out as exceptions to the rule. Indeed, some such moments have become well known as part of Elton legend. One example is the "what's his color, I don't care, he's my brother" line from "Border Song"—a spontaneous shout-out to guitarist and old friend Caleb Quaye, but a line that came to play a key role in that song's history (to which we shall return in a later chapter). But the examples that produced love songs (loosely defined) are the most illustrative.

One example whose origins are wrapped in contested contradictions is the 1985 John/Taupin worldwide smash—Top 10 in two dozen countries, #1 in a third of them—"Nikita." A mid-tempo unrequited-love ballad, the song describes a crush on a border guard whom the singer craves but can never know. Were the lyrics inspired by an unrecorded song, named "Natasha," submitted to the same company that published Taupin/John songs at the time? (The allegation was rightly dismissed in court.) Were the title and words the product of Bernie's imagination, neither he nor Elton aware that Nikita is a man's name in Russian? (Unlikely, despite Elton's claim to that effect in some interviews at the time.) Or did the song's idea, and its title, come from John, after he was smitten by a male border guard during his recent travels in the Soviet Union? (Most likely, and an inside joke shared by George Michael, who sang backing vocals on the song, as well as by Ken Russell, whose video turned the guard into an East German woman.) Despite my opinion as to the "real" story behind "Nikita," what really matters is that its origins and meanings are layered, because of the John/Taupin method, with John's non-musical contributions—whatever they were—only serving to highlight the multifaceted connotations of their love songs.

Another example—another exception that proves the rule, "an odd man out" (in Taupin's account of the song's creation)—is one of John's signature ballads, "Sorry Seems to Be the Hardest Word." The song comes from a well that is a little deeper than, say, "Nikita." There are two different versions of how its birth differed from the usual John/Taupin song partum. Elton's version is that he came up with the first line, "What have I got to do to make you love me?" ("the fallout from another disastrous infatuation with a straight guy"), and then with the opening chords, inspiring him to write either very little or most of the song (accounts vary), with Bernie finishing it. Bernie remembers Elton coming up with just the opening melody, and Bernie then saying, "Don't do anything more to that, let me go write something"; and Bernie returning minutes later with the rest of the lyrics, to which Elton then composed the rest of the music.

If that sounds like an authorship disagreement, it isn't. Their versions have over time moved up and down a spectrum, often overlapping, and both agree on the creative context: sitting around a piano in someone's apartment in Los Angeles, not planning to write a song, but going with the flow of it when their parallel emotional states sparked their creative partnership. Both men were experiencing agonizing endings to relationships, that "heartbreaking, sickening part of love" when you "want to save something from dying" but you "know deep down inside that it's already dead" (in Taupin's words). This is Taupin too, but it could have come from John, remembering how the song came together: "It was actually pretty immediate, the title and first couple of lines came into my head in a way that I guess I felt they were already there and just needed a little prompting."[†]

But does any of this matter? Don't songs like "Tiny Dancer" and "Sorry" and "I'm Still Standing" resonate with us not for how they reflect Elton's and Bernie's lives, but because they articulate some part—however large or small, on the nose or indirect—of *our* emotional existence? Isn't "Your Song" *our* song? Of course. But that transposition is facilitated by the ambiguity of the John/Taupin partnership: Who is still standing? Who wants whom to hold

---

[†] The only John song that was written entirely by him, lyric included, is "Song for Guy," whose one line is "Life isn't everything"—sung repeatedly in the background starting more than five minutes into what is otherwise a seven-minute instrumental. It was a #4 hit single in the UK but was poorly promoted in the US and failed to crack its Top 100. Perhaps Americans misheard the song's title the way that Gianni Versace did: years later, when the two were friends, Versace told John it was his favorite Elton song and a wonderfully brave one; he thought it was titled "Song for a Gay."

them closer? Whose situation is sad, sad? Recognizing Taupin's role as the other half is more than a simple acknowledgment of songwriting method; it is an appreciation of how the intricacy of that method is crucial to the impact of their most resonant songs.

Perhaps the last word on the John/Taupin partnership should go to them. After all, if the partnership strikes us as a complex friendship expressed through intricate creative methodology, how does it feel to them?

In a 2013 interview, John talked about "We All Fall in Love Sometimes," the *Captain Fantastic* track that uses the medium of a romantic ballad to convey the concept of John and Taupin as creative soulmates. I considered using the song to open this chapter, but in the end, it seemed to me that "I'm Still Standing" best introduced the complex way in which John/Taupin songs can simultaneously convey both one and two separate meanings, one and two individual emotional states. "We All Fall in Love Sometimes" is a precious gem within the catalogue, best appreciated with its other half, "Curtains" (whose lyrics lend my next chapter its title). In contrast to "I'm Still Standing," it speaks directly to the partnership, expressing it in terms deliberately simple to reflect its youthful origins. "Naïve notions that were childish," as Taupin describes his early lyrics (echoed in the "Curtains" lyric, "such childish words for you"), paired with (the line that follows) "simple tunes that tried to hide it."

So, what did John have to say about "We All Fall in Love Sometimes"? It is worth quoting at length:

> I cry when I sing this song because I was in love with Bernie. Not in a sexual way, but because he was the person I was looking for my entire life, my little soul mate. We'd come so far, and we were still very naïve. I [realized I] was gay by that time, and he was married, but he was a person that, more than anything, I loved. And the relationship we had was so odd because it was not tied at the hip. Thank God it wasn't tied at the hip because we wouldn't have lasted. That relationship is the most important relationship of my entire life.

And what of Taupin's perspective on the relationship? In Taupin's recent 400-page autobiography, John plays a briefly prominent role at the start (the third chapter is titled "The Ballad of Reg and Bern"), but thereafter is a spectral presence, somehow always yet never present. On the final page, Taupin turns to the subject of Elton while—significantly—not actually naming him, admitting that he is "in absentia for much of this narrative." And yet he also admits that through his adult life, "He's been a staff to lean on, a most excellent musical conduit, and comes replete with massive benevolence." "Alike we are not," Taupin stresses, "but that is our magic." The relationship has worked as "two sides of the same coin," inseparable or "integrated," yet with the yin and yang "split." "Still," Bernie concedes in the final line, "he is an eternal love and perhaps the reason I got to write this book."

2

Once Upon a Time

Elton and Bowie, Part 1

"Someone Saved My Life Tonight" (6:45, 1975)

"As long as Elton John can bring forth one performance per album on the order of 'Someone Saved My Life Tonight,' the chance remains that he will become something more than the great entertainer he already is and go on to make a lasting contribution to rock." What was it about this song that so inspired critic Jon Landau in his *Rolling Stone* review of the track's parent album, *Captain Fantastic and the Brown Dirt Cowboy*?

Landau was hardly alone. Reviews of both song and album were generally stellar. *Captain Fantastic*, upon its release worldwide in May 1975, was an immediate smash. In the US, it became the first album to be certified gold prior to its release and to enter the Billboard charts at #1, selling 4.1 million copies stateside in the first four days. The only single from the album was "Someone Saved My Life Tonight," released a month after its parent, helping to keep the album atop the US charts for seven straight weeks.

At 6'45", "Someone Saved My Life Tonight" defied the conventional wisdom that radio stations would never play a single that long, thus dooming it to flop. Record company executives supposedly asked for it to be edited down for 7" release, which Elton refused to do. The same story has become part of the legend of Queen's "Bohemian Rhapsody," consolidated by its telling in the 2018 biopic of the same name. The epic Queen track was released just four months after "Someone Saved My Life Tonight," which was actually fifty seconds longer. The length of the Queen song did not stop it from hitting #1 in the UK (for nine weeks, no less) and #9 in the US. In fact, that narrative of artists insisting a long song be untouched is a much favored (and surely often apocryphal) anecdote in pop music history. Its apparent and irresistible moral is that consumers will endorse the artistic integrity of musicians in unified opposition to money-grubbing corporate philistines.

Certainly, record label executives regularly requested shorter versions of tracks for 7″ release. But they also knew that there periodically existed long hit singles. "Hey Jude" hit #1 in 1968 (UK and US), despite being 7′11″. Don McLean's "American Pie" was a huge 1971 hit (US #1, UK #2), at a whopping 8′42″ (although it was split in half on the single, one half on each side, and radio stations often played one half only). And a 6′54″-edit of The Temptations' "Papa Was a Rolling Stone" was #1 in 1972 (#14 in the UK; the album version was over 12 minutes). Whether anyone at DJM or RCA tried to make John and his producer Gus Dudgeon edit "Someone Saved My Life Tonight" or not, it was played plenty on the radio, reaching #4 in the US and #22 in the UK (a reflection of John's relative chart success in this era, a topic to which we return in a later chapter).

Its unusual length, therefore, helped it stand out. After all, if long songs were not typically hits, then one that *was* a hit must be exceptionally good. Oversized hits had oversized reputations—see the above three examples that preceded the John song—and that allowed "Someone Saved My Life Tonight" to acquire some immediate legendary luster. The length also supported the impression given by the lyrics, by Elton's delivery of them, and by the steadily building rock-ballad production: this was a serious song on a big topic. John and Taupin made it clear during the promotion of *Captain Fantastic*, starting before its release, that it was a concept album about their origins and rise as a creative pair. Each song therefore had a story behind it.

"Someone Saved My Life Tonight" narrated an incident that soon became well known. The version reflected in the song, supported by publicity at the time of its release, was that in 1967, before Reg became Elton, before he and Bernie really got started, Reg met a girl at a Bluesology gig in Sheffield; her name was Linda Woodrow. Linda moved down to London, they became engaged, and Reg moved in with her. He brought Bernie with him. The relationship was never consummated, "which Linda took as evidence of old-fashioned chivalry and romance on my part," John later mused, "rather than a lack of interest or willingness." They lived together for six months, during which time Reg allegedly composed nothing, steadily feeling more and more trapped, and then suicidal over his inability to undo the mistake he realized he had made. One night, in stepped Bernie and "came to my rescue," persuading his friend to flee the flat and the engagement. He saved his life, certainly metaphorically but perhaps literally.

The lyrics were a twist, therefore, on the usual arrangement; this was Bernie writing about Elton's life, but seen from Bernie's viewpoint, for Elton to sing about. The partnership is still intact—this isn't John writing his own story—but now Bernie is channeling Elton's emotions, and in turn Elton is channeling those words into his emotional response to his own story. That layering of emotion and friendship was irresistible to listeners. It smacked of a kind of authenticity—a term that was very much in vogue in the 1970s, driving the singer-songwriter wave at the turn of the decade (of which Elton's first few albums were a part). Indeed, the concept of popular music authenticity, as flabby as it was, remained in vogue even as it shored up the punk reaction to stadium rock later in the decade.

John's delivery in the first part of the song was so intense that producer Gus Dudgeon kept pushing him to do another take, less sensitive and more forceful. As Dudgeon later remembered it, guitarist Davey Johnstone eventually leaned over and murmured to the producer, "He's talking about attempting suicide!" Then Dudgeon got it, quickly grasping how to use his production skills to underpin the despair and anger voiced by John as the song built to its climax and then its orchestrated finale. Taupin heard not a note of the music until it had been composed, recorded, and mixed; when Dudgeon played him the completed song, Taupin was so overwhelmed by its emotional punch, he had to leave the room.

Was the story quite that simple, however? And how real was that suicide attempt? For as John later admitted, decades before his 2019 autobiography, but he puts it well there:

> I'd not only put a pillow in the bottom of the oven to rest my head on, I'd taken the precaution of turning the gas to low and opening all the windows in the kitchen.... There wasn't enough carbon monoxide in the room to kill a wasp.

Also, was the rescuer really Taupin, or was it Long John Baldry—John's former bandmate and old friend, the mentor from whom he had taken half his name (a fact later rewritten to feature John Lennon)? In one version of the story, three weeks before the wedding, Baldry sat Reg down in the Bag O' Nails (a 1960s live music club in Soho, London) and talked him out of it; two days later Reg's stepfather Fred showed up in his Ford Cortina (turned into "a truck" in the song) to return him home. And was young Reg saved from marrying the wrong woman—as readers and listeners were led to believe in

1975—or from marrying any woman at all? After all, Baldry was openly gay, at least to the extent that openness was possible in the 1960s (when it was still a crime in Britain) or the 1970s (when he was more "out," and his career, not coincidentally, stalled).

Elton would in fact marry a woman, nine years after the song in which Taupin or Baldry "saved my life tonight." Not until thirty years after the song was first released would Elton marry a man (a 2005 civil partnership, becoming officially a marriage in 2014 when UK law made it possible). By the time of the *Rocketman* biopic and the *Me* autobiography (both 2019), the ambiguity surrounding John's salvation from the unfortunate Linda Woodrow had been edited out. "You're gay," Baldry tells Reg in the *Me* version. "You love Bernie more than you love her." Fans had been given one origin myth in 1975. In the twenty-first century, they were given an updated one. "Someone Saved My Life Tonight" has served as an enduring—and evolving—cornerstone of Elton's origin mythology, of his genesis story.

Rock stars need to reinvent themselves, not just to be different from the rest of us mere mortals, but also to highlight the contrast between their own mortal past and their immortal present. In doing so, their humble origins must be reimagined; a mythology of origins, leading to a rebirth, needs to be created and nurtured. "Just like us, you must have had, a once upon a time," sang John on "Curtains"—from the *Captain Fantastic* origin-story album. Yet unlike us, Elton's once-upon-a-time has evolved and repeated, in a cycle of rebirth befitting the mythical genesis and semi-divinity of a rock star.

The transformation of Reginald Dwight into Elton John has been told often, including in that hit biopic, *Rocketman*—and indeed the ubiquity of the tale is central to the point here. Whether the details of that transformation are repeated as biographical scene-setting, or in less straightforward terms as legend or fantasy (as in *Rocketman*), there is still an emphasis on "fact." I suggest that we can better understand John—from his conversion from Reg to Elton to the full sweep of his career, complete with ups and downs—by emphasizing the ongoing and performative nature of his transformation. To do that, to understand John's origins and success in an original and insightful way, I'd like to compare the phenomenon with David Jones's evolution into David Bowie.

Both men came from similar origins at the same time and place (the London suburbs, both born in 1947), and both remade themselves into someone new. More importantly and more interestingly, their mythological metamorphoses were not singular events. In parallel and contrasting ways, John and Bowie managed repeated rebirths across half a century. Bowie's rebirths were marked by a more conscious branding—a self-confessed actor, he created, named, and performed personas such as Ziggy Stardust and the Thin White Duke—and are thus better known. But John also invented and embraced a series of alter egos, insufficiently appreciated as such. He has typically been portrayed (including by his own self) as merely *reacting* to his own psychological struggles (with his sexuality, e.g., and with addiction) as well as to external forces, such as trends in music and popular culture.

While his self-branding has been far less overt and obvious than Bowie's was, John has nonetheless *actively* and deliberately forged over five decades an evolving mythology of rebirth and reinvention. In striving to turn the self-perceived ugly duckling into a bedazzled swan, he has created multiple manifestations of that swan (complete with the endless swan song of a four-year "farewell" world tour). Through his albums, genre choices, extravagant costumes, public persona, and the public projection of his private life, John has morphed from Reginald Dwight into singer-songwriter Elton John, from a rock star to a has-been to a pop star to a Broadway composer, from Elton the addict to Sir Elton the philanthropist, from a punching bag for tabloid homophobia to the exemplar of a gay married man with children.

Cultural theorists have observed that identity is, or can be, performed—that is, expressed in how we dress, speak, and present ourselves in person and in social media. For rock and pop stars, that includes, or is built around, the kind of music made and how it is packaged and presented.

There are two further dimensions to the performativity of identity that are relevant here. One is that such identities are not static; in fact, arguably, they never are. Rather than assuming that a person's identity is "an already accomplished fact," as one theorist argued, "we should think, instead, of identity as a 'production,' which is never complete, always in process, and always constituted within, not outside representation." The other relevant aspect of identity as an evolving production is that it obfuscates "real" identity—partially disguising it but also calling into question its very existence.

In this century, in which musicians reach audiences and make a living by selling themselves more than records, artists have become "artist-brands" (as one communications scholar has phrased it). Image is the medium that conveys the music, and image must be mass marketed in ways that allow artist identities to be as produced, performative, and multifaceted as ever.

This is all relatively new, but not *completely* new; its scale and totality are recent, but the culture of artist-brands goes back to the moment when rock and pop stars were first emerging—when Elton John and David Bowie were beginning to construct their brands.

Let us detour for a moment, then, to consider Bowie's origin mythology. Davey Jones grew up in Bromley, a suburb in the southern swathe of London's Green Belt, "a drab, featureless dormitory town" (as one biographer put it), not unlike Pinner, where Reg Dwight was growing up during the exact same time.[*] But Jones had been born in Brixton, living there for the first five years of his childhood; as Brixton was then far less bland, more gritty, multiracial, and working class, Bowie frequently claimed that it was where he had grown up. On occasion, he also claimed to have spent a significant part of his childhood in the romantic, rural setting of Yorkshire.

The evidence reveals the Jones family and young Davey to have been "cushioned by a comfortable level of middle-class privilege" (one biographer's words). But Bowie preferred anecdotes of a grim, fractious upbringing, against which he rebelled by being "outrageous" and "camp since I was seven." Many of those who knew him when he was still Jones took their cue from such tales, confirming how "cold" and "soulless" his home life was—even while seeing providential signs of his future stardom, from the midwife's claim that the angelic newborn David had clearly "been on this earth before" to assertions that as a child he'd pose under the coaching-lantern of the Crown pub in anticipation of the *Ziggy Stardust* cover image.

Such imaginative and contradictory stories were part of the general pattern of "jokes, provocation and outright lies" that Bowie delivered to interviewers over the years. That pattern was deftly dissected by Bowie scholar Will Brooker, whose phrase that is ("jokes . . ."). But Brooker also noted that "the nature of research and writing" is "not just the discovery of information but the way we join it up; what we omit, as well as what we include." That is true of this book (whose structure I have designed to make that process more transparent), as it is of all John and Bowie biographies; and it is especially true of how Bowie presented his own origins, as if talking about himself was a research exercise in preparation for a creative writing

---

[*] If we take Hyde Park Corner as our central London pin-drop, Bromley is about eleven miles to the southeast, Pinner about thirteen miles to the northwest. Originating in the 1930s, the Metropolitan Green Belt was designed to create a ring of protected, undeveloped space around outer London; in the face of Green Belt development, the zone has been constantly expanded and redefined ever since.

project. "Some writers have struggled to put all this in a logical sequence," Bowie told one of them. "I wouldn't bother if I were you."

Through his teens, as he sought to transform himself into someone else, someone better poised to achieve stardom, his name changed from Davey Jones to Dave Jay to Davie Jones to—at the age of eighteen—David Bowie. But that didn't do it. Stardom did not come until, aged twenty-five, he became Ziggy Stardust. Behind the name changes of that long struggle was a series of experiments with media of artistic expression, musical styles, public images, and sexual identities. "Living in Bromley, fed and clothed and funded by his parents," Jones/Bowie imagined into existence new worlds to surround his own self-inventions, like a teenage "suburban correspondent filing a story from the field"—and like Dwight and Taupin creating characters and stories in their suburban bedroom.

The difference was that Dwight understood he needed to become John in order to channel the music he loved into his own music; the metamorphosis was a means to an end. (And Taupin, as backstage sidekick, didn't need to remake himself at all.) But for Jones/Bowie, the metamorphosis *was* the end; the liminality of simultaneously being himself and someone else, of being both comfortably safe and dangerously out on the edge, was the very place he wanted to be. To achieve that, he needed to remain "unguessable as an individual"—a shapeshifter, elusive, always on the move.

The Aztecs used a concept they called *nepantla* (roughly meaning "in-betweenness" or "in the middle" in the Nahuatl language). To become *nepantla* was a survival strategy at a time of cultural change. Bowie was *nepantla* for that exact reason, but with a twist; his use of that strategy accelerated the process of cultural change. One of Bowie's friends who was caught up in that change, and who suffered for his failure to adopt a strategy to survive it, was Marc Bolan (he is one of the threads that links musicians who feature strongly in this book—Bowie, John, and Rod Stewart—all of whom attended Bolan's funeral in 1977). "What Bowie understood, and Bolan didn't, was you present a moving target," English music writer Charles Shaar Murray once said. "Bolan was a one-trick pony. Kept trying to do his single one trick even after he got too fat to jump the hurdle."

That trick was the sound and look of glam rock, which dominated teenage pop culture (and thus the singles chart) from 1971 to 1974 in the UK (but not in the US).[†] John co-opted elements of glam, most notably in hits like

---

[†] Glam is sometimes broadly defined to include its US cousin, but that phenomenon had a different label ("glitter rock"), was New York–focused rather than national (at least in its early years),

"Saturday Night's Alright for Fighting" and in his stage costumes. But he never became a primarily glam artist, and his costumes (especially the ornate, oversized glasses) were too unique—too *Elton*—to be simply labeled as glam. And while Bowie commandeered glam, deploying and developing it in service to his Ziggy persona, he did so with deliberate impermanence. As music writer Chris Charlesworth has noted, both John and Bowie were "part of the glam-rock movement" but ultimately "transcended it." Bolan, on the other hand, was perceived as one of its—if not *the*—key founder, and he was inescapably associated with it, shackled to it as it suddenly faded in 1975.

At the time of Bolan's accidental death, John too had become a moving target. As we shall see in subsequent chapters, Reg's Elton persona struggled to jump the hurdles from around that date through the 1980s, evolving in the 1990s as a new persona, Sir Elton. But that was in the future: in 1975, as the Thin White Duke was emerging (or "returning," in a very-Bowie sleight of hand) from the ashes of Ziggy Stardust, "Someone Saved My Life Tonight" and *Captain Fantastic* were Elton's latest global hits. But more than commercial and critical successes, they also worked well to promote the particular version of John's origin mythology that had been building in the press for several years. Like Bowie's origin legend, its various pieces were not easily reconciled with each other.

One such piece was the legend of a childhood shaped by "conflict and anxieties in his own home," an upbringing under "tense, restrictive conditions." This version of Reggie saw him as an only child in a house of four conservative adults—a cold, domineering father, a repressed mother, and his mother's parents—in cold, conservative Pinner. Those adults were so uptight, in John's sometime telling of it, that they wouldn't even let him wear Hush Puppies. That nerve-wracking childhood became "tragic teen years" (see Figure 2.1), marked by a broken home and a father of whom "I was afraid" and who disdained his son's musical ambitions.

Another core aspect to John's origin myth, however, runs rather against the grain of his strict upbringing and tragic youth. It is the enduring legend of little Reg as a piano prodigy. His father's antipathy toward rock 'n' roll was hardly unusual for a man of his generation, but it did not stem from a dislike of music. On the contrary, in his younger days Stanley Dwight had

---

and featured US acts like early Alice Cooper, the New York Dolls, and later, Kiss. So, while US glitter rock is certainly part of the larger glam story, it does not speak directly to John's massive US success during the glam years.

ONCE UPON A TIME 27

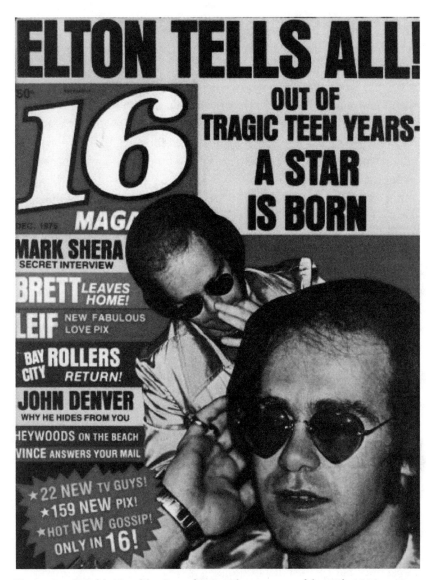

Figure 2.1 Double Trouble. One of many Elton covers of the US's *16 Magazine*; this December 1975 issue came less than a year before his 1976 *Rolling Stone* cover story resulted in his permanent banishment from *16*. Was Elton really a star born "out of tragic teen years"? In 2024, copies like this sold on eBay for roughly ten times the original (inflation-adjusted) cover price.

played trumpet in a swing ensemble called the Millermen. In Reg's home there was a radio, a record player with many records—including those by pianists such as George Shearing, by jazz balladeers like Nat King Cole, and by country singers of the Tennessee Ernie Ford kind. "I was three or four when I first started listening to records like that," John would recall. Later, his mother brought home the latest sounds, such as Elvis Presley's "Hound Dog." There was also an upright piano, which little Reg took to playing in imitation of the music heard on the radio and turntable—something he was encouraged to do.

Indeed, one piece of "family lore" has Reg, at the tender age of three, repeating Émile Waldteufel's "The Skater's Waltz" on the upright, having heard the record playing in the other room. By some accounts, the new upright bought when Reg was four was a gift to *him* (that detail was even used to underpin "The Boy and the Piano," a 2018 two-minute TV commercial for British retailer John Lewis, using footage from John's best-known performances to suggest that a career like his could stem from the right Christmas present). At seven, his parents started paying for piano lessons. At eleven, he won a Royal Academy of Music scholarship.

Reg's father's irritation over him practicing piano licks by Little Richard and Jerry Lee Lewis, instead of Bach and Chopin exercises, is perhaps understandable. But such details, real or apocryphal, helped to contrive an uneasy squaring of the legend of a terrible childhood with that of the home that nurtured a musical prodigy—whereby Reg "found refuge" in music, an escape from grief (his grandfather died when he was five), neglect (his father's discipline and even—so his mother claimed decades later—dislike of his son), and conflict (his parents fought, divorcing when he was fifteen). "I used to find solace in music when my parents used to argue," John has often said. Such context has served to embellish the prodigy legend: not because of a musical home and professional training, but *despite* them, Reg turned into the extraordinary pianist that is Elton.

The narrative theme of our hero facing great obstacles, but finding redemption and resurrection, is a classic and irresistible one. Bowie took it to extremes, constructing his own repeated resurrection. Not surprisingly, then, it is also threaded through John's origin mythology. For example, young Reg Dwight gamely pursued through his teens a dream of being a professional musician, forming bands that failed (the Corvettes, Bluesology), playing to unappreciative audiences in a local pub (at the Northwood Hills Hotel), and realizing he could never be a real songwriter because his lyrics were terrible. His destiny seemed, at best, to be a session player, the unheralded keyboardist behind other people's success. But it was too late to give up and pursue the kind of comfortable middle-class career his father wanted for him—in insurance or banking, for example—as he had dropped out of school, aged seventeen, right before taking his final exams. He'd made perseverance at the piano his only option.

Central to this spin on his youth is the emphasis on the young Reg/Elton's appearance: the "overweight, bespectacled thing" (his own words) was "a model of mediocrity, plain and artlessly simple" (a biographer's words). He said he had sausage fingers. He could play and sing, but he didn't look like a rock star—not even close. Long John Baldry's temporary takeover of Bluesology as his backing band symbolized the problem: Baldry was tall and debonair, his charm (patently camp, in retrospect) made women swoon, and his 1967 UK #1 was titled "Let the Heartaches Begin."

In origin-myth tradition, such obstacles are overcome by a combination of sheer, transformative grit and the intervention of fateful good fortune and guardian angels. In John's case, such an angel took the unlikely form of a grubby seventeen-year-old from rural Lincolnshire. Remember that 1967 Liberty Records newspaper ad answered by Bernie (with his mother's help; or not)? The emerging Elton John answered it too; and the young A&R man, Ray Williams, who had placed the ad (another unlikely angel, the same age as Elton), saw how well they complemented each other's strengths and weaknesses. They "hit it off right away," Williams later said. "They were like an old couple." Bernie's marriage at the start of their rise to stardom helped squash any suggestion that there was a "deviant" side to their closeness; and it had the added effect of painting John in the mildly tragic light of an eligible bachelor in need of the right girl. In the early 1970s, the formerly tragic teen found success but not love—a narrative that was catnip to young fans.

The same year that Fate brought him Taupin—1967—Dwight realized that in order to become the performer he was not but wanted to be, to become someone else, he needed someone else's name. With Baldry's takeover of Bluesology, there were some personnel changes, including the replacement of the saxophonist with Elton Dean (1945–2006), a jazz player who would go on to play with Soft Machine. One night on the tour bus, Dwight asked Dean if he could borrow his name. "Fuck off, Reg!" he replied. Dwight, only half-deterred, took half of Dean's name, adding to it Baldry's given first name.

The choice of two first names subjected John to some ribbing over the years (although Reginald and Dwight were arguably also two first names). But that very fact worked for how Reg Dwight built Elton John, drawing attention to the metamorphosis in a way that was flavored with just the right amount of self-deprecation. When Groucho Marx showed up to a party in Malibu that John threw for his friend the movie director Bryan Forbes, John was too shy to ask Marx for his autograph; a third party made the request, explaining it was for Elton. "Who the fuck is Elton?" asked Marx. Told he was the host, who had earlier played his yet-to-be-released new album on the piano (in its entirety, according to one account), Marx retorted "Oh, the *piano* player. What's his name?" "Elton John." "What a stupid fucking name. His last name is where his first name ought to be," he snapped, styling his autograph "To Elton John—Marx Groucho." In a different version of the story, John witnesses the exchange, and retorts, "Don't shoot me, I'm only the piano player!" Whatever the details, John made that line the title of his next album (the very one he had played at the party), its cover referencing the exchange by including a poster for the 1940 Marx Brothers' film *Go West* (see Figure 2.2).

Marx's role in the story is more deprecatory than witty, yet John leans into it hard. As he would for decades. In 1991, he was interviewed live on stage by British comedian Rowan Atkinson, as part of a benefit for the UK AIDS charity the Terrence Higgins Trust. Atkinson began by asking the origin of his "funny name," wondering if he'd ever considered "John Elton," and returning to the topic repeatedly for the whole six-minute interview (had he considered changing his lyricist's name to Taupin Bernie? Did he envy Ben Elton his name? And so on). John played along marvelously, struggling not to laugh while performing a growing irritation, finally pretending to shoot Atkinson and getting the last line—"what a head dick!" The British press sensed echoes of the skit seven years later, when John was knighted by the Queen, and the Lord Chamberlain accidentally introduced him as John Elton.

Armed with his new name back in 1967, it took Reg/Elton a few years before he understood how to add a new image to go with the new name. The Reg-to-Elton transformation was not one of rags to riches (although vast wealth and excessive conspicuous consumption would come), but one of ordinary to extraordinary, the metamorphosis of (to repeat the metaphor one last time) an ugly duckling into a dazzling (and bedazzled) swan. The legendary turning point, when Elton started to go from awkward to exuberant, was his August 1970 week at the Troubadour. Reviewing that performance

Figure 2.2 What's His Name? The cover of 1973's *Don't Shoot Me I'm Only the Piano Player*, with one "movie" poster showing John playing the album and another poster of the Marx Brothers' 1940 movie *Go West*. The reference to an exchange with Groucho Marx at a party was explained numerous times, with various versions of the story evolving over the years.

in the *Los Angeles Times*, Robert Hilburn mused that "there is a certain sense of the absurd about John as a performer that is reminiscent of the American rock stars of the mid-1950s." According to guitarist Caleb Quaye, who was close to Elton from when he was still Reggie and through the 1970s, John "really went after it and really pursued his craft, not only in the development of his piano playing and singing, but his showmanship as well, his performance."

The reaction of audiences and critics to the Troubadour gigs "was the first time I knew something really big was happening," John later said. "That was really when I became Elton." The exterior transformation—the key pounding, the kicking away of the piano stool, the handstands on the keyboard, then later the elaborate spectacles and costumes—all came easier and quicker than the internal one. "I'm a tubby little singer and I can't understand why people scream at me," he was still telling interviewers after his star had risen. "There must be a reason, but God knows what it is." Whereas Bowie seldom said anything that was not deliberately artful, John lacked artifice in that way. As disingenuous as his early-1970s insistence that "I'm plain" may seem—in light of teen-idol hysteria, as well as record, concert ticket, and magazine sales—I perceive sincerity. His self-image was far more Reg, the vulnerable, self-doubting mortal with a receding hairline and inelegant fingers, than it was Elton, the godlike magic-fingered superstar.

By revealing the Reg beneath the Elton, he showed his humanity, and for that he was adored. The more he sought to compensate for what he perceived as his inadequacies, with increasingly elaborate costumes, absurd headdresses, and outrageous glasses, the more fans loved him. His stage get-ups weren't a single look that he inhabited; they do not appear on a single one of his studio album covers, for example. Whether seen as "a joke . . . affectionally parodying the rock 'n' roll business" (as John claimed in 1975), or as an expression of the "huge Hollywood glamour attached to him" (as Charlesworth has put it), or as compensation (that "really went too far"; John again) for his self-conscious complex over his receding hairline, fluctuating weight, and need for corrective lenses, the baroque costuming was always clearly just Reg/Elton dressing up "for the occasion." Unlike Ziggy Stardust, this wasn't a persona that eclipsed the real person inside, one that consequently had to be destroyed and replaced in order to maintain Bowie's human continuity. Rockstar Elton of the 1970s was a persona that still permitted views of Reg, humble, stumbling, all too human—a precedent that has proved as essential to John's survival as a pop culture icon as Bowie's endless series of personas were to his. Bowie is loved for his commitment to being *nepantla*, right to the very end. John is loved for not using Elton as a disguise, for always also being Reg.

Stars tend to "mythologize how they became stars in the first place. Mythmaking plays a vital role in creating their public image, but the process must be deeply personal to them as well. How did I get here? Why was it me this happened to?" That observation was made by a music writer who had in mind Donna Summer and her memoir. Looking back from the late-1990s, Summer made "sense of her often-torturous path through the trials of stardom" by glossing "each twist and turn with a magical significance," with her fate presaged by omens and facilitated by guardian angels.

The point applies to others too, including Bowie and John. Bowie never published an autobiography, so we cannot be sure which version and what details of his own mythology he believed—or in later life wanted others to believe. But perhaps that is why such a book was never written (or completed); he wasn't sure either, and he understood that the contradictions and ambiguities were essential to that mythmaking, which was itself essential to his immortality as a star. But whereas Bowie relished ambiguity and life's liminal zones, John has relished linear narrative and tropes of redemption as a way to escape those gray zones. It makes sense, therefore, that John would publish an autobiography that embraces his own origin myths (leaving myth-busting to Taupin's meandering autobiography). Its title, *Me*, is deceptively simple, but only mildly so, as its linear narrative, complete with origin mythology and a trajectory of rise, fall, and resurrection, can easily make sense of the "me" sequence of Reg, Elton, Sir Elton, and Uncle Elton. A similarly titled Bowie memoir would have needed to be called *Mes* or *Me's* or *Me?* or . . . well, it just doesn't work, which is of course the point.

Cynics might raise eyebrows at Summer's frequent mention of "God's plan," at Bowie's use of mendacity as a promotional tool, and at John's unambiguous consolidation of his own legend. But those strategies for making sense of stardom are inseparable from the stars themselves.

3
Starmen

Elton and Bowie, Part 2

"Rocket Man" (4:42, 1972)

His second hit "Rocket Man" proved that 1970's "Your Song" had not left Elton stranded in the borderlands of one-hit wonders. A 1972 Top 6 hit in both the UK and US, it carried parent album *Honky Château* to #2 in the UK and #1 in the US. It was also his first global smash. While he had achieved critical acclaim but only modest commercial success before "Rocket Man" boosted his career, by the mid-1970s, John was the biggest-selling recording artist in the world. The print advertisement that MCA used in the US for the song's launch (a pun used liberally) anticipated the metaphor of a rocket taking Elton into the stratosphere of stardom (see Figure 3.1). Far from being lonely out in space, he would be on top of the world.

"Rocket Man" has had a long and revealing shelf life, both as a song and as a branding device. Elton has sung the song in concert thousands of times. The fantastic ten-minute version that he has often performed was the closing number, complete with fireworks, of his already-legendary Glastonbury show in 2023. Its forlorn subtitle ("I Think It's Going to Be a Long, Long Time" in parentheses) remains officially attached to it, but is often forgotten, overshadowed by the increasing ubiquity of the song's title—used, for example, to title a chart-topping *Definitive Hits* compilation in 2007 (styled *Rocket Man*) and to title the 2019 "biographical musical fantasy" film (styled *Rocketman*). Its bleak lyrics ("Rocket man burning out his fuse up here alone") have been buried by positive associations; John performed the song live at the 1998 launch of the space shuttle *Discovery*, for example. In this century, the song has steadily climbed the ranks of lists like *Rolling Stone's* "500 Greatest Songs of All Time," reaching that one's #149 in 2021. It is the heart of John's #1 hit "Cold Heart," the upbeat and

Figure 3.1 Space Cowboy. Record label MCA's promotional print ad for "Rocket Man," accompanying its "launch" as a single in April 1972. Elton John's outfit suggests that the stars in his future are not in outer space.

danceable Pnau creation that dominated club and radio play all over the world and all through the autumn of 2021, just as it was at the triumphant center of the John medley to which Nathan Chen skated to Olympic Gold in 2022 (again, despite its lyrics).

Meanwhile, the word "rocket" alone has been so closely associated with John as to serve as a parallel branding term. Within a year of the song's rise up the singles charts, John and his inner circle—including Taupin, Dudgeon, and Reid—launched Rocket Records, their own label. It was used to help launch comebacks for artists that Elton admired and was keen to mentor, just as they had inspired him in the 1960s—such as Kiki Dee, Neil Sedaka, and Cliff Richard (a topic to which we shall return in a later chapter). The first Elton John album on the label was *Blue Moves*, but most subsequent albums were not on Rocket. In other words, the label's role has been expansive, seldom used as an outlet just for John's own music, existing today primarily as a management company. *Rocketman* was produced by Rocket Pictures, the film and TV arm of the enterprise, established in 1996. In parallel, the official website's highly active fan club is called the Rocket Club. Elton's streaming "radio" show or podcast is called "Rocket Hour." An initiative begun in 2023 to raise funds for the Elton John AIDS Foundation is dubbed the Rocket Fund.

Meanwhile, the space agencies of this century have adopted "Rocket Man" as one of their theme songs, something in which John takes great delight. "Good morning, *Atlantis*, this is Elton John," began his wake-up message to the STS-135 astronauts in orbit in July 2011. "We wish you much success on your mission. A huge thank you to all the men and women at NASA who worked on the shuttle for the last three decades." The following year the European Space Agency played "Rocket Man" on the International Space Station, amazing Elton with a declaration—from André Kuipers, a Dutch medical doctor and astronaut who shared the ISS mission with a Russian cosmonaut and a NASA astronaut—that "this song has been an inspiration to many people who are interested in space, and especially those who wanted to become astronauts, including myself. It is certainly one of the most played songs here on the ISS, and we know it will accompany more astronauts into space in the future."

All this makes it unsurprising and fitting that in 2016, at a tribute concert to David Bowie, who had died weeks earlier, Elton sang "Rocket Man," merging it with a partial cover of "Space Oddity." The two songs seemed to perfectly match the yin/yang of funerals—with Bowie's expressing the mournful side and John's the hopeful. The moment seemed to work; Bowie's death had sent shockwaves through the pop cultural universe, and John's effort to connect to him seemed poignant. But skeptics sensed something else going on, something that I do not believe was intended by John—although I can see the argument made that a little dig was buried in the song choice. For the relationship between the two songs had not always been so harmonious as Elton's mashup. They have had extended shelf lives, but as sibling rivals, reflecting the uneasy relationship between their creators—the starmen, John and Bowie—and their respective catalogues.

"Space Oddity" was written in 1968 and recorded the following year, at a low point in Bowie's career. His debut album, 1967's *David Bowie* (released, later famously so, on the same day as *Sgt. Pepper's Lonely Hearts Club Band*) had failed utterly, as had the singles that preceded it and were drawn from it. Inspired by his viewing of Stanley Kubrick's 1968 movie, *2001: A Space Odyssey* ("I went stoned out of my mind, and it really freaked me out, especially the trip passage," Bowie later confessed), "Space Oddity" was a stab at a song that was musically more complex than his earlier compositions, yet still deploying some of the lyrical catchiness that characterized his debut album. The difference was that Bowie—depressed over his stalled career and breakup with Hermione Farthingale (whose name would grace the next album's track listing)—was in no mood for the humor that marked many of those earlier songs. That somberness did not stop Tony Visconti, the producer of the next album (and many future ones), from grumbling that "Space Oddity" was a "novelty record" and "a gimmick to cash in on the moonshot." Although an early demo of the song had been crucial to Bowie winning a new record contract, Visconti had rehearsed and sequenced a full album of songs when he was asked to add "Space Oddity" as the lead single for the album. He refused.

"There was a man who had just been in orbit a few weeks earlier," Visconti later explained. The topic and timing were just too much of "a cheap shot." Another producer recorded the single, which Philips rushed out on July 11, 1969. Ten days later, Neil Armstrong would be the first person to set foot on the moon. Yet, despite Visconti's gripe, the single made no initial impact, selling very slowly in the UK, taking four months to reach its #5 chart peak in November. In the US, it failed to make it into the Top 100. A Visconti-produced version of the song was squeezed in as the first track to the album, again given the title *David Bowie*, released in the UK the week after "Space Oddity" peaked on the singles chart. The album flopped. Released the following year in the US as *Man of Words/ Man of Music*, it flopped there too.

But there's a twist. In his annoyance over the last-minute addition of "Space Oddity" to the 1969 *David Bowie* album, Visconti had passed production duties to an in-house sound engineer at Decca, an accomplished twenty-seven-year-old who had already worked on Bowie material (he later admitted he was the gnome's voice on "The Laughing Gnome" and "responsible for some of the terrible jokes on it as well"). The engineer's name was Gus Dudgeon. Upon hearing how Dudgeon had produced the song, the twenty-two-year-old Elton John requested him for the album he was scheduled to record in the opening weeks of 1970 (to be released as *Elton John*). Thus, in addition to producing Bowie's first hit single, Dudgeon would also do the same for John (with "Your Song")—going on to produce John's run of ten successful albums of 1970–1976.

That meant, of course, that Dudgeon also produced "Rocket Man," a fact that only contributed to the notion that the song was a cheap knock-off, a "low-grade photocopy of the blueprint" of "Space Oddity." It isn't clear whether that was Bowie's own, immediate reaction, or whether the idea was planted in his head by a music journalist. "Other people can sing about space, too," Angie Bowie told her husband. But he apparently remained chagrined, and as a result, John and Bowie soon became "avowed frenemies." "We didn't exactly become pals," Bowie remarked after the two met when "Rocket Man" was still in the charts, "not really having much in common. Especially musically." A testiness would soon creep in. When Bowie referred to John in an interview as "the Liberace, the token queen of rock 'n roll," John retorted that "Bowie's a little crazed," that he "was obviously high" at the time, and that "he's a silly boy." Later John was more blunt, remarking that Bowie's snipe was "a cunty thing to say" (adding, "but then he's a cunt anyway").

There were, in fact, other factors at play in the development of the "passive-aggressive rivalry" between the two (to which we shall turn in due course). But the press and fans took to the notion that Bowie and John were two sides to the same coin of elaborately costumed rock stars, one arch and cool, the other goofy and gauche; and they saw that divide symbolized, even initiated in, the contrived rivalry of "Space Oddity" and "Rocket Man." For Bowie partisans, John's hit was a rip-off, a pale pop mimicry of the ever-modish original. To this day, Bowie writers still refer to "the 'Space Oddity'–indebted 'Rocket Man.'" After all, "Space Oddity" had come first. It was obvious, wasn't it?

Not quite. In the months following the 1969 moon landing, numerous space-themed songs had charted in the UK, US, and elsewhere—from Van

Morrison's breakthrough album *Moondance* to "In the Year 2525," which hit #1 on both sides of the Atlantic for Zager and Evans. Facing one-hit wonder status, that American duo broke up in 1971, and by 1972, Bowie also appeared to be a one-hit wonder. Furthermore, Bowie's one hit had only been a modest UK novelty success, failing to chart anywhere else except Ireland (where it reached #13). Why, therefore, pick on Bowie's old song as the one being ripped off?

By chance, in April 1972, a week after the release of "Rocket Man," Bowie put out the lead single from his new album, *Ziggy Stardust and the Spiders from Mars*. Titled "Starman," the song trailed "Rocket Man" into the UK charts: John's song entered the Top 10 in the first week of May, reaching its peak of #2 by month's end. In June, as "Rocket Man" slipped down and "Starman" slowly crept into the Top 50 and then Top 30, the two songs passed each other. On July 6, Bowie mimed "Starman" on *Top of the Pops*—the performance that is widely hailed as launching him to stardom in the UK, and even "changing the course of music forever" for its impact on future musicians (including a thirteen-year-old Kate Bush, who consequently pasted Bowie-as-Ziggy "on my bedroom wall next to the sacred space reserved solely for my greatest love, Elton John"). Two weeks later "Starman" reached its #10 chart peak.

Only in the wake of the success of "Starman," then, was the idea born that the hit that had immediately preceded it, "Rocket Man," had filched its concept from a much earlier Bowie song. "Starman," its parent album, and Bowie's new Ziggy persona drew a rapid and fervent fanbase that perceived Bowie as claiming a monopoly on the space metaphor. Asked about Bowie's newfound stardom at the time, John clearly understood that the rivalry was really about "Starman." "I know David has always wanted to be Judy Garland," he sniped—a reference to the octave-leap in the chorus to "Starman," reminiscent of (or borrowed from) "Over the Rainbow."

And what of the creative origins of "Rocket Man"? Any similarity between it and "Space Oddity" lies in their lyrics, and because Taupin/John songs originate with Taupin's words, the origin of "Rocket Man" must lie with Bernie. According to him, the title came to him from two sources: Ray Bradbury's 1951 short story "The Rocket Man" and a 1970 song of the same title by a psychedelic folk band from Florida, Pearls Before Swine, written by singer Tom Rapp (1947–2018) on the very day that Neil Armstrong set foot on the moon. Rapp lived close enough to Cape Canaveral to see NASA's rockets taking off. Having read Bradbury's story as a boy—as had Taupin—Rapp used the story as the narrative underpinning of his song.

All this was in Bernie's head late in the summer of 1971, as he drove from London to his parents' house in Lincolnshire, the stars visible on a clear night. As he later recalled:

> Driving the back roads, I began writing a song in my head about the drudgery of being an astronaut. As I thought about how to start the song, the first verse came to me at once: "She packed my bags last night pre-flight / Zero hour 9 am / And I'm gonna be high as a kite by then." But I didn't have a pad or pen in the car. I also couldn't dictate the words or call someone to take them down. That technology didn't exist yet. So, I repeated the lyrics over and over. I was trying not to lose my train of thought as I raced to my parents' house. When I arrived, I rushed in without saying hello. I was hunting for a pen and paper. I had never written that way before. Usually, I'd come up with a line and build from there. In this case, words to an entire verse fell out of my mind and onto the page.

A few months later, Taupin and John gathered with the band at the Château d'Hérouville. "Rocket Man" was the first song recorded for the new album. Early on their third morning in the château, Maxine placed her husband's typed-up lyrics on Elton's piano. While the band were eating breakfast, John found a melody in the Gm9 and C9 chords, expressing musically the sense of melancholy and isolation conveyed by Taupin's lyrics. Davey Johnstone finished eating and asked John to play the melody again, then picked up his guitar and instead of suggesting "a solo or anything that a regular lead guitar player might do," John later recalled, "he used a slide and played odd, lonely notes that drifted around and away from the melody. It was great." Dee Murray contributed a melodic bass line. Subtle drums and a quartet of acoustic guitar parts were added. The band—Johnstone, Murray, and drummer Nigel Olsson—sang backing vocals, intended by Dudgeon as a stopgap measure, only to discover that the lads made "the best in-house backing vocalists that anybody's ever had on record." The song was finished that afternoon. And the rest is history.

Only history, of course, changes. Past events aren't really set in stone because our perception of them constantly evolves. In retrospect, the notion of "Rocket Man" ripping off "Space Oddity," despite its long half-life in the Bowie universe, is plain silly and easily debunked. The competition was really between "Rocket Man" and "Starman," and even that was manufactured, a blinkered way of looking at two pop songs emerging at a time when space travel was a massive political and cultural phenomenon. Perhaps it mattered a little in 1972 because the notion seemed to irk both Bowie and John, and their fans; it served as an expression of a burgeoning rivalry between the two rising stars, even if much of that rivalry (like that between John and Rod Stewart, in reality close friends) was invented and stoked by the music press.

But it matters now for how the parallel metaphors of a Rocket Man and a Starman evolved to define Bowie and John, for how they both became starmen, but in revealingly different ways. Indeed, the metaphors are so important to their respective careers and ongoing cultural significance that it is almost impossible to understand either star without them. Over half a century later, the two songs most closely associated with space/stars are "Space Oddity" and "Rocket Man," which routinely top such lists.* In turn, the songs have shaped how Bowie and John are seen, although the stark difference in how they each used the metaphor has tended to be ignored.

As Bowie's following is so fanatical, fans and writers have listed and sorted and analyzed his catalogue of roughly 400 songs in many ways. Struck by the impression that space was not the obsession it appears to be, I made my own analytical lists, and sure enough, roughly twenty songs—just 5 percent of them—are space- or star-oriented. Even if we discount a few that don't use the metaphor—like "The Prettiest Star," a straight-up love song to future wife Angie—and include songs that lack space-related titles but reference the subject or metaphor—"Ashes to Ashes" being the most obvious—the total percentage remains about the same. For most of his career, Bowie wasn't focused on the space and star metaphor at all; from 1985 to 2001, for example, across eight albums only three songs make use of it. So why is the perception so prominent that Bowie's creative world was out in space?

The simple answer lies in the historical details: the vast majority (over 80%) of those space songs were released in the earliest (1969–1972) and latest (2002–2015) years of Bowie's career; and in the wake of his 2016 death, much of the focus was naturally on his swansong album (titled *Blackstar*, rendered as a black five-pointed star) and on breakthrough early songs, most

---

* A typical example is a list of some 400 such songs compiled by Frans von der Dunk, a Dutch law professor who holds the Chair in Space Law at the University of Nebraska. Over a number of years, student contributions were used to rank the songs: "Rocket Man" was consistently #1, with "Space Oddity" at #2 (and in 2016, after Bowie's death, a very close #2, with "Starman" climbing to #12).

notably "Space Oddity," "Is There Life on Mars?," "Starman," and "Ziggy Stardust." Major Tom, the protagonist of "Space Oddity," only returned momentarily, on "Ashes to Ashes," but as that was a #1 hit in 1980, the reference became magnified. That was in the UK; the song failed to chart in the US (as is often forgotten, Bowie did not place a solo single in the US Top 60 between 1975's "Golden Years" and 1983's "Let's Dance"). Major Tom's second return, in 1996's "Hallo Spaceboy," was not Bowie's doing at all; the fictional astronaut was added by Neil Tennant in the Pet Shop Boys remix that was released as a single.

But perception is everything, and in his final years and, especially, since his death, the perception has deepened that Bowie was not only heavily invested in the space metaphor, but that he was in essence an alien to be loved, a Starman waiting in the sky, "an otherworldly being who descended to our planet in January 1947 and departed it in January 2016." Fans have turned Bowie's early and later interest in the space/star metaphor into a "career-long fascination with outer space," extending it "into a comforting image" of him not really dead (as he sang on *Blackstar*'s "Lazarus," "look up here, I'm in heaven").

That said, Bowie's quest for his own brand only took off when he invented Ziggy Stardust as an androgynous star man persona. Despite the effectiveness of his killing off the persona, it lasted through four albums. Even after Ziggy seemed well buried by the rise of the Thin White Duke in 1975, Ziggy seemed to return the next year in a different form as the alien whom Bowie played in *The Man Who Fell to Earth*. The Thin White Duke made 1975 a far bigger year in the US for Bowie than all the Ziggy years, and the pop persona behind *Let's Dance*—then, and still, Bowie's best-selling album anywhere—made the early 1980s his peak period of global recognition and stardom. Yet Ziggy Stardust endured as the most deep-rooted and lasting persona, the one used to make sense of *Blackstar*, to make sense of his premature passing, to adorn his image with immortality. In the age of avatars and emojis, Ziggy's facial lightning bolt promises to persist as *the* icon representing Bowie, the Starman who fell to earth.

When Bowie sings, on the title track to his final album, "I'm a blackstar," he clarifies the metaphor with a series of denials of star identities. "I'm not," he repeats, "a white star," "a gangster" (gang-star), "a flam star," "a film star," or "a popstar." As Brooker notes, "Among all these negatives is a single positive": as Bowie explains, "I'm a star star." The expansion of the metaphor of alienation and regeneration in outer space, with Bowie descending as a Starman and then ascending to become a star in space, contrasts starkly with John's career-long doubling down on his image as a successful star man who rockets up the charts rather than into space.

Between these divergent visions of space and stardom, Bowie's was a more apt, postmodern reflection of the increasing diffusion and aimlessness of anything from the space program to celebrity culture to Western civilization—we could choose. But, for John, the star metaphor remained anchored to its Hollywood origins. His use of the metaphor grew lighter—as Bowie's grew darker. John's use of it became more broadly appealing and enduring, helping to reinforce a positive popular association between stardom and space flight.

But that association was also stretched far enough to be almost lost, with Elton becoming a very different category of "star star." The association of entertainment celebrity with celestial stars dates from the early days of cinema, while the space race of the 1960s and the simultaneous rise of the rock star gave it an added dimension. The music business was fully established as an industry by the time of John's imperial phase of 1971–1976, so that in 1973, when he was riding high in the charts all over the world, Joni Mitchell could write a song about David Geffen and pen the immortal phrase, "the starmaker machinery behind the popular song."

John's use of the white-star motif predates "Rocket Man," suggesting a vague constellation reference. Beginning in 1970, variants on that pattern appeared in John costumes for decades, and while it is tempting to see them as an overt "Rocket Man" reference, that is clearly not necessarily the case (see Figures 3.2–3.3). Furthermore, the simple, shiny white or golden five-pointed star evoked another image for the Americana-obsessed John and Taupin—the sheriff's badge of the old American West. The American sheriff's badge, in the form it developed in the nineteenth century to reference the stars on the US flag and to distinguish it from older sheriff's badges going back into medieval England, had seven points. No matter. The five-pointed star on the costume chosen for the launch of "Rocket Man" appeared again in various forms over the years, including when John received his Hollywood star on the sidewalk of the Walk of Fame in 1975; even with the cowboy hat replaced by a bowler hat, the visual references are overwhelmingly the old sheriff's badges (with the names of actors and directors of old Hollywood Westerns attached to the star badges) and the Hollywood star on the ground, with the stars of outer space too distant to be consciously evoked.

Figure 3.2 A Star Full of Stars. Elton John wore outfits decorated with stars as early as 1970 and continued to do so through 1975, when he received his own star on Hollywood Boulevard's Walk of Fame (photo credit: Wikimedia Commons).

In contrast to the lyrics of "Rocket Man," then, John and Taupin have since tended to eschew terminology and imagery that is unambiguously about outer space, instead turning the metaphor into one about terrestrial stardom. John's 1973 Hollywood Bowl concert, now considered one of his legendary shows, might have leaned into the imagery of his recent rocket-themed hit, but instead it was conceived as a spectacular homage—five pianos, a sixty-foot staircase, Elton's massive marabou-feathers headdress—to classic Hollywood and stars like Marlene Dietrich. By this time, John's onstage costumes had become outrageous and luxuriant, a unique blend of influences ranging from Liberace to the UK's glam fashion to the clothes used by the Black American acts he had backed in the late 1960s—including Patti LaBelle, who in 1973 reciprocated the influence when her Labelle trio donned silver space suits that, à la Elton, evoked stars on stage more than life in space. In the cultural world of Elton John, the term "star" has always referred overwhelmingly to celebrity rather than astronomical objects.

The effect is paradoxically to embrace the concepts both of launching up into the sky and being terrestrially resplendent. The name of John's private touring airplane during his 1970s imperial years—*Starship*—illustrates the

Figure 3.3 A Star Still Full of Stars. John wore star-decorated outfits throughout the 1970s and 1980s. By the time of this 1986 example, ornate head gear and costumes had long been an Elton tradition (photo credit: Pictorial Press Ltd / Alamy Stock Photo). In all cases, the stars evoke celebrity stardom more readily than they do outer space.

trick. The word "starship," originating in the 1880s but spreading rapidly as the space age dawned in the 1950s, refers to a vehicle for interstellar travel. But John's *Starship* jet was a vehicle to convey an earthly star from one arena of thousands of fans to another, and also to serve as a sign and symbol for that stardom. The star in his starship wasn't the destination, but the passenger.

The *Starship* always landed before too long, and the star metaphor tends to always take us back down to earth. That is even true of Bowie. In the years of struggle between "Space Oddity" and "Starman," Bowie wrote and released another song that seemed to use the star/space metaphor: "Life on Mars?" Considering the rhapsodic way in which the song is now acclaimed, it is hard to imagine that at the time it was simply a track buried on *Hunky Dory*, which failed to chart at all upon release in 1971, just as the album's only single, "Changes," likewise failed to chart. However, in the wake of the explosive success of *Ziggy Stardust*, its predecessor did start to sell, eventually reaching #3 in the UK in late 1972. In the US, *Hunky Dory* would eventually climb to #57 and "Changes" would reach #41—but not until 1974. Meanwhile, in June 1973, to ride the *Ziggy* bandwagon, "Life on Mars?" was released as a single in the UK (not in the US, where "Space Oddity" had been reissued instead). It also reached #3. Another Bowie space hit; but did it mine the same metaphor as the *Ziggy Stardust* songs?

Let us return briefly to Hermione Farthingale, the middle-class girl whom Bowie met and fell for at a mime workshop run by Lindsay Kemp in 1968. By August of that year, David and Hermione had moved in together, and with a mutual friend they soon formed an experimental folk trio. Called Turquoise, and then Feathers, the trio was not a success, and Bowie moved on to making a short film to showcase new songs. *Love You till Tuesday* was an amateur affair (often generously called "avant-garde" by Bowie biographers) that included a planned sequence for an early version of "Space Oddity," featuring Hermione as "a seductive space maiden" (as one writer later put it). But before the sequence and its song could be completed, Bowie and Farthingale had a row over her friendship with a Norwegian dancer—resulting in her leaving Bowie for the dancer (who then worked with Farthingale on a film called *Song of Norway*). (As Dwight/John had moved back to his childhood home after his breakup with Linda Woodrow, so too did Bowie briefly move back home after the Farthingale breakup.)

"I was totally head-over-heels in love with her, and it really sort of demolished me," Bowie later confessed. "It set me off on the 'Space Oddity' song." In other words, a song that had been already drafted as a song about an astronaut now took on deeper meaning as one about loss and isolation. And while songs written about Farthingale while they were together would appear on the parent album for "Space Oddity" (1969's *David Bowie*)—most notably "An Occasional Dream" and the beautiful gem, "Letter to Hermione"—that metaphor would be soon used for a new song. For "the girl with the mousy hair" in "Life on Mars?" was Farthingale, who was by then no longer living and working with Bowie, but instead "hooked to the silver screen."

The lyrics are packed with surreal images, making them open to various interpretations. Is the girl the main protagonist, seeking escape in the cinema from the crowded, media-saturated modern world? Bowie himself has said as much, although Farthingale denied that the girl could be her (on the rather spurious grounds that her hair wasn't mousy, and "I didn't live a fantasy life in films"). It seems clear to me that Bowie is both making a comment on media saturation *and* having a dig at Farthingale and the context of her "escape" from him to work in a film with her new boyfriend—"the film is a saddening bore" and it won't spare her disappointment. The point here is that the source and meaning of the song prevents its title from connecting to the space/star metaphor; it expresses, albeit very artfully, a very down-to-earth everyman sort of story. Similarly, the "God-awful small affair" of his breakup with Farthingale (or of her new relationship with the dancer) was set to dramatic music by Bowie, as if it were all a big affair. And that music was Bowie's angry poke at Paul Anka and Frank Sinatra: in 1968, Bowie was asked to write an English version of a recent Claude François hit, "Comme d'habitude," but his work was rejected and Anka rewrote the song as "My Way," which was a huge hit for Sinatra in 1969; "that really made me angry for so long," said Bowie, who fumed, "I can write something as big as that, and I'll write one that sounds a bit like it." Rejection, anger, inspiration, resurrection, all very human and terrestrial and not very space-like or star-related at all—although, of course, one could argue that such things are precisely what Bowie's star/space metaphor is *really* about.

This is where you expect me to produce a new theory about how "Rocket Man" is actually about an early moment of Taupin heartbreak. I cannot do that, I'm afraid. But let us consider two cover versions of the song by way of bringing it too back down to earth.

Kate Bush, who (as we've seen) has often cited Elton John as her first musical idol and the inspiration behind her piano-based songwriting, recorded a cover of "Rocket Man" in 1991. Her version is strangely affecting, more beautiful and poignant than the original, and yet more contradictory. Released as a single, it hit #12 in the UK, #2 in Australia, and was included on the tribute album *Two Rooms*. But the best way to appreciate it is through Bush's mimed performance on the BBC TV show *Wogan*. Because she doesn't alter the lyrics, she is the gender-bending rocket (wo)man who misses his wife; s/he is alone out in space, yet swaying and pouting as if seduction is on her/his mind; and the piano part, which one would expect to be highlighted as the Kate/Elton contact point, is absent, with her playing a ukulele (or pretending to) and the band playing a reggae rhythm. The ukulele playing was intended to evoke Marilyn Monroe in *Some Like It Hot*, as Bush recorded a cover of "Candle in the Wind" for the single's B-side, but the reference is a tad obscure, requiring that explanation.

Exactly where this version by Bush is taking us is not clear, but space has nothing to do with it. What she does make clear is the surprising elasticity of the song, suggesting that its increased use over the decades as something upbeat, positive, even celebratory, is not as paradoxical as it might seem.

And then there is the cover—if it can be called such—by William Shatner. It is a spoken word version, blessed not by John, as far as I can tell, but to some extent by Taupin, who introduced its live performance at the 1978 Science Fiction Film Awards. The context of the ceremony is obviously space, and Shatner delivers Taupin's words rather as if he were Captain Kirk. But Shatner and Kirk were always versions of each other. He overacts the lines, squinty-eyed from his own cigarette smoke, leaning forward in his dinner jacket, leaving us unsure if it is all a brilliant parody (with Taupin in on the joke) or the absurdly pretentious butt of future parodies (as it became); Taupin leaves us unsure by dismissing it (in his autobiography) as "an inexplicably surreal reading of the song." (Shatner himself has said it was "a joke" intended only for the live audience, and "not my proudest moment"; the version he later recorded for one of his albums, however, was not that different.)

But then, near the end of Shatner's rendition, he reveals a meaning to "Rocket Man" that has been staring us in the face all along. Just for a few seconds, he does a groovy, goofy little dance while pronouncing the title phrase as "rock-it man" and then "rock it, man!" And that, of course, in the end, is the significance of the song and its long life. Rock it, man, indeed!

4

Pride

Elton and David

"Philadelphia Freedom" (5:38, 1975)

Legendary tennis champion Billie Jean King is one of the few living people for whom John and Taupin have written a song, not a song about that person but one composed as an act of friendship. The context of that friendship, its nature and timing, are thus significant. "Philadelphia Freedom" was written for King in 1974, when she was the coach and leading player of a pioneering mixed-gender tennis team called the Philadelphia Freedoms. John gave the song an upbeat pop-disco vibe, imagining it as an anthem for the team, and he attended most of their home games, wearing the uniform and cheering on his friend the coach. But Taupin, asked by John to come up with words, was a little stumped. He only met King (whom he later called "a force of nature") through John, after the song was written. He knew nothing about tennis, nor was he very familiar with Philadelphia. The lyrics he delivered were consequently neither about the game nor the city—and anyway, by the time the song was released, the following spring, the team had moved location and become the Boston Lobsters.

No matter. "Philadelphia Freedom" was a worldwide smash. It was especially huge in the US, where it hit #1, helping to keep the momentum rolling on John's imperial phase, as the fourth of six consecutive #1 singles. It also caught a rising tide of American patriotism in the buildup to the Bicentennial, with its title phrase, and its chorus line—"from the day I was born, I've waved the flag"—as seemingly relevant and resonant country-loving buzzwords.[*]

---

[*] In the UK, the single did less well, peaking at #12, which some have argued was because John had refused to have the string section re-recorded for the British release, in accordance with Musicians' Union rules. More likely, I suspect, was the fact that the imagined Bicentennial connection did not resonate in Britain. Although I may be overanalyzing, as John's chart showings in the US were

Thus the very ambiguity of Taupin's lyrics—a vague ode to a free life—allowed the song to become an anthem of civic and nationalist pride in the mid-1970s. And yet the words also helped the song to grow into a different kind of anthem. As both King and John went from being closeted to out and vilified, and then to out and respected philanthropists, "Philadelphia Freedom" became gradually claimed—or recognized—"not simply as a gay anthem, but a pride anthem. It's a song about what it feels like when we manifest our truest, fullest, and freest selves."

Interestingly, the initial cultural context for the meeting of John and King was not homophobia, but sexism. Bobby Riggs, a former #1 tennis pro, winner of four Grand Slam titles, in his early fifties in the early 1970s, was very vocal in his belief that women did not belong on the tennis court at all; their place, said Riggs, was the kitchen. He could beat any woman of any age, he claimed. Billie Jean King quickly accepted the challenge, and in September 1973, she vanquished Riggs in straight sets (6–4, 6–3, 6–3) at "the battle of the sexes" in Houston's Astrodome. Elton John was there, and afterward they met. A few months later they played tennis together at a charity event (she went easy on him, unlike her handling of Riggs), and John offered to write a song in support of the team then managed by King, the Philadelphia Freedoms. "We talked and talked, and listened to music," King recalled, until John "finally said, 'I'd like to write you a song.'" Or perhaps it was the other way round: on different occasions, John confirmed that he made the original offer, but he has also said that it was King who asked him to write a song; "I couldn't refuse; I adored Billie Jean!" (see Figure 4.1).[†]

Taupin agreed to write the lyrics, but reluctantly, lacking the requisite knowledge and having been handed no more than a title. That title was "Philadelphia Freedom," without the "s" on the team's name, which seems to have been a tiny error with large consequences, as it encouraged Taupin to think more expansively. At the time (August 1974), John and Taupin and the band were at the Caribou Ranch studio in Colorado, writing and recording the *Captain Fantastic* album. Taupin's head was therefore full of words telling stories about his and John's origins (as we saw in Chapter 2).

---

consistently higher than in the UK during his 1970–1976 imperial phase (as discussed later; also see my Discography).

[†] Sources differ slightly on whether John and King met for the first time a few weeks before the Riggs match, or right after it; as they do on the detail of when the conversation took place that led to the song (was it at the 1974 Wimbledon Championship, e.g., or after it?).

Figure 4.1 Acoustic Set. Elton John and Billie Jean King, holding tennis rackets like guitars, in a classic Terry O'Neill photograph from the time of "Philadelphia Freedom." (Photo credit: Terry O'Neill / Iconic.)

Not surprisingly, then, he delivered lyrics that expressed Elton's liberation from being Reg in Pinner, leaving behind "the good old family home" (with he, Taupin, having done the same). Philadelphia became merely a metaphor for the freedom of a life cut loose from those roots: "I like living easy without family ties," Taupin had John sing. As conceived by Taupin, the song has nothing whatsoever to do with tennis, with the city of Philadelphia, with the battle of the sexes, or with gay liberation. Which was fine, Taupin later insisted, "as fifty percent of the people who liked it never even listened to the words"; they just loved that "it's got a good beat, man." Of course, for John, it could be composed, sung, produced, and promoted as if it were about any or all of those things.

To begin with, John decided the song should be excluded from *Captain Fantastic*. (I always thought that was a shame, and in my early teens I taped my own version of the album, with "Philadelphia Freedom" kicking off Side Two, and the rather grating "Better Off Dead" dropped to make room for "Freedom." I still think that makes for a better album. But there's no accounting for taste. And, after all, it is *his* album.) John wanted the song to be released as a stand-alone single, rightly convinced it would be an instant hit. Furthermore, he wanted Dudgeon to mix it as if it had been recorded in Philadelphia, an homage and echo of the "Philadelphia Sound" or "Philly Soul" sound that had been developed by Black Philadelphian songwriter-producers Kenny Gamble, Leon Huff, and Thom Bell. Gene Page—who had worked with Barry White, Aretha Franklin, the Temptations, and the Four Tops—was brought in for the orchestral arrangements. As Philly Soul was one of the cornerstones of disco, the song was the closest that John had yet come to making a disco record; it would certainly be the most successful. After it was recorded, but before it was released, John played a tape of it to King in the Philadelphia Freedoms locker room before a Denver match. At the end, he asked if she liked it. "I don't like it, Elton," she exclaimed. "I love it, love it, love it!" On the back of the single, John inscribed, "With love to B.J.K. and the music of Philadelphia."

If "Philadelphia Freedom" can lay claim to being one of John's great pride anthems, if not *the* such anthem of his, while neither being conceived nor initially received as one, so was John: that is, neither in his own mind (until he was about twenty) nor in the public's general perception (until he was about thirty) was he gay. The line connecting those points to Sir Elton being, in his own words, "the most famous poof in the world," was, of course, far from direct, straight, and easy.

"My friend wasn't in the slightest bit camp," Bernie has recalled of his early years with Reg. Admitting that in the late 1960s they were both virgins with virtually no understanding of human sexuality, Taupin noted that the era's "grating stereotypes" of homosexuality had no bearing on the "hardcore soccer fan," with "eclectic musical tastes"; the Reg who was "tough as old boots." Insisted Taupin, "Reg was everything that screamed 'not gay.'" Nonetheless, there was an early, clumsy pass made by Reg, at which Bernie laughed, and they moved on—their creative bond already strengthened by the fact that they were *not* "sexually like-minded." And just as well. For otherwise, their friendship and working relationship would have "eventually crashed and burned."

But whereas Taupin had the freedom, as a straight, white man, to explore his sexuality and channel its highs and lows into his creative outlet, John was trapped. As Dwight transformed himself into John, he began the agonizingly protracted process of coming to terms with his own sexuality and determining how to present himself (or selves) to the outside world. It took about twenty-five years. That was in part because Elton John was a created character, promoted as a teen idol and rock star, with an incompatible homosexual identity relegated to Dwight's secret, private life. Even if the secret was an open one in the industry—Elton's manager, John Reid, was his domestic partner from 1972 to 1976—the pressure to present oneself as straight and single was relentless and wretched.

It was also because the pop and rock industry in the 1970s and 1980s, along with the culture it fostered and fought to defend, "was dominated by white men at record companies and radio stations and onstage," targeting "white men and boys," and celebrating "heterosexual love" (in the words of Madonna's recent biographer). Some Black artists broke through to reach white audiences, thus receiving "crucial industry financial support" (because they made the industry money). Women were admitted too, "expected to be sexy but not sexual, with an aim of titillating an audience raised on looking at women, not listening to them." And if "gays and lesbians wanted to make music, there were two rules; they could not be out, and their lyrics had to be so obtuse as to render them indistinguishable from heterosexual material."

As the danger of being "out" affected women as much as men, "women performers who chose to be open about their lesbianism invariably lost the chance to reach a broader audience," Gillian Gaar noted of the 1970s and 1980s. Elton was keenly aware of this, not only from his female friends in the world of sport, like King, but also from friends in the music business. Because gay women were obliged to be closeted, or at least reticent and ambiguous in talking about their private lives, all women who were similarly reticent were assumed to be covert lesbians.

Kiki Dee—whose career John revived in the 1970s with new albums on Rocket Records and with their #1 duet "Don't Go Breaking My Heart" ("Keek, darling," John still calls her)—is one example. She lived for a while in the 1970s with John's guitarist Davey Johnstone but has never married or had children, and she has been close to Elton for the last half century; and so "a lot of people think I'm gay," she said in 2008, but "I'm not." Nonetheless, the perceived ambiguity surely hurt her career. Similarly, Detroit rocker Suzi Quatro, who is also not gay, dressed like a biker in the 1970s and found that her chart success as a leather-glad glam artist in the UK and Australia could not be replicated in her home country; there her image as "a tomboy, lank-haired, tight-bottomed and (twice) tattooed" (as Philip Norman put it in 1974) ran against the acceptable stereotype of pop/rock women. *Rolling Stone* dismissed her as a "pop tart" and *NME* called her "punk *Penthouse* fodder," but Quatro would not give in to the male wishful thinking that she sell herself as sex-on-stage—the path that artists from Donna Summer to Kate Bush found themselves placed upon, and from which they then fought hard to escape.

Female artists were thus caught between homophobia and sexism. As Gaar put it, "at a time when male performers such as David Bowie, Elton John, and Queen's Freddie Mercury were toying with personae that freely questioned acceptable 'masculine' and 'feminine' behavior, such freedom for women came at a high price." Fair enough, but Bowie is the odd man out on that list in a way that matters much to the Elton story. John was forced into living a tortured life of identity ambiguity. Bowie, as a straight man, enjoyed the luxury of testing the waters of androgyny and bisexual ambiguity. John rather resented him for that, for as a closeted gay man, John was obliged to sing another man's straight love songs, or to sing disguised gay love songs.

It is worth spending another moment with Bowie, in order to understand how the story of his alleged sexuality in the 1970s and early 1980s would have struck somebody like Elton John. "I'm gay and always have been, even when I was David Jones," is the famous line in the 1972 *Melody Maker* interview, taken by Bowie apologists to be a "self-outing" of great "courage." But was it? First, the word "gay" was still mainly understood in Britain in 1972 to mean "happy" or "bright." Its modern use in the gay community was decades old, but that community and its culture was largely unknown to the general public; homosexuality had only been decriminalized five years earlier. That's not to say that he meant "I'm happy" or expected the comment to be read that way; but the concept was far vaguer and the confession less absolute in 1972's Britain than it would be even five years later. In other words, this was another case of Bowie trying to be *nepantla* (see Chapter 2).

Indeed, that takes us to the second point: at the time of the 1972 interview, Bowie had a wife and "baby son," both discussed, making the confession really one of bisexuality; and later that year he told Cameron Crowe in *Rolling Stone*, "It's true. I am bisexual. But I can't deny I have used that fact very well," and he went on to tell a shocking story of bringing home from school "some very pretty boy" to be "neatly fucked on my bed upstairs." From the 1970s through to his second marriage in 1992, Bowie would be associated with many women, but the stories about dalliances with men were all or mostly that—stories—and like the one he told Crowe, they strain credibility, partly because Bowie seems to be so transparent about their purpose as publicity fodder. He shocked when he could and felt the need, but as one biographer noted, "the fair-weather bisexual Bowie would distance himself" from such confessions "when the mood hit him"—something that "actual gay stars" could not do so easily, if at all.

Third, therefore, the 1972 confession was arguably a kind of performance piece, a "set up" (in Shaar Murray's words), timed with the end of the recording of *Ziggy Stardust* and as part of the preparation for its release. The "superstructure" of Ziggy comprised the album and concerts; the media events, like that interview and its "seismic" impact, were "the real masterpiece artwork." Asked by *Newsweek* in the autumn of 1972 about his sexuality, he called it "irrelevant. I'm an actor, I play roles." As Bowie's tour manager Tony Zanetta later observed, "David sensed that there was something attractive about being a sexual outlaw," and he made that part of the Ziggy character, in order to appeal to "alienated kids all over the world, like the fat girls and the gay boys that didn't fit in." In 1993, Bowie admitted that he had "wanted to imbue Ziggy with real flesh and blood and muscle" and "be him," but Bowie himself was neither gay nor "a real bisexual," and that the Ziggy persona made Bowie "a closet heterosexual."

So, not surprisingly then, Bowie sought to backpedal the confession over the years. "I was quite proud that I did it," he later said, "but I didn't want to carry a banner for any group of people. . . . Being approached by organizations. I didn't want that." He told *Rolling Stone* in 1983 that "the biggest mistake I ever made" was his 1972 claim "that I was bisexual." For some, the 1983 interview was "a really devastating moment." In the age of the rise of AIDS and its stigmatized gay victims, many in the gay community felt betrayed by Bowie's dismissal of his youthful experimentation ("Christ, I was so *young* then; I was *experimenting*"), a perceived perfidy that seemed apiece with his conservatively male *Let's Dance* persona. He has ever since been called "an opportunist," a pretender who "trafficked" in gay culture, even "a closet homophobe who cynically manipulated his own sexuality."

Cultural critic Camille Paglia understood the context of that "censoriousness" but objected to it on the grounds that Bowie was an artist. He therefore "has no obligation to say, 'I'm gay,'" she said. "His only obligation is to his imagination." More recently, with the rise of terms and concepts articulating "a fluidity of sexuality," Bowie has been defended as an explorer of such concepts, rather than a manipulator, "one of the first famous gay allies." "Bowie gave me permission to be me," Boy George has said. "To hell with whether he disowned us later," said Tom Robinson (one of Britain's first openly gay musicians, who co-wrote several songs with Elton at the turn of the 1980s); intention didn't matter, as "even a cynical appropriation of gay culture can open doors for others."‡

Regardless of how generous we wish to be with Bowie, or how much we are willing to dismiss the details and focus on the positive impact of any influential gay icon, it is hard not to see how Elton did not see him as a bit of a chancer. With every passing year of John's imperial phase, there was increasing pressure to keep the lid on something that John increasingly wanted to let out. The resulting "ever-changing mood swings" were the result of Elton being "angry and unhappy inside" (in Bernie's words). It is even possible, albeit not evidenced, that in 1976, seeing Bowie's star having risen in the US despite his bisexuality confession four years earlier, John imagined it safe for him to follow suit (even if he resented him for it). If so, he surely

---

‡ This debate is hardly just about Bowie, or one restricted to the previous century; in the mid-2020s, there is fierce discussion over Taylor Swift's LGBTQ-friendly signaling. Is she thinly masking her bisexuality, or making bold—or misguided—attempts at "allyship," or (echoes of the Bowie critique here) "a straight woman co-opting queer aesthetics and narratives to promote a commercial product"? I imagine there might be some truth to all three.

did not know what Bowie himself would not articulate for years, that the bisexuality confession was not "a mistake in Europe, but it was a lot tougher in America." Talking to an interviewer and fans in 2002, Bowie continued, "America is a very puritanical place, and I think it stood in the way of so much I wanted to do."

Certainly, Bowie-as-Ziggy had limited success in the US; the albums did fairly well, but the singles—a mark of radio play and mainstream popularity—did not, most tanking completely and none rising higher than #64. Significantly, only when Ziggy was well dead and Bowie became the Thin White Duke, with an album of white "Philly Soul" called *Young Americans*, did he crack radio and the charts ("Fame" even went to #1). That impression of American homophobia correlating with chart success is confirmed by the reaction to the interview Elton gave with *Rolling Stone*'s Cliff Jahr in New York in the autumn of 1976 (see Figure 4.2).

John had been sold to the American public as straight for years—and as available to young female fans, his single status explained by his shyness and his busy schedule as a star. His outrageous stage costumes, the "flamboyance and kinkiness" of his performance persona, was seen as part of rock's new excess, the "straight rock audience" clutching him with "an embrace that hovered somewhere between acceptance and ignorance"—but in the US far more the latter. In 1975 alone, *16 Magazine* gave him three covers, with headlines like "ELTON—SHY GUY!" and "ELTON HOT SECRETS" (flip back to Figure 2.1). At first, his interview with Jahr seemed to be on point, as he spoke of his loneliness, having only "my vinyl" to fall in love with at home; "I crave to be loved." But then he blurted out, "I haven't met anybody that I would like to settle down with—of either sex." Seeing an opening, Jahr asked if that meant John was bisexual. He said he was, that "there's nothing wrong with going to bed with somebody of your own sex. I think everybody's bisexual to a certain degree. I don't think it's just me. It's not a bad thing to be."

Rolling Stone editor Jann Wenner (who would not himself come out until the 1990s) asked John if the interview could be run, and as a cover story. John approved. It had an immediate negative impact in the US—"tectonic ramifications," as one biographer put it. John's records were burned in public, and his songs were banned from radio stations, especially in the US South, where DJs received calls demanding they stop playing records by "faggots." He was dropped permanently by *16 Magazine*, and offended readers wrote offensive letters to *Rolling Stone*, decrying the "decrepit morality" of the "gross perverter of the sacred." John's imperial phase was over; his sales in the

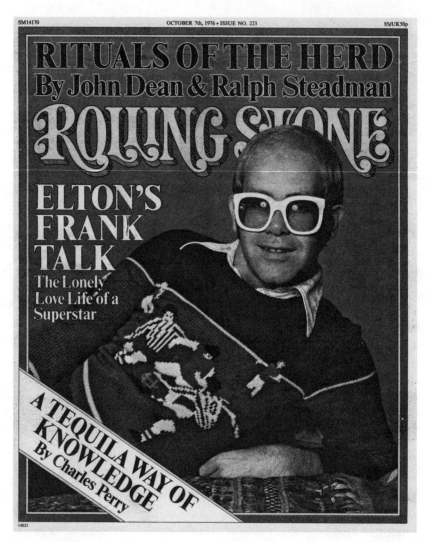

Figure 4.2 Frank and Elton. The cover of the October 7, 1976, issue of *Rolling Stone*, in which Elton confessed to being "bisexual"—to the extended detriment of his career in the US.

US would never recover (as we shall see in more detail later). It was a "monumental revelation," his friend Rod Stewart said, that created "a turning point in his career."

For the next fifteen years, John existed in a miserable middle space—not Bowie's carefully manipulated *nepantla* status, but a liminal zone where he suffered the worst of both worlds, both mocked for being gay and denied the

Figure 4.3 Nutty Butty. The January 16, 1978, *People* cover that showed an attempt of sorts to walk back the confession of sexual orientation that Elton had made in *Rolling Stone* eighteen months earlier.

full freedom of being out. Efforts to backpedal the 1976 confession only made him more of a possible figure of fun (see Figure 4.3). In Britain, his sexuality was tolerated—it seemed to have little impact on record sales, which more closely tracked the quality of the product—but was at the same time ridiculed.

He had become chairman of Watford Football Club in 1976. And so for years the crowds greeted him whenever he was in the owner's box with rounds of "Elton John's a homosexual," to the tune of "John Brown's Body." "He's bald! He's queer! He takes it up the rear!" chanted football (soccer) fans. Watford became the "poof" team. When they played away, rival teams sang—to the tune of "My Old Man Said Follow the Van"—"Don't bend down, when Elton's around, or you'll get a penis up your arse."

He had anticipated all this in the interview with Jahr, saying (with a laugh), "It's going to be terrible with my football club. It's so hetero, it's *unbelievable*. But I mean, who cares!" But when it happened, over and over, did he care? Witnessing the chanting at games, another interviewer asked John, did it bother him? "Very nice when it's sung by fifteen hundred Halifax supporters and it echoes around the stadium," he sighed; but no, "I can take all that until the cows come home."

No doubt he could take it, but as he detailed with poignant good humor in his autobiography, he didn't see that he had much choice. And the homophobic weaponization of his half-out status by the press and public was clearly a factor in the deepening of his addictions. His records, meanwhile, revealed here and there the ambiguity of his status. This was particularly the case in the very five years or so after the 1976 *Rolling Stone* interview, when John and Taupin were on a hiatus (the songs written with Taupin had tended to mask the issue, as it was common knowledge that Taupin wrote about his own straight sex and love life). "Big Dipper," one of the tracks on 1978's *A Single Man*, whose lyrics were all penned by Gary Osborne, was so overtly and joyfully gay that it was cut from the version of the album released in the Soviet Union. It was hard to miss the camp humor of the song; the Russians didn't, and presumably neither did the Watford football team, who chanted the backing vocals.§

One of the songs co-written with Tom Robinson, titled "Elton's Song," was a "melancholy depiction" (John's phrase) of unrequited love. (Written in 1979, it was included on 1981's *The Fox*.) The lyrics were not gendered, but the press seized on the identity of the lyricist and on the video—directed by Russell Mulcahy and banned on British television—in which both protagonists are schoolboys. "ELTON'S GAY VIDEO SHOCKER," ran the tabloid headlines. The next album, *Jump Up!*, included another John/Osborne song

---

§ Russian censors also chopped "Part-Time Love," retitling the album, now just nine tracks, *Poyot Elton John* (Elton John sings).

that was gay-themed, but its video was not. That was enough, it seemed, to permit "Blue Eyes" to be a worldwide hit (Top 10 in numerous countries, #12 in the US) and to earn a Grammy nomination. All that, even though a photograph of the subject of "Blue Eyes"—Vance Buck, "a sweet blond boy from Virginia," as John remembered this ex-boyfriend of his who tragically succumbed to AIDS—was included on the album's inside cover, right under the lyrics to the song. A few years later, 1985's "Nikita" pulled off the same trick. As mentioned earlier, this love song to an East German border guard was not gendered in the lyrics, allowing the video to turn the guard into a woman in the video—and the song to be an even bigger hit than "Blue Eyes."

Meanwhile, less than a decade after singing that his life had been "saved" by being persuaded not to marry the unfortunate Linda Woodrow, John went to the altar with a woman. In December 1983, the John team began to assemble on the island of Montserrat in order to record in the new year the album that would become *Breaking Hearts*. German tape operator Renate Blauel was promoted to sound engineer. Although Elton had his current boyfriend, Gary, with him, he found himself enjoying Renate's company more and more, and the two became fast friends. By the end of January, he'd proposed, and she had "understandably laughed it off" (as he recalled). When the team relocated to Sydney the next month, to mix the new album and start touring, he proposed again. Elton's friends and team members were stunned when one night he and Renate came back from dinner with an engagement announcement—which was "greeted by a sea of aghast faces, not least Gary's" (Elton again).

Bernie recalled that in the 1980s, Elton was "in the habit of flying his infatuations in and out of whatever location we found ourselves in. He seemed to be in love with someone different every week." But the objects of his affection were usually young men. Despite grave misgivings, John's friends went along with the wedding; the pair of best men were his manager and ex-boyfriend John Reid, and Taupin. John called Rod Stewart the next day: "I've got married, dear. To a woman." "The only possible response," Stewart later said, "was 'What the fuck?'" Explained Elton, "I just thought it was the right thing to do, dear."

That was Stewart's memory of it. In John's version, Rod, too tied up to attend the wedding, sent a telegram referencing his friend's recent hit: "You may still be standing, dear, but the rest of us are on the fucking floor." The marriage was inevitably not a success, which John insists was entirely and obviously his fault, "down to me and me alone," the cocaine-fueled and rotating-boyfriends lifestyle continuing unabated through the decade. Their 1988 divorce "was the right thing to do, but it was a horrible feeling. I'd broken the heart of someone I loved and who loved me unconditionally, someone I couldn't find fault in in any way."

That repeated phrase—"the right thing to do"—stands out. In the 1980s, it haunted John. Having thought it justified marriage to Blauel, it then seemed to fit the divorce. Meanwhile, his lifestyle made him one of the favored punching bags of Britain's tabloid press. When they couldn't find new stories with which to mock John, they made them up. The homophobic slander of "ELTON IN VICE BOYS SCANDAL" was followed by "ELTON'S SILENT ASSASSINS," which added allegations of animal abuse to the stew of smears. He sued, winning a £1 million judgment against *The Sun*, and a front-page headline the same size as the original slander: "SORRY ELTON." Then he sued *The Daily Mirror* over their "ELTON'S DIET OF DEATH" story, winning £850,000. "You can say I'm a talentless, bald old poof, if that's your opinion," John later said. "But you can't tell lies about me. Or I'll see you in court."

All sums won in court were given to charity; doing the right thing. Of course, only once he was out of rehab and his lifestyle shifted did the press begin to treat him differently. Changes in the law and the precedent of lawsuits like those won by John were also a factor, but the emerging new Elton, then Sir Elton, of the 1990s gave the piranhas of the press far, far less on which to nibble. John describes his journey into and out of rehab in 1990 with such eloquence that it would do it a disfavor to summarize it here. And the point for our purposes lies not in all the details, but in the fact that four events combined to transform John, to rehabilitate him in multiple ways, and lay the foundation for the final long phase of his career.

The first was that successful completion of rehab, and the emergence of a sober Dwight/John. The second was his reaction to the plight of Ryan White—an American teenager who contracted AIDS through a blood transfusion and was ostracized and abused by his hometown of Kokomo, Indiana. White was victimized by such shocking bigotry that John was inspired to help and befriend Ryan and his family, thereby setting John on the path to helping himself and then others, a path that led to the Elton John AIDS Foundation (EJAF). Third, he met Canadian filmmaker and advertising executive David Furnish; John's sobriety made their stable relationship and eventual marriage possible, in turn supporting John's sobriety and his career (Furnish became John's manager and EJAF chair).

Finally, John may well have agreed to write the music for *The Lion King* if none of the above three things had happened (and he actually met Furnish between taking on the soundtrack job and the film being released). But I cannot help imagining that the final product would not have been as successful; it remains the highest grossing animated film of all time, and the soundtrack has sold over 18 million copies worldwide, outselling all John's albums since his 1974 *Greatest Hits*. More important, it became a cornerstone to John's new image. It would have been hard to reconcile the John of the 1980s with the composer of music for a children's animated film; in the 1990s, it was not, and *The Lion King* in turn helped make that change permanent.

In the 1990s, then, John was able to push gently against the era's "don't ask, don't tell" culture by being out—but in a way that defied gutter press stereotypes regarding "gay star" debauchery (over which John had suffered in the 1980s, along with Boy George, Freddie Mercury, and others). That is, the "out" John was a conservative figure. He became, and remains, the post-rehab-sober founding president of a massive charitable organization, committed to a monogamous relationship with Furnish (the David of the chapter's title), to whom he is still married, with two sons. His disguised "gay" songs have faded away, replaced by songs about mature love (unconcerned with sexual orientation). At the same time, John has enthusiastically embraced a new professional identity as a composer of scores for Broadway and Disney musicals—something often associated with gay artists, rightly and wrongly, but no longer with the stigma of earlier decades (see the next chapter).

Elton John's sexual identity has always impacted and influenced the twists and turns of his career—when he was closeted, when he was agonizingly half-out, and as someone fully and happily out—in complex and often surprising ways.

In September 2022, on the South Lawn of the White House, President Joe Biden presented Sir Elton John with the National Humanities Medal. The pretense under which John and the assembled audience gathered is not clear, but he seemed genuinely surprised and moved to the brink of tears. Biden's speech hit the notes that one would expect from a politician, emphasizing public service and family. "Throughout his career, Elton found his voice, not only his voice but his voice to help others, and help them find their voice,"

declared Biden. He briefly mentioned the influence of American genres of music on John, and how John's music in turn impacted America. "To David and the boys, thank you for sharing your husband and Dad with us," he ended, "And to Elton, on behalf of the American people, and I sincerely mean this, thank you for moving the soul of our nation."

Sitting at a grand piano, John called out "the heroes" who have helped "my AIDS Foundation" and those who work "on the frontline, teachers, nurses" and others who help fight the disease. He then played "Your Song," whose lyrics, birthed in minutes by a teenage Taupin, bear a clumsy naïveté that has permitted the song a universality of appeal and application. It was thus the ideal signature song to soundtrack a ceremony that symbolized who and what John had become.

A year later, the UK government expanded opt-out HIV testing. In another public ceremony, Sir Elton was there, giving a small speech, urging Britain's politicians to fight to make their country the first in the world to end new AIDS cases, "to defeat this awful virus." He explained how his embrace of his own identity had led him to take up a leadership role in this particular battle:

> The reason I started the Elton John AIDS Foundation in 1992 was because in the 1980s when AIDS was so prevalent everywhere in America and Britain and starting to spread globally, I did the odd benefit here and there, and I thought I was doing my bit. But I wasn't doing my bit. I was a gay man who wasn't marching with ACT UP in Atlanta or New York. I was letting my brothers and sisters down. I was ashamed of myself. And I thought, I've got to do something for people that have died, my friends, people who are living with this horrible disease.

Set up "at my breakfast table in the kitchen in Atlanta," the charitable foundation would go on to raise over half a billion dollars by the time it was thirty years old, making a significant impact on the battle against the disease. No other charity has raised as much for this cause. Chaired by Furnish, the EJAF has leveraged the steady fame of its founder into a consistent expansion of fundraising efforts and cooperative partnerships with governments and other organizations. In 2023, for example, the Rocket Fund became the latest such campaign, aimed at using the "rocket man" aspect of Elton's brand to raise $125 million in three years.

Meanwhile, the friendship between King and John forged through the success of "Philadelphia Freedom" has lasted for decades, with the pair supporting each other's causes in various ways. Since 1993, they have annually co-hosted a celebrity charity tennis event called Smash Hits—a reference to both of their careers. Some of the biggest tennis stars in the world compete for Team Elton against Team Billie. For years, "competitive as ever" by his own admission, Sir Elton did his best to take part. By this century, the event was routinely raising a million dollars a year for the EJAF.

Herein lies one of the keys to understanding Elton John as a public and pop culture figure—to understanding both how he has survived so well as such, and how his story reflects the larger changes in society. For consistency's sake, let us consider Bowie for a moment. As one biographer put it, "Someone as sexually active as Bowie"—"one of rock 'n' roll's most heroic pansexual substance abusers"—"must have had a there-but-for-the-grace-of-God attitude throughout the AIDS crisis." Having survived, he then entered "a middle age marked by marriage, sobriety and fatherhood." So too, of course, did John, but with the difference that he set about using his "money and power to help combat the disease in part as a sort of extended gesture of gratitude" for having been spared the fate of friends like Freddie Mercury, "despite similar debauchery."

In other words, John's mature persona left behind his earlier lifestyle, but not its defining context. When Bowie became a middle-aged family man, he ceased performing sexual identities, or even discussing them—and indeed, after a serious health crisis, he ceased performing identities or personas of any kind, retiring for a decade to a degree to which John is clearly incapable. But as John became the conservative figure that he now is, he remained "the most famous gay man on the planet" (as activist Mark Segal called him in 2004; or, as John himself put it the same decade, and quoted above, "the most famous poof in the world!"). His spouse is a man, and his charitable foundation has for decades confronted the stigma of a disease that was marginalized by public health policies because it was "the gay cancer." But he has incorporated that aspect of his identity and life into being the fundraising president of a charitable organization, a highly affluent corporate CEO, married with children—all without contradiction. How has that been possible? Arguably, it has been possible because of society's shifting attitudes toward homosexuality—specifically, its increased acceptance as a variant on heterosexual lifestyles, rather than a stereotypically gay or countercultural lifestyle. But I don't think it is being too generous to Elton John to claim that he has also helped make that change possible.

5

For All Seasons

Elton and Rod

"Electricity" (3:30, 2005)

The last Elton John solo Top 40 hit in the UK (so far) was "Electricity."* His 63rd such entry in his home country, it peaked at #4 in 2005. But its significance goes beyond the chart history that matters so much to him (a topic to which we turn in a later chapter). In addition to being a fine example of late-period Elton pop—added in 2005 to his 2004 country-tinged pop album, *Peachtree Road*—it also saw him enter his second decade as a highly successful composer of songs for musicals, starting with 1994's *The Lion King*.

"Electricity" was part of the score for *Billy Elliot: The Musical*—a film-based stage musical for which John wrote all the music. The lyrics for John's musicals have not been written by Bernie Taupin, but instead have come from collaborators in the world of musical theater: Tim Rice was lyricist for *The Lion King*, for their 1999 *Aida*, and for the 2000 animated film *The Road to Eldorado*; Lee Hall wrote the screenplay and lyrics for *Billy Elliot*, as well as the script for *Rocketman*—a jukebox musical that I suggest should be seen in the same creative category as John's musical theater work. This pattern of collaboration with lyricists marked a break, then, from John singing about his and mostly Taupin's personal lives. His work in musicals thus represents both a genre evolution, an arrival at a destination that seems natural to him for various reasons, as well as the completion of a full circle—back to his origins as a composer-for-hire of piano melodies. Indeed, that circle was

---

* Emphasis on "solo," and one might add "original," as Elton was #3 in the UK in 2009, but as a featured artist on Ironik's hip-hop hit "Tiny Dancer"; #1 twice in 2021, but with Dua Lipa and Pnau ("Cold Heart") and with Ed Sheeran ("Merry Christmas"); and #3 in 2022, but with Britney Spears ("Hold Me Closer"). His last solo original Top 40 hit in the US Billboard Hot 100 was 1995's "Blessed"—but he has since had collaborative US hits and appeared on specialist Billboard charts.

loosely referenced by the choice of B-side to the UK "maxi-single" release of "Electricity": "Your Song," that first hit and his most enduring tune.

What is "Electricity" about? *Billy Elliot* was based on the 2000 movie of the same title, also written by Lee Hall. The musical stage version premiered in London's West End in 2005, its success spawning productions all over the world, from Broadway to Sydney, Spain to Korea. The plot centers on a motherless eleven-year-old boy in working-class County Durham, who, against the violent backdrop of the 1984–1985 UK miners' strike, starts taking ballet classes with the girls—unknown to, and then against the wishes of, his father, a striking miner. "Electricity" is sung toward the show's end, when Billy auditions for the Royal Ballet School in London. The song and its parent work are thus about overcoming obstacles in order to fulfill one's dreams. The song's title refers specifically to the feeling Billy tries to express when he is dancing: "Electricity sparks inside of me and I'm free, I'm free!"

Billy Elliot offers a relatively sympathetic indictment of working-class masculinity while celebrating the right to fight gender stereotypes and hegemonic norms—the right to be yourself. That theme, set in England no less, resonated in obvious ways with Elton John. The fit seems right, just as Elton on stage in a tutu celebrating the musical's success seems like a happy ending not just to the play, but to Elton's own personal and musical journey (see Figure 5.1).

As an Elton song, therefore, "Electricity" succeeds because John infuses Hall's words with his own emotion—just as he has done for decades with Taupin's words—turning that feeling from one about dancing to one about singing, playing the piano, and performing music. The song is an exemplary one in the John canon, expressing his relationship to all the genres he has explored, while also representing the genre that is, in the end, his natural home: musical theater pop.

That is a very far cry from where Elton began. Indeed, what genre of music *does* he make? For his oldest fans, he is—or once was—a rock star. For others, he writes great pop songs. For fans who were just the right age when *The Lion King* came out, he writes songs for children's films and musical theater. For some fans of those musical theater numbers, John also has a catalogue of older songs that fit right in—regardless of whether or not other people call them classic rock. Put the question to an internet browser, and the answer will be pop and country. He even has an association with R&B (a topic that is the focus of the chapter to follow). There may be no simple answer, but there

Figure 5.1 Tutu Too. On various occasions, in theaters in multiple countries—as here, in the Victoria Palace, on the third anniversary of the play's London run—Elton John has donned a tutu and joined the *Billy Elliot the Musical* cast on stage for the curtain call. (Photo credit: PA Images / Alamy Stock Photo.)

are two lines of argumentation that combine to offer a complex but revealing explanation.

One is to emphasize John's identity as a pianist, one who composes and performs at the piano, permitting him to explore a particular range of genres—to be, to borrow a phrase from John/Taupin's "Idol" (an absolute gem from 1976's *Blue Moves*), "a man for all seasons." The piano has permitted John to be, for example, a pop singer and balladeer who compares revealingly to Billy Joel—with whom he toured on and off for sixteen years starting in 1994 (the Face to Face Tour pairing of the "Rocket Man" and the "Piano Man" was the most lucrative concert duet tour in music history). But

Joel has roots in rock—in his late teens he was in the psychedelic rock bands the Hassles and Attila—and he often cites Little Richard's rocking piano style as a key inspiration. As indeed does John, who has talked of Liberace and Little Richard as muses on different points along the piano players' pop/rock spectrum. But whatever the roots and the routes taken, the piano is omnipresent and in the center.

John's instrument is thus one illuminating way to approach the question of genre, albeit an approach that tends to bury the question. From start to finish—from those famous photographs of a little Reggie sitting at the family upright with his signature grin (peek ahead to Figure 9.3), to the somewhat portly septuagenarian wearing the same grin at his piano stool during his *Farewell Yellow Brick Road* concerts—Elton has been attached to the piano. The other common instruments of popular music have dominant genre associations: electric guitar with rock, drums with jazz and rock, saxophone with jazz and pop. In contrast, the piano's roots in classical music and its presence at the dawn of all genres lend it a kind of pan-genre ubiquity. Elton can thus move between pop and rock, country and R&B, AOR and musical theater, as long as he remains attached to his piano—in terms of both composition and performance. (That is largely why *Victim of Love* is his greatest failure of an album; he neither composed its music on piano nor played a note on the album.)

The other line of argumentation is to take a more historical perspective, and that is our focus in the rest of this chapter. John moved through genres from the end of the 1960s into the twenty-first century. His motivation was partly personal, a drive to explore his influences. But he also responded to the surrounding shifts in popular culture and music, seeking to navigate the choppy waters from 1970s rock through the upheaval of disco and punk to the pop 1980s and beyond. Elemental to those changes was the way in which popular music reflected homophobia, misogyny, and racism—and efforts to counter those deep-rooted social phenomena. John's own genre history, therefore, became intertwined with the history of his public sexual identity. In which case, how did he pull it off? How was he able to go from "Saturday Night's Alright for Fighting" to "Electricity," both hits a mere three decades apart, and somehow still seem to be the same musician? And how might the parallel story of one of Elton's oldest friends (Rod Stewart), as well as that of one of their close mutual friends (Long John Baldry), help us to answer that question?

"You can be Rod Stewart, and be Clive Davis's dog, and have a career at the expense of your artistic soul," remarked Daryl Hall in a 2007 explanation of why he no longer worked with a major record label. "I have nothing but negative things to say about that, because I respect him as a singer, and I hate what he does. He sold his soul. And I take that personally." What exactly had Stewart done that prompted Hall to make such a biting critique? And does this mean that Elton John also became Davis's dog, or a canine subordinate to some other label honcho? Or does the Stewart story offer an illuminating contrast with Elton's journey through genres?

In the opening months of 1971, Elton John and Rod Stewart went into two separate studios to produce the two separate sides of a new record by Long John Baldry. It was titled *It Ain't Easy*, after the Ron Davies song that Baldry recorded on the Stewart-produced side (and which was far more famously recorded by David Bowie later the same year, included as the sole cover song on 1972's *Ziggy Stardust*). The Stewart-produced side features some classic blues numbers by the likes of Huddie Ledbetter and Willie Dixon, and the band is excellent (Ron Wood, of the Faces and then the Rolling Stones, plays guitar, e.g., along with others who had just finished playing on *Every Picture Tells a Story*, the Stewart solo album that would hit #1 later that year in the UK and US). But Baldry's Stewart-produced version of the much covered "It Ain't Easy" is less compelling than Bowie's, and Baldry's spoken word intro to the Stewart side is funny but wears thin.

In the end, the John-produced side is better, comprising four sterling songs—by Randy Newman, by Lesley Duncan (who also sings backing vocals in two songs), by John and Taupin ("Rock Me When He's Gone"), and by Stewart, Lane, and Wood (a fine cover of "Flying," included on the Faces' eponymous 1970 album).[†] This side works better because of the song choices—the four comprise half a coherent, contemporary album—and because Elton plays piano on all of them. Stewart's magical power is his voice, which is absent from the record; John's is the trifecta of his voice, his compositional talents, and his playing, and the last of these is essential to the enduring unity of the side he produced.

Above all, however, the record is a labor of love—a love letter from Stewart and John to Baldry. Baldry, nicknamed Long John because he was 6'7", was

---

[†] "Rock Me When He's Gone" was written specifically for Baldry, and when John recorded his own version during the *Madman across the Water* sessions later the same year, it was left off the album (much later included on 1992's *Past Masters* and on the 50th Anniversary reissue of *Madman*). I prefer the Baldry version (with John on piano and Caleb Quaye on organ).

the pioneer of electric blues in England, working throughout the 1960s with English musicians who would in many cases become far better known than he would—although that wasn't obvious when he hit #1 in the UK in 1968 with "Let the Heartaches Begin." Two of those musicians were Stewart and Dwight. Baldry's 1964 band, the Hoochie Coochie Men, featured Stewart on vocals. His 1965 band, Steampacket, also included Stewart (they toured with the Rolling Stones). In 1966, Stewart left Steampacket to sing for the Jeff Beck Group (and, in 1969, the Faces, in parallel with a solo career), while Baldry turned to a group of mostly teenage blues-playing Londoners, Bluesology, to be his backing band.

The keyboardist and part-time singer in Bluesology was a nineteen-year-old Reginald Dwight. As we saw, it was from two other members of this iteration of Bluesology that Dwight crafted his new name (saxophonist Elton Dean and Baldry). But this was the birth of Elton John in other ways. Just as Stewart would later testify to the essential role Baldry had played in his career formation, so would Dwight/John.

Here is Rod: "I owe so much to Long John Baldry. He discovered me—on a bench in a railway station, as the perfectly accurate story goes—and he turned me into a singer and a performer, but that's really only the beginning of it. I loved him while he lived and was distraught when he died." And here is Elton: "He was many things to me. He was a dandy and a gentleman who liked a good time and loved his music. That, for me when I was young, was all I needed to be influenced by him. He literally saved my life, and I loved knowing and working with him."

Baldry not only "discovered," "saved," and helped launch Stewart and John, he was a glue that helped stick them together. It was Baldry who nicknamed Stewart "Phyllis" and Dwight/John "Sharon"; Sir Rod and Sir Elton call each other by these names (or just "dear") to this day less as a camp affectation, more as an echo of the affection shared with a much-missed mentor.[‡] Rod and Elton have been pals ever since, a genuine and abiding friendship complete with occasional disagreements that the British press have always tried to frame as a feud. They "had football in common, obviously," in Stewart's words, and respect for each other's "opinions about music" (see Figure 5.2). Stewart admitted that he "quietly envied the way that gigantic-selling popular melodies seemed to come to him in such a constant flow."

[‡] Note the contrast to the nicknames that Bowie and Eno gave each other in Berlin—Derek and Clive—in reference to the distinctly un-camp, vulgarian personas created in the 1970s by comedians Peter Cook and Dudley Moore.

Figure 5.2 What Soap? The famous photograph of Rod Stewart and Elton John in the baths of the Watford Football Club, taken November 7, 1973, for the UK's *Daily Mirror*. Their passion for football helped bond the friendship between the two English rock stars. It was also part of their early branding and marketing. The photograph's enduring appeal also lies in its ambiguity as both innocent and homoerotic. (Photo credit: Trinity Mirror / Mirrorpix / Alamy Stock Photo.)

It Ain't Easy was intended by Phyllis and Sharon to resuscitate Baldry's career. It would be his most successful album, reaching #83 in the US—producing a single that likewise briefly visited the Billboard charts, peaking at #73, the Stewart-produced "Don't Try to Lay No Boogie-Woogie on the King of Rock and Roll." But that very modest critical and commercial success would never be matched. Stewart and John did Baldry the same favor the following year, producing a side each on 1972's *Everything Stops for Tea*. John and Stewart contributed some backing vocals, but no songs. The album "repeats the formula, but it falters," as one music writer recently opined, "because the songs simply aren't as strong." It reached #180 in the US. Its 1973 sequel failed to chart completely. Baldry moved to Canada, battled depression and drug addiction and gout, and occasionally made records, but made his living doing voice-overs for films and television shows until his death in 2005.

Baldry's career challenges were, to be fair, partly to do with the unflinching way in which he embraced his homosexuality: he was as out in the London of the 1960s as it was possible to be without being arrested, prosecuted, and jailed (a very real risk until 1967); and his 1979 album *Baldry's Out!* was a bold public statement that very few artists were then willing to make (and one that pretty much marked the end of his music career).

But Baldry's challenge was also one of genre. His one big hit was very much late-1960s pop, not a genre that could be easily repeated. His true passion, the genre of almost all his touring and album songs, was the blues. But while a white Englishman covering Black American blues artists was a revelation in 1960s London, it was in subsequent decades seen as both old hat and inauthentic (and, eventually, appropriation). The way forward for English blues artists of the 1960s was to turn American blues into British rock, achieved with greatest success by the Rolling Stones and Led Zeppelin. But it was also achieved slightly less obviously by Rod Stewart, who channeled R&B more than blues and whose Black American idol was Sam Cooke far more than Muddy Waters. And it was achieved, albeit even less obviously, by Elton John, who channeled his omnivorous taste for all genres of American music into a new pop/rock. (Perhaps Baldry should have just covered Stewart and John songs.)

Before we circle back to Elton and his genre journey from Bluesology to "Electricity," what of Rod's more troubled genre history? Stewart is a couple of years older than John, and his breakthrough came a year or two before John's 1970 arrival. Rod then entered his imperial phase just months before Elton did—with *Every Picture Tells a Story* holding the #1 or #2 slot in the UK and US throughout the autumn of 1971 (while *Honky Château* hit #2 in the UK's spring of 1972, and #1 for five US summer weeks). *Every Picture* was the first of five UK #1 albums, the first of an unbroken run of twenty-nine Top 11 albums in the country of Stewart's birth. His US album chart history has been less consistent, but twenty-two of the albums beginning with *Every Picture* reached the Billboard Top 20. Stewart has sold almost 50 million albums in the US and over 120 million worldwide.

It is hard, therefore, to believe that any of Stewart's career twists and turns were missteps, or that he made mistakes as he navigated for half a century the turbulent waters of popular music genres. And yet he has had to battle the perception that he did just that: first, by breaking up the Faces in 1975 with his selfish sellout of a solo career (so the allegations went); second, that same year, "betraying" the land of his birth, as the British press put it, to live in Los

Angeles (even Elton called Rod "a traitor" when he broke the news in John's Windsor house, playing Elgar's "Pomp and Circumstance" so loudly that it drowned out Rod's defense of his decision); third, that he embraced disco in 1978, betraying his rock fan base in order, yet again, to sell out; fourth, that his 1980s records were half-hearted meanderings through whatever pop and rock sounds were fashionable, as he sought to maintain sales rather than artistic credibility; fifth, that his hit *MTV Unplugged* album in 1993 was a shameless copying of other former rockstars (Elton had done it in 1990, Paul McCartney in 1991, Eric Clapton in 1992—Clapton's being the best-selling live album of all time); and sixth, that his five 2002–2010 *American Songbook* albums were the ultimate, shameless sellout ("Clive Davis's dog").

All these positions can easily be dismantled. For example, Ron Wood leaving Faces for the Stones was as much a cause for the Faces' breakup as was Stewart's solo career. And Stewart moved to Los Angeles to evade high UK income taxes, as numerous other rock stars had done and would do (Joe Cocker and Clapton, claimed Stewart, left the very same month he did). It was not an easy decision, very different from Taupin's ready embrace of the "Americanism that was always in my soul." In fact, Taupin later mused on how "Rod was part of that quirky breed of Englishmen who emigrate to the US then proceed to fervently cling to every bit of Britishness they can."

As for "Da Ya Think I'm Sexy?" (frequently misspelled and auto-incorrected), it is a brilliant glob of ear candy, a rock-disco hit (#1 in the UK and US) that was only a tiny bit more disco-sounding than "Miss You." The Stones hit from earlier the same year was "a rock band's take on disco," noted Stewart, "that really appealed to me," and was the inspiration for "Da Ya Think I'm Sexy?" And if "Sexy" was rock disco rather than pure disco, its parent album, *Blondes Have More Fun*, wasn't disco at all. It comprised Stewart's usual mix of rockers and ballads, and the only track other than "Sexy" with a distinctive disco bass line was a cover of the Four Tops' "Standing in the Shadows of Love," which was still more rock than R&B, let alone disco. But "Miss You" was on *Some Girls*, which rocked more consistently than *Blondes*.

The Rolling Stones had also rocked more consistently than Rod Stewart, whose solo albums had mixed (in Rod's own words) "a bit of rhythm and blues, a bit of folk, a standard, some rock 'n' roll," and "I had only sustained a light wounding as a result of these tactics. But disco was clearly regarded in some places as a dash too far." Stewart regretted alienating fans such as those "from the *Gasoline Alley* days"—referring to the 1970 album often hailed by fans as his pre-superstardom master work—who "felt truly let down." But he also lamented how badly and bitterly music fans were divided by the "battle lines in those days" between genres, "all in their separate trenches with bayonets drawn."

In the context of that music culture war, timing mattered. Other rock artists who had veered into disco had done so earlier, when it was still new to the mainstream, rather than right at the point when *Saturday Night Fever* fatigue began to combine with rockism's resentment of a genre that triggered its racism, misogyny, and homophobia. John's "Philadelphia Freedom" and Bowie's "Fame" were released in 1975, for example, as was Roxy Music's vaguely disco-ish "Love Is the Drug." *Blondes* and "Sexy" were released in 1978, at the peak of disco after *Saturday Night Fever* had reshaped the chart landscape. So the timing was ok, but not ideal: the single topped the UK charts in December, and its month at #1 in the US was February 1979, at the start of a disco backlash that would clear disco from the US charts that summer. The backlash was one of those examples of a hate-filled minority ruining things for the rest of us, with songs like "Sexy" a target because most people liked them. That hit remains, to this day, *the* most commercially successful song written or recorded by Stewart; when he dropped it from his set list in the 2000s, fans complained so much that he permanently reinstated it.

But it was also, to paraphrase Stewart, a pink toilet around his neck. Of all the disco or disco-ish songs by non-disco artists, only Stewart's drew attention to him in such a blatant way, one that could so blatantly be misunderstood. That is, people ignored the lyrics (the verses are written in the third person) and took the title to mean, "don't you think I, Rod, am sexy?" (As Stewart explained, "It wasn't *me* asking every Tom, Dick, and Harriet in the world if they thought *I* was sexy.") Rather as John's "Ego," a 1978 stand-alone single that stalled at #34 in the US and UK, was supposed to poke fun at "the silliness of rock 'n' roll stars," in John's words, but was taken literally as a hubristic expression of egoism by John.

The next criticism—of Stewart's search for direction in the 1980s and 1990s—is likewise a failure to grasp the historical context. Rod has always liked hits, as much as Elton, but both of them were too distracted in the 1980s for that to be their driving, calculating goal. By Rod's own admission, he experienced "a bit of a loss of focus" for the same reasons as his hard-partying pal Elton: the three tightly interrelated factors of too many drugs and drinks (Rod pointed specifically at "booze" and "recreational cocaine"); a relentless schedule of massive tours and yearly albums; and an unstable personal life (Rod has fathered eight children by five women, a cycle of relationships and marriages that did not settle down until he married his current wife in 2007). Rockism was also still rampant, buoyed by what it perceived as its vanquishing of disco. Its bigotry ran so deep that even a straight, white male like Rod was a target for mockery. "Sexy" was "only a pop record" (said Stewart), but music critics ensured it would cast a shadow over the 1980s for its creator, who had thereby exposed his love for the enemy, "led astray forever by the glitter of the disco ball."

As for *MTV Unplugged*, hundreds of artists have appeared on the show, many releasing albums; Stewart was the forty-second to appear since its 1989 inception. Enough said. And finally, those *Songbook* albums: I admit that I never choose to listen to them, and I understand the vehemently negative reaction by old fans of Faces-era Rod; I'd rather listen repeatedly to his thrilling 1971 version of "(I Know) I'm Losing You," for example, than a whole *American Songbook* album.

However, I also admit that the albums are well done, and the songs are an interesting medium for his gently aging rasp of a voice. All artists must be allowed to experiment, without fans turning into genre police, and if an experiment reaches a new audience, why not make them happy with a whole album series? I also find persuasive Stewart's own account of how the idea was his own, that it was then developed with veteran producer Richard Perry into a set of demos, and that those were shopped around and rejected by several labels (including the one to which Stewart was signed) before Clive Davis offered him a two-album contract (as opposed to the story that Davis suggested the albums as a way to cash in his soul and revive a stalled career).

Furthermore, a close listen to Stewart's entire catalogue reveals a less tidy pattern than the initial impression, a pattern that doesn't totally fit that sellout narrative. While blues and rock numbers feature far more heavily in the early years, they crop up for decades; and while pop songs dominate later albums, there is pop throughout—especially if by pop we include ballads. Stewart's core influences were American blues and the R&B of the late 1950s and 1960s, mixed in with British folk music, and those genres are channeled throughout his six-decade career. Even the decision to record standards was not totally unprecedented. His latest album (released in 2024, as I write) is another kind of "standards" project (*Swing Fever*, with Jools Holland), but the previous four records (2013–2021) are pop albums appropriate for a septuagenarian rockstar. Most of those 2010s songs—and the videos, with Rod surrounded by beautiful young blonde women, a decades-long tradition albeit one getting too May-December for comfort—are close in genre and feel to his ballads and pop hits of the 1980s (and even, adjusted for production differences, the 1970s).

This takes us back to the chapter's core questions. John's catalogue fits into what genre or genres of popular music? And if his genre identity really has evolved as dramatically as the contrast between the two Top 10 hits mentioned above—1973's "Saturday Night's Alright for Fighting" and 2005's "Electricity"—how did he manage to avoid permanent career collapse (like Baldry) or career-long accusations of betrayal (like Stewart)? After all, his genre history is just as varied, even dramatic, as Stewart's, if not more so. Why did John not get the same flak for going into musical theater as Stewart did for recording old standards—most of them originally written for musical theater (stage and film), no less? There are several, overlapping ways to answer.

First, my questions are arguably misleading, as John *has* suffered audience abandonment. But it did not simply result from a change in genre, despite the common claim that in 1976 he did just that (shift genre and lose fans). In fact, it has as much been the other way round, with John's genre evolution coming after and even resulting from audience shifts.

As I have argued before, one of the great Elton myths is the perception that his 1977–1979 career slump (or even 1977–1990 slump) was due to a genre shift from rock albums to the "impossibly weepy" and "desperately pretentious" *Blue Moves* of October 1976. It is true that the double album is more sophisticated than John's previous four-sider, the hits-filled *Goodbye Yellow Brick Road*, and moodier than the unchallenging album that came before it, *Rock of the Westies*. John was a rock star, especially in the US, and fans expected more rock; the slow-building opening of "Your Starter For"/"Tonight" was orchestral and poignant, very different from the arena-rock slow-build thrill of "Funeral for a Friend"/"Love Lies Bleeding." Yet for all of Bernie's gloomy *Blue Moves* lyrics about the collapse of his marriage, the album is less obsessed with morbidity than is *Yellow Brick Road*, and none of the women on *Blue* is dirty, deceitful, or doomed to be murdered as they are on *Yellow*. As for *Westies*, it was not a great album, as is now generally recognized ("not to everyone's taste," as Taupin later noted), whereas *Blue Moves* is, in retrospect, the pivotal masterpiece of the John/Taupin creative career. It rivetingly explores the three elements with which John and his team had redirected the evolution of popular music—piano-playing troubadour, orchestral pop, and full band rock. It manages to capture all the subgenres of pop and rock that John had channeled into his work to date, while still being coherent and compelling. My opinion may be more favorable than most, but I would still maintain that, viewing it as objectively as one can, *Blue Moves* is far from being a "career-freezing mess."

In fact, the freeze on John's career had multiple causes (many detailed further in other chapters). The demands of his imperial phase had left him utterly exhausted, prompting a series of attempts to retire in 1977 and through 1979. During those years, he launched no major tours of the kind that had made him the world's biggest rock star. Taupin took a break too, writing for Alice Cooper and others. John's studio efforts were patchy, some unfinished. Having recently dropped DJM, the British label that had launched his career, he found his new material constantly fighting for airtime and chart space with recycled hits from his imperial years.

Meanwhile, John's spontaneous confession of bisexuality, as half-hearted as it was, proved devastating to his career in the US. As we saw in the previous chapter, the record-burning and banning of his music, especially in the US South, was part of an extreme negative reaction. And while the burning and banning did not last long, the long-term impact on his status in America can be seen in his chart history. During the imperial years of 1970–1976, the average peak of John's albums was 2.6 in the US, but 6.3 in the UK. Six studio albums in a row hit #1 in the US, three of them in the UK. That pattern reversed dramatically for 1978–1989, when his album chart average dropped to 29.5 in the US, while he maintained 12.8 in the UK. That difference softened for 1992–2021, when his numbers rose again as Elton became rehabilitated in multiple senses, but the US average (11.8) was still lower than in the UK (5.4). Since 1989, three John albums have been UK #1's, but none have hit the top spot in the US. In the 2020s, John's sales of tickets and hits compilations suggest he is as popular as ever in the US, with the impact of his serial "outings" well in the past. If so, that recovery was a long time coming.

A further factor behind John's 1977–1979 career crisis takes us closer to issues of genre. A few weeks after the release of *Blue Moves*, the Sex Pistols made their first British TV appearance, with seismic impact on the pop music scene. Punk was born. And although it would burn itself out by the decade's end, paralleled by the continued rise and then collapse of disco, the choppy waters of music genres in those years were hard to navigate (that was some crazy water, to borrow a *Blue Moves* song title). "Johnny Rotten called me an old fart," Stewart recalled, "on a British television show. I was thirty-two." John came in for the same criticism, but whereas Rod was defiant,

Elton internalized the accusation that he was suddenly a dinosaur. He found the new music exciting; but sitting in his mansion in Windsor (as he later admitted), "I thought, Yes, you *are* a lazy, fat cunt."

John's 1980s were too complex a mix of contradictions to sum up easily—the rollercoaster ride of album quality, his ill-advised marriage to a woman, his addiction-soaked lifestyle—but he did not attempt to rebuild himself as a rock star. Instead, he adapted the 1970s Elton rock persona to be a 1980s Elton popstar. Even the marriage fitted the very-1980s open secret of his sexual identity. Stewart tried to make his 1970s genre formula fit the new era; John simply made pop records. He shifted the balance between Jerry Lee Lewis and Liberace to be far more of the latter (the "glam Liberace," as Barney Hoskyns put it, was now even more "shameless"). Stewart seemed to be struggling with the new era; John embraced it and, despite the uneven success of the records, helped to shape it—for better or worse.

Likewise, in the 1990s he adapted the Elton pop persona to be its final manifestation as Sir Elton, veteran pop star and pop musical theater composer. Whereas Stewart's later knighthood was simply an honor—it did not change his image or persona—Elton's was the culmination and official recognition of a process begun in 1990. His emergence from rehab and the dawn of his relationship with his future husband were crucial milestones in that process. But in terms of genre, the key event was his accepting *The Lion King* assignment—and its massive success. In contrast to the changes of the late 1970s, when he faced burnout, homophobia, and musical self-doubt, unsure how to be who he really was and express that musically, the *Lion King*-era John was energized, supported, and free to embrace who he was by making music that reflected that. That doesn't mean he created a whole new persona, or that his music changed dramatically, or that he started making "gay music"; rather, all those things occurred, but in the subtle way that gently shaped Sir Elton (as he became, officially, in 1998).

This brings me to my next point: timing. The crisis of 1977–1979 may seem like a case of bad timing, especially for *Blue Moves*, but John's career has been marked as much by good timing as it has by the struggle all popular musicians faced during the turbulent music culture era of *Top of the Pops* (1964–2006). In the end, that era's changes worked well for him, partly by design, partly by luck.

Elton emerged at a moment when pop and rock were very far apart, with pop far more narrowly defined than it later became. That helped determine what genre John would fall into with the three albums he released in just eighteen months between April 1970 and November 1971.[§] Competition was steep, but it also brought people into record stores, and it gave the three John albums a context in which rock leaned toward folk and country, as well as into the rock end of the singer-songwriter genre. For example, just in the few months prior to the release of *Madman across the Water*, the last of that John trio, the following arrived in the shops: John Lennon's *Imagine*, David Bowie's *Hunky Dory*, Don McLean's *American Pie*, T. Rex's *Electric Warrior*, and *Led Zeppelin IV*. Earlier in the year, *L.A. Woman* by the Doors, *Every Picture Tells a Story* by Rod Stewart, and *Sticky Fingers* by the Rolling Stones had all come out, as well as now-classic albums by Joni Mitchell, the Who, Black Sabbath, and the Beach Boys. No wonder that Hepworth has repeatedly called 1971 "unquestionably the annus mirabilis of the rock album"—even writing a book-length case to support the claim.

Also helping John's emergence as a rising rock star, not pop star, was his weak presence on the singles chart. Aside from "Your Song," which on its own suggested John might have tilted either way, John was completely absent from the UK singles chart until "Rocket Man" came crashing in during the spring of 1972. In the US, he had only a couple of minor hits from *Madman*, and they were less pop than "Your Song" ("Levon" reached #24 and "Tiny Dancer" #41, both in 1972). *Tumbleweed Connection*, dropped in the autumn of 1970, single-free and loosely a concept album, did a great deal to establish John as a serious rock artist. Before long he would have hit singles, lots of them, and some of them unabashedly pop, but in the US in particular his rock identity was too well established to be shaken—not yet at least.

Then, in the very years that John's star rose with astonishing rapidity, first in the US and then worldwide, pop and rock music became "about performance as much as about sound." The effect was to widen the gap between rock and pop, or at least admit pop when it was secondary and leaning toward rock. Rock operas and increasingly massive concert festivals were less and less venues for pop stars. And as tours became bigger and bigger, going from theaters to arenas and stadiums, they projected rock's blunt masculinity ("its phallic substitutes and the jackhammer rhythm of the male climax"), with visual experiences "that ran the gamut from the sublime to the absurd."

That was perfect timing for Elton, who during those very same years was discovering the joy and efficacy of pomp and theatricality on the concert

---

[§] There were actually five albums, all of which reached the US Top 40, if we count the *Friends* soundtrack and the live album *17-11-70* (UK)/*11-17-70* (US).

stage, from the sublime to the spectacularly absurd—for personal reasons (as we've seen) stemming from his self-perception and need to turn un-star-like Reg Dwight into rock star Elton John. His breakthrough had come in the US, and in 1970 it was still possible to become one of the new rock stars in America without audiences understanding (or caring to understand) that star's true origins and identity. And for the promoters and music critics who did know of his origins, he could be seen as both an exotic import and—more important—someone discovered for the first time by *American* audiences.

In the UK, the overdressed showmanship and humorous spectacle of John's performances made him glam-like (albeit outside the glam pantheon of Bowie and Bolan, Slade and Sweet). But that was irrelevant in the US, where glam so failed to get a look-in that it could not even have served as a negative association for John. Slade and Sweet were routed in the US, Bowie did not become big there until his post-glam *Young Americans*, and US glam rockers like Suzi Quatro found success only in Britain, while by 1973—"glam's annus mirabilis" in the UK—John was already a chart-ruling imperial-phase rock star in America. Ironically, the camp element to John's theatricality, surely more heartfelt by him than by all the straight men who made up glam bands, was lost on US concert goers.

The US was the largest market in the world, and those who made money off bands—managers, promoters, label executives—worked hard to persuade or coerce artists into "breaking" that market. But whereas in the UK a following could be built through the music papers, of which there were many, most with impressive distribution, the vast US market required grueling touring and painstaking publicity efforts paired to innumerable concerts. British bands were not used to "audiences such as the ones in Moose Droppings, Ohio, who couldn't read your social and cultural references, didn't read the *NME* and just expected to be won over" (as Hepworth has put it). As a result, some never tried, and most of those who did came home exhausted and defeated.

Elton John, however, was uniquely positioned to be an exception—a British artist who not only "broke" America but was bigger there than at home, precisely in the decade *between* the two British Invasions (of the mid-1960s and mid-1980s). This was for two reasons beyond the fact that his breakthrough moment occurred not in England, but in one of the two predominant music industry cities in the US, Los Angeles. First, John was willing to build on that moment by touring relentlessly, responding to his growing fanbase by increasing the number of concerts and the size of the venues, culminating in the unprecedented, record-breaking legendary series of shows in LA's Dodger Stadium during August 1975. This seemingly superhuman ability to tour in the US eventually took its toll on John, but that implosion did not occur until 1977. By that time, his position in the market was so deep and secure that he was still benefiting from it a half-century later.

And second, there was Taupin's boyhood fascination with a kind of romanticized, country-and-western vision of America, which he translated into lyrics that resonated with US record-buyers. John shared that fascination, and he contributed to its impact in his adoption of Southern American accents in singing Taupin's more "Americana" lyrics. In retrospect, some of those stylings seem parodic today, but that is largely because we know the full story. In the early 1970s, many Elton fans in the US assumed he was a compatriot. The other members of the new singer-songwriter movement were all North American (from US and Canada), so it was logical to assume that so was Elton John.** After all, he sang like an American often about American things and seemed always to have an upcoming concert in an American city.

When that all changed, it wasn't because John alienated his fan base by breaking up a much-loved band from which he had emerged (there was no such band), or by moving abroad, or by suddenly and inexplicably embracing disco. It changed because there was a pop culture shift beneath John's feet, while homophobia pulled out the rug beneath him. When he tried disco, therefore, nobody much cared. When he returned as a pop star, it made sense. It wasn't that Elton was changing on us, it was that we were trying to keep up with who he was—almost, but of course not really, like Bowie.

In fact, I argued in an earlier chapter that John has pursued with success a highly modified and muted version of Bowie's sequence of personas. If that opinion seemed to stretch John's evolution too far, consider the case of Stewart, who sits at the opposite end of the image spectrum from Bowie. Rod Stewart is his birth name. His signature hairstyle and bad-boy-lover image, developed before he became a star, has been consistent across a career almost sixty years long. Maintaining an image deep into old age is now more common than not, a necessity in a music marketplace where artists are brands, making Stewart far from rare in this regard. Yet few have maintained the image so tenaciously. The cover of his 2012 autobiography omitted his surname and most of his face; all it needed was the word ROD, his spiky

---

** John is the sole non–North American in the list by music historian Ted Gioia of twenty of the most prominent new troubadours, as he calls them, of the turn of the 1970s—from Joni Mitchell and Carole King to Don McLean and James Taylor.

blond hairdo, and those bedroom eyes. It is too late to change the brand now, of course, and Stewart's ongoing popularity and sales figures would make even considering such a change absurd. Yet, as anyone who has been to a Stewart concert in this century knows, the static image awkwardly functions as a big tent for the very different fans of bad-boy-rocker Rod, Rod the MOR pop-rockstar, and suave Rod the songbook crooner. So, the image's rock-solid consistency both works (he still sells tickets and records) and has not worked (different genres with the same image can foment disaffection).

If Stewart and Bowie are at the ends of that image spectrum, one never changing, the other always shifting, it therefore finds John somewhere in the middle. That place has allowed him not only to be a singer-songwriter, a global rock star, a pop singer, a cheesy balladeer, a songwriter for children's animated films, and a musical theater composer, but to be all those things at once.

We saw earlier how *The Lion King* work proved crucial for John in various ways; the point to be added here is that, in terms of the success of the project and the readiness of audiences to accept John's association with musical theater and children's animation, the timing could not have been better. The 1990s witnessed Disney Animation "on one of its most remarkable hot streaks." From 1989's *The Little Mermaid* through 2000's *The Emperor's New Groove*, mainstream animation was dominated by Disney, making the release of each new feature film a pop culture event. When a Disney cartoon movie was a hit—and most of their animated features during those dozen years, at almost two a year, were hits—it was massive, to the positive exposure of all those involved. And *The Lion King* was the biggest hit of them all.

As one scholar of musical theater has remarked, "*The Lion King*—an updated, more politically conscious *Bambi* (with echoes of *The Jungle Book*), and insanely successful—was something of a transition to more modern or even post-modern styles." Those new styles gave more importance to superheroes, and less to the music, than traditional styles, while drawn animation gave way to digital. Disney's "hot streak" ended due to various factors: the rise of rival studios (which Disney tended to buy—Pixar in 2006, Marvel in 2009—but not dissolve into its own animation studio); the explosion of the internet and, later, the streaming revolution; and the undermining of US monoculture by the culture wars.

Indeed, not coincidentally, it was toward the end of this period that Disney's progressive LGBTQ policies began to attract attacks from extreme right organizations. "Gay Day" at Disneyland had started quietly around 1990, but by 1995 it was drawing over 30,000 attendees, and in that year, Disney began offering domestic-partner benefits to same-sex couples. "Walt Disney might have been horrified," opined the *Orlando Weekly* in 2000, by which time right-wing groups such as the Southern Baptist Convention, Focus on the Family, and the American Family Association had attempted to organize boycotts. They failed: Disney thrived, their policies unaltered, and by the early 2020s, the event had become a long weekend of "Gay Days," drawing some 180,000 participants. When Florida elected the aggressively homophobic Ron DeSantis as governor in 2019, his attacks on Disney, beginning in 2022, and prompting a 2023 lawsuit by Disney, were widely seen as a determinant factor in his failure to win the Republican presidential nomination in 2024.

Had *The Lion King*, with Elton as song composer, been created thirty years later, would his sexual orientation have been a vaguely irrelevant fact, neither an open cause for celebration nor grounds for boycotting the brand? There are so many other factors relevant in such a counterfactual speculation, that it is hard to say. But while excremental opinions would certainly have been thrown around the troll-world of the internet, I suspect that *the* crucial and abiding factor would have remained the same: the five John/Rice songs were both a perfect fit for the film and elastic enough in their lyrics and musical style—especially "Circle of Life" and "Can You Feel the Love Tonight"—to be pop hits that transcended their context.[††] As soon became evident from their incorporation onto John's set lists and hits compilations, they are above all Elton songs, a manifestation of a genre impulse that has been in his catalogue all along; the US edition of the 1995 *Love Songs* compilation began with "Can You Feel" and ended with "Circle of Life," a symbolic framing of his previous ballads. So, whether John had an impact on musical animated film or not, it surely had an impact on him, helping him to become more himself than ever before.

Far from leaving the past behind—in terms of genres and the catalogue—that meant continuing to work in musical theater while continually looping back into past songs and weaving a complex self-referential tapestry. Two soundtrack projects came out in 1999: an instrumental track (with one John/Taupin song) for the forgettable film *The Muse*; and, far more successfully, another John/Rice collaboration, the music for a Broadway

---

[††] The exception that proves my point is "Hakuna Matata," which was also nominated for an Oscar up against the above two hits ("Can You Feel the Love Tonight" won); its association in the film with a farting cartoon warthog tied it too closely to its source for it to be incorporated into John's canon, especially his love-songs catalogue.

adaptation of Verdi's *Aida*—for which John and Rice won a Tony, with John's duet with LeAnn Rimes ("Written in the Stars") becoming incorporated into his subsequent hits compilations. The next animated musical film for which John wrote music—as with *Lion King*, with lyrics by Tim Rice, and the score by Hans Zimmer—was the 2000 Dreamworks feature *The Road to El Dorado*. Because the movie bombed, the two singles were not hits, but the underappreciated soundtrack showed that *Lion King* was no one-off outlier in the John catalogue, but merely the start of a rich vein that John was now mining. A John/Taupin soundtrack for *Lestat*, a musical theater interpretation of Anne Rice's *The Vampire Chronicles*, was a flop, but, as we've seen, *Billy Elliot* was a huge and enduring success. As I write, 2022 theatrical productions with music written by John are opening in London (*The Devil Wears Prada*) and on Broadway (*Tammy Faye*).

Critics wondered why he'd not been writing such soundtracks all along; rather than unpacking the complex explanation of John's prior discomfort with his public identity, and the possibility that he may not have been psychologically "free" to dive into musical theater until being sober and out, critics tended to blame the failure of the 1971 film *Friends*, for which a young Elton wrote songs.

As for that self-referential tapestry, it was created in three ways. One comprised some clever contemporary branding. Examples are the reworking of "Sorry Seems to Be the Hardest Word" with British boy band Blue (a #1 hit in 2002) and videos for *Songs from the West Coast* singles that featured "shrewd referencing of Elton's glory years and cross-branding with a new generation of pop stars" (Justin Timberlake played a young Elton persona in "This Train Don't Stop There Any More," and Mandy Moore was a 1970s Elton fan for "Original Sin"). A second strategy lay in the way that John's twenty-first-century albums referenced his imperial phase—most obviously *The Union*'s collaboration with his early 1970s idol and touring partner, Leon Russell, and *The Captain & the Kid*'s composition and promotion as a sequel to *Captain Fantastic and the Brown Dirt Cowboy*. Finally, a steady series of new compilations and set lists incorporated the musical theater hits into the canon—from a 2000 live hits album on CD and DVD (*One Night Only*), and the 2003–2009 Las Vegas residency, *The Red Piano*, to the 2002 *Greatest Hits* CDs, the 2007 *Rocket Man* compilation, the extravagant multidisc *Diamonds* compilation, and the great 2018–2023 Farewell tour.

We have taken something of a meandering yellow brick road through genres and potted pop histories to get to a straightforward conclusion: Stewart prompted a Clive-Davis's-dog reaction to his *Songbook* albums because that isn't who he is; John's work in *Billy Elliot* and other musical theater and film elicited no such reactions because that is clearly who he is. That is not who we thought he was much earlier, but we see now that in fact he was that person all along—Reg, Elton, Sir Elton, Uncle Elton (we are coming to him soon) are not different personas, just the evolution of the same one.

Again, perception is everything: the stage antics and outrageous costumes, perceived as appropriate rock bombast in the 1970s (see Figure 5.3), were perceived as spot-on pop pomposity in the 1980s; toned down in the 1990s, they were perceived as a suitable echo of musical theater, with a touch of nostalgia for the 1970s; in this century, they were largely gone, reserved by the time of the four-year Farewell Yellow Brick Road tour for backscreen images of younger, wilder Elton—a heavy dose of nostalgia.

Figure 5.3 No Skyline Pigeon. One of Elton John's famous feathered costumes, this one for his 1977 appearance on *The Muppet Show* television series. He sang "Crocodile Rock."

Decades ago, John's old touring partner Billy Joel gave up attempting to navigate genre; he stopped making new records and settled into a highly lucrative residency of nostalgia gigs in Madison Square Garden.‡‡ He was, it turns out, somewhat ahead of his time. Today, genres have collapsed in on each other, along with cultural time. Our sense of "linear development" has been swamped by "a strange simultaneity" (as music critic Mark Fisher put it). Genre trends are lost in the swirl of streaming. Elton John, selling compilation records and endless-farewell concert tickets by the boatloads, can traffic in the same kind of nostalgia while—in his senior-singer rendition of songs from across his career—he can be very au courant in his mashup of genres.

Perhaps that is why, having been cool for a few years a half-century ago, and then decidedly uncool for many, many years, he is now, once again, rather cool.

---

‡‡ At the Grammy Awards in March 2024, Joel revealed his first new song in three decades, "Turn the Lights Back On," conceding in interviews that "I'm just dipping my toe in the water"; by the time you read this, there may therefore be a new Joel album out, but I suspect that new song will prove to be the exception that proves the rule of his timelessness—his catalogue neither old nor new, rendered through repeated performance into an exercise in presentist nostalgia.

6

Fantasies of Difference

Elton and Aretha

"Border Song" (3:22, 1970)

Among the various songs in the John discography with milestone status there sits one that has had significant and complex resonance for over half a century. "Border Song" is a John/Taupin track nestled into the second side of *Elton John*, his second LP (but first to be released in the US). The song was not John's first hit. But it was the first of his singles to chart anywhere in the world (peaking at #29 in the Netherlands and #34 in Canada) and his first to chart in the US (it spent a week at #92).

For Eltonologists, the single is a milestone for inspiring enough interest upon its UK release in March 1970 to warrant John's first appearance, on April 2, on the legendary BBC television program *Top of the Pops*. For John, that moment mattered because one of his idols, Dusty Springfield, introduced herself to him in the dressing room, offering to mime backing vocals. But the *Top of the Pops* appearance did nothing for the single on the UK charts. Indeed, it only squeaked into the US Top 100 in October on the heels of "Your Song," which became John's first hit, and which he would mime twice the following year on *TOTP*.[*]

More significant, the song was covered the same year by Aretha Franklin, whose version embraced the gospel/R&B potential of the song, adding "Holy Moses" in parentheses to its title. That phrase begins the song and is

---

[*] All performances during this era of *Top of the Pops* were recorded earlier in the day and then fully mimed during the evening broadcast. It is hard to overstate the significance to British pop culture and pop music history of the BBC TV program, especially in its 1970s–1990s heyday (as mentioned earlier, it broadcast, in one form or another, from 1964 to 2006). For a *TOTP* appearance not to boost the sales of a song was rare, although less rare for artists making their first appearance. John would feature on the program a total of 106 times between 1970 and 2006, 39 of those being original appearances (as opposed to showings of videos, previous recordings, etc.).

sung six times, prominent in the three verses and the bridge (the song has no chorus); the bridge begins with "I'm going back to the border," but the title phrase "Border Song" is never voiced. Franklin's parenthetical addition thus tied the song tighter to its lyrics while emphasizing its gospel potential. Any awkwardness embedded in two white English boys indulging in a Black American genre—even if it was more likely to be seen in 1970 as an homage than as a parody or appropriation—was eliminated by Aretha singing it and singing it as if it were her own.

Franklin's recording was a far bigger hit than John's, peaking at #37 in the Billboard chart, getting yet further airplay and attention when it was included as the closing track on her Grammy-winning 1972 hit album, *Young, Gifted and Black*. In addition to repositioning the song's genre through its "near-spiritual arrangement" (as *Cash Box* put it), Franklin's recording also drew attention to its final verse. Taupin's lyric had been about his homesickness as a young country boy in London, a sentiment that jibes with the first two verses. But in the studio, John had thrown in some extra lines at the end, inspired by Caleb Quaye—the Afro-Londoner who played with John in Bluesology in the late 1960s and then in John's band for much of the 1970s. Thus "there's a man over there / what's his color, I don't care / he's my brother, let us live in peace" was John's rather clunky embrace of racial harmony (think McCartney and Wonder's "Ebony and Ivory"). That last line was repeated three times, closing the song. In Franklin's hands, the clunkiness is gone. Its impact was further highlighted by the sequencing of the track on her album, where the lyric served as a powerful way to bring *Young, Gifted and Black* to a climax.

Elton John's career took off in the US before it did in the UK, and he was more successful stateside throughout his 1970s imperial phase than he was in his home country—as we have seen. That was partly because John and Taupin were obsessed as young songwriters with a kind of stereotype of American culture, which they channeled into the Americana and country elements of their 1970s records. But they were equally obsessed with African American artists, acquiring their records whenever they could, and jumping at opportunities to back them on stage during UK tours in the late 1960s.

As much as John was taken by the pop-rock styles of white American pianists—he would, in particular, go on to channel the antics of Jerry Lee Lewis and the fabulous flair of Liberace—it was Black American pianist-singers like Little Richard and Ray Charles that would capture his imagination the most. Combined with what seemed to be the unique ability of Black American women to express emotion in song, the R&B records that reached the UK from the US in the 1950s and 1960s had a huge impact on Dwight/John. It has been a lasting one. "I feel an affinity for Black music like no other," he said in 2011, "and I feel sometimes when I'm playing it that I'm channeling something." It would be easy to overanalyze (and criticize) such a claim, but John's "something" strikes me as an attempt to soften the claim. He's enthusing about his influences, saying that he is a conduit for great music, not pretending as a white Englishman to understand or express the history of suffering and survival behind African American music.

Indeed, John and Taupin had both been fascinated in their formative years by the way that white American musicians had absorbed Black American music (again, we might today think of it more as an appropriation). "There were white musicians making soul music without covering 'In the Midnight Hour,' or doing something that was just a pale imitation of what black artists did," John later wrote. "It was a revelation." On top of that came direct inspiration from artists that John backed on tour. American R&B artists were warmly received in 1960s Britain; many even had their own local fan clubs, including those backed on piano by young Reg Dwight, like Doris Troy and Patti LaBelle and the Bluebelles. Thus, early compositions like "Take Me to the Pilot" and "Border Song," John would later say, "had a sort of funk and soulfulness that I'd picked up backing Patti LaBelle and Major Lance, but they also had a classical influence that seeped in from all those Saturday mornings where I'd been forced to study Chopin and Bartók." It was hardly surprising which influence predominates, particularly on the likes of "Border Song"—one influence the result of reluctance and obligation, the other derived from childhood fascination and direct contact with accomplished musicians, some of whom, like LaBelle, befriended the young Englishman. And underlying it all was the fact that, as has been well noted, "Blackness often appeals to whiteness as a fantasy of difference."

The foundation was thus laid for an enduring but somewhat uneasy relationship between John and his music on the one hand, and US R&B artists and their music on the other. Although I think "Border Song" prompts the theme best, the elephant in the room is "Bennie and the Jets," and its relevance here is worth a detailed digression.

During the era of John's imperial phase, one of the few female music directors in North America was Rosalie Trombley (1939–2021). Immortalized by the Bob Seger song named "Rosalie" after her, she developed a reputation in the 1970s as a hitmaker, predicting what songs would be hits—and sometimes fulfilling her own prophecy. She worked for Windsor, Ontario–based CKLW, but the station had reach throughout neighboring Detroit and even beyond into adjacent US states. When she pulled "Bennie and the Jets" from *Goodbye Yellow Brick Road* and spun it on CKLW, it was therefore heard in Detroit, and then picked up by two stations in that city. One of them, WJLB, was an R&B station, with a historically Black following. Before long, "Bennie" had risen to #1 on that city's "Black" music airplay chart.

Elton had protested at first when his North American label, MCA, planned to release the song as a single. "I think you'll be an R&B artist as well as a pop artist," MCA's Pat Pipolo told a very skeptical John. But Pipolo was "tenacious and savvy" (in Taupin's words), and his efforts, combined with word of the song's reception in Detroit, convinced John to drop his objections. Released in February 1974, "Bennie and the Jets" went to #1 in both the US and Canada.

Was "Bennie" no more than the "fluke crossover hit" that it has typically been called? The most obvious connection that it had to other songs, in terms of both its genre of music and its lyrics, was to "Ziggy Stardust"—yet another example of Bowie lurking in the wings. This was obvious in Britain, at least, where glam rock swamped the singles charts between 1971 and 1974. Bowie's Ziggy Stardust persona and albums were elemental to the genre's success; he was, while he was Ziggy, a glam rock artist. By dramatically abandoning the genre after 1974's *Diamond Dogs*, he ensured himself a post-glam career (and, some would argue, ensured glam would fade rapidly from favor)—unlike entirely glam artists like Gary Glitter, Mud, Slade, and Sweet. Similarly, toe-dipping artists who drew upon glam in terms of their image, enjoying some glam hits but who were not primarily branded in the genre, were unaffected by glam's demise—the most prominent artists in that category arguably being Roxy Music, Queen, Rod Stewart, and Elton John.

The parent album to "Bennie and the Jets," *Goodbye Yellow Brick Road*, came out in October 1973, and the release of "Bennie" on 7" (as an A-side in North America, a double-A with "Candle" in Australia, but only a B-side in the UK) came the following February—all in glam's peak period. So, how did the song become a Black radio hit in the US, taken by such listeners to be a hit by a new Black American artist? Because Black and white music in America existed in their own silos, separated by artists and audiences, radio stations and genre sections in record shops (or the shops themselves). WJLB's program director, Donnie "The Love Bug" Simpson, had thus not previously played John songs; Simpson's listeners knew nothing of Elton himself, allowing them to hear the music without that artist filter.

The explanation also lies in a larger context, in the differences between the UK and US music scenes in the 1970s. The First British Invasion of the 1960s and the Second British Invasion of the 1980s only make sense as phenomena because of the music culture divide in between. British glam acts never made it big in the US, and even Bowie did not place higher than #64 on the Billboard singles chart until his post-glam *Young Americans* album and singles. Americans were far less likely than Britons to spot that both "Bennie" and "Ziggy" were self-conscious or meta songs about fictional sci-fi glam bands, with androgynous lead singers, rendered in a glam style.

The other explanation lies in how John put Taupin's lyrics to music. "Bennie" is not Elton at his most musically glam (that would probably be "Saturday Night's Alright for Fighting," a worldwide hit in the summer of 1973, also taken from *Yellow Brick Road*). It lacks the guitar riffs that are a sonic hallmark of glam, instead leaning—not surprisingly—on Elton's piano playing. That playing here echoes R&B in two ways. First, in the verses, Elton deployed the honky-tonk soul sound inspired by Leon Russell (one of John's idols, to whom we'll return later, Russell was a white Oklahoman who worked in multiple genres—notably R&B, blues, and gospel). Second, in the choruses, John favored the downbeats with his fingers, syncopating his notes with the bass and drums. So, it all depends on cultural context, on what the listener knows or doesn't know of the artist, on what the listener brings to the song. "Bennie" can be glam or soul, neither or both.

The song's appeal among Black American listeners in Detroit spread to other markets across the US. Eventually, "Bennie" reached #15 on Billboard's *Hot Soul Singles* chart (spending eighteen weeks on the Billboard Hot 100). As a result, John was invited to perform on the TV show *Soul Train*. (Accounts differ as to whether it was John or Don Cornelius, the creator and producer of *Soul Train*, who initiated the invitation.) John recalled that Cornelius "took a shine" to the "huge lapels and brown and bold pinstripes" of Elton's outfit, asking, "Hey, brother, where did you get that *suit*?" That moment brought John full circle from when he was still just Dwight, backing Black American artists who amazed him with "the way they dressed ... such style, such panache."

John found the whole *Soul Train* experience to be "an unreal thing, seeing my name in among the singles by Eddie Kendricks and Gladys Knight and Barry White. I may not have been the first white artist to do that, but I can say with some certainty I was the first artist from Pinner." John was right; he was not quite the first white musician to appear on the show (that was Dennis Coffey and the Detroit Guitar Band). But that myth has become part of the Elton legend.†

And rightly so. The episode was taped and aired in March 1975, when John was at the peak of his imperial phase, just as Cornelius and his show (which he hosted from 1970 to 1993) were enjoying huge success. "The episode was an important moment for cultural relations," the Roots' drummer and journalist Ahmir "Questlove" Thompson has written. "It stated to me that if your music was quality, you would be embraced by *Soul Train*. Talent transcends all, no matter what color you are. Elton was a prime example."

As John was so productive during these years, by the time of the *Soul Train* appearance he was several singles and an album or two further along from "Bennie." But that meant that his latest single, released just weeks before, was "Philadelphia Freedom," which Dudgeon had crafted to sound as if it had been produced by Gamble and Huff—the Philadelphians who had written "TSOP (The Sound of Philadelphia)," a 1974 #1 hit that was used at the time as the theme for *Soul Train*. "Philadelphia Freedom" was thus perfect for the show, and John taped a version of it to perform on the same episode as "Bennie and the Jets."

It was in fact the success in the US of "Bennie and the Jets" that had encouraged John to think of contemporary R&B, and specifically the Philly Soul sound, as a direction to consider. "It took me to a whole new audience," he reminisced in 2014. "I love Black music more than any other music—gospel music, soul music, and blues music—so to have that"—the success of "Bennie" in Black America—"was just an essential for me. It did me a lot of good, confidence-wise, to be accepted by that area of people buying records."

Inevitably, John was consequently inspired to think in terms of recording a whole album that was R&B inspired, or in the style of R&B or soul or disco, or produced by Gamble, Huff, or another Philadelphia Sound producer

---

† The myth is a fungible one, one easily embraced by writers keen to display the cultural significance of their subjects, and inevitably that includes Bowie—"one of the first white performers ever to appear on *Soul Train*" (as one biographer proclaimed). Bowie did indeed appear on the show, eight months after John.

like Thom Bell—or all of the above. And, in fact, he soon did, but with unfortunate—even disastrous—results.

In the autumn of 1977, he went into the studio with Bell, recording six new songs, only two of which were John compositions. The studio was in Seattle, but Bell finished the mixes back home in Philadelphia. Disappointed in how they sounded—more "saccharine" than soulful—John shelved them, canceling the follow-up session. In January 1979, John remixed three of the tracks with his longtime sound engineer Clive Franks, and a few months later they were released in the UK as an EP simply titled *The Thom Bell Sessions*. It flopped, and a single release of "Are You Ready for Love" did only a tad better, peaking at #42.

That summer, John tried again, flying to Munich for a day to spend eight hours laying down vocals on seven tracks, one of them a disco remake of Chuck Berry's "Johnny B. Goode," the other six cowritten by Pete Bellotte and members of the German team responsible for launching Donna Summer's disco career. Sequenced as a continuous half-hour of driving beats and melodies that were "at best, pedestrian," the tracks were released as *Victim of Love*—the biggest commercial and critical failure of John's career.

Why did both these attempts to make all-soul or all-disco albums crash and burn? The shortest answer—that the material was weak—only gets us halfway there. For it was also to a significant degree a question of bad timing. In 1977, when the Thom Bell tracks were created, disco fever was at its peak on both sides of the Atlantic. By 1979, the backlash (as mentioned earlier) had taken effect (in fact, in the US, it took place very rapidly *during* the summer of 1979). Soul and disco still charted, but the songs had to be far better than two years earlier. And they needed to sound like 1979, not 1977, disco with a hint of rock (like "Da Ya Think I'm Sexy?" and "Miss You"). There was clearly great potential in the Bell sessions, with two of the tracks in particular future John classics. In the US, "Mama Can't Buy You Love" was #1 on Black radio and #9 on the Billboard charts; it took all summer of 1979 to get that high, but it did it, and it even earned John a Grammy nomination for best male R&B vocal performance—the exception that proved what was possible with the right song at the right time. Its success rubbed off a little on the weaker "Victim of Love," which limped up to #31 in the US that autumn. John's label in the UK, meanwhile, flubbed it; seeing "Mama Can't Buy You Love" finally make it across the pond, they pressed it for a British release, then changed their minds and instead put out "Victim of Love"— which flopped completely. "Are You Ready for Love" did eventually hit #1 in the British charts (and #1 on the US Dance charts), but that was in remixed form (neither the Bell nor Franks mixes) and in 2002—long, long after those issues of timing ceased to apply.

The timing was also bad in other ways. In the final few years of the 1970s, John was burned out and exhausted, repeatedly retiring and returning to the stage and studio and retiring again. His "coming out" in the autumn of 1976 had been unplanned and half-hearted, as were efforts to retract the confession, creating double layers of stress. And he and Taupin were on hiatus; just when Bernie might have served as a restorative muse, he was tied up in Los Angeles working with Alice Cooper. In the 1980s, the John/Taupin magic would resurface, just as John would resurface on the charts as a productive popstar—albeit with mixed results, fueled by drugs and alcohol. Elements of soul, R&B, and even hints of disco would likewise surface on his 1980s albums, but never as successfully as on 1970s hits like "Bennie," "Philadelphia Freedom," or even the frothy pop-disco of 1976's summer smash "Don't Go Breaking My Heart."

Then, in 1988, John made a final attempt, this time in collaboration with Taupin, to channel into a whole album the love the partners had for 1960s soul. John took specific songs by Franklin, Ray Charles, Sam and Dave, the Drifters, and similar artists and suggested them to Taupin as inspiration for lyrics, which were then written and given to the pianist. "The concept," said John, was "of harking back to the songs that really inspired us when we first met." The results were "not rip-offs," said John; those old songs were just used as "seeds" for the tracks that ended up as 1989's *Sleeping with the Past*. The idea both worked and didn't. Far from a "rip-off," the album sounds like a John/Taupin record, and few listeners would even guess at the concept without being told of it. But it's a good album, John's first to reach #1 in the UK since 1974's *Caribou*, marking the start of his 1990s comeback.

Meanwhile, there were two further dimensions to John's relationship with American R&B. The first predates the success of "Bennie" in the US, and in some cases even predates or was contemporaneous with Franklin's release of her "Border Song" cover: the mining of the John catalogue by R&B artists. I have not attempted to make a comprehensive list of such cover versions, but I suspect there are dozens stretching through the 1970s and into the 1980s, many of them deftly and imaginatively extracting the soul potential of the John/Taupin compositions. For example, Eugene Pitt and Jyve Fyve, who had enjoyed success in the 1960s as a doo-wop group named the Jive Five, covered "Come Down in Time" in 1971. In the words of Hope Silverman, a music writer who surveyed some of these covers in an online study of soul covers of MOR songs, the Jyves "inject the dreamy ballad with a whole lot of fire, reshaping it into an intensely urgent, horn-fueled beast full of emphatic wailing." As much as I love the *Tumbleweed Connection* original, I think the Jyve Fyve version is better; it is certainly more compelling and, yes, soulful.

Other examples are Mary McCreary's transformation of "Levon" into a gospel banger, included on her 1974 album *Jezebel*. At the time she was married to John's idol and former touring mate Leon Russell, a connection that surely introduced her to the original. She makes the song her own, rendering it wonderfully close to unrecognizable as a track from *Madman across the Water*. Less successful, but irresistible for its eccentricity and ambition, is Walter Jackson's 1976 cover of "Someone Saved My Life Tonight," the angst of the original turned into totally believable soulful anguish. Jackson's closing mention of "white powder" (as in, someone saved Walter from a cocaine overdose) is poignantly ironic; an overdose was not the danger to John in the song's original story, but, by the time of this cover version, it was beginning to be so.

The other dimension of the John/R&B story is his collaboration with Black American artists; his interaction with those already mentioned was part of a larger trend in which John sought out and seized upon opportunities to work with Black musicians he admired—or, put another way, those who more directly and authentically represented the African American musical traditions that he believed influenced him. A glance at the contributors to John's duets albums, non-album singles, live shows, and backup vocal credits reveals a list that reads like a US R&B primer. The women alone are an astonishing group; in addition to Aretha, the list includes Mary J. Blige, Millie Jackson, Gladys Knight, Dionne Warwick, Sister Sledge, and the Labelle trio of Patti LaBelle, Nona Hendryx, and Sarah Dash.[‡]

The highest-profile collaboration with such legendary divas was "That's What Friends Are For," the Bacharach/Bayer-Sager song originally recorded by Rod Stewart, released in 1985 under "Dionne Warwick and Friends"—the friends being Elton John, Gladys Knight, and Stevie Wonder. A worldwide hit, #1 in the US, Canada, and Australia, and winner of two Grammy Awards,

---

[‡] Labelle offers another example of John's mentorship/friendship loops (to which we turn in detail in Chapter 9): not only did Dwight/John back the Bluebelles, but the co-creator and manager of Labelle, Vicki Wickham (by some accounts Nona Hendryx's romantic partner for half a century), was also close to Long John Baldry.

the song raised over $3 million for AIDS research—all Warwick's initiative, and one that would in time influence John and his embrace of that cause.

John, Knight, and Wonder would go on to collaborate again; a Wonder composition, "Go On and On," appeared on 1993's *Duets* as a John/Knight pairing but with Wonder's backing vocals so high in the mix (he also produced the track) as to make it a trio. In fact, by this point, Elton and Stevie had known each other and collaborated on and off for two decades, a history on which it is worth briefly dwelling. Their first real meeting, as peers in the business, has become part of the canon of legendary John anecdotes. One October night in 1973, John boarded his tour jet, *Starship*, to fly to Boston for the next gig. Keen to rest at the front of the plane, Elton grew increasingly irritated by a "cocktail pianist" playing keyboards at the back of the plane. Demanding the pianist be stopped or even thrown off the plane, John was instead dragged back to meet said pianist—who turned out to be one of his idols, Stevie Wonder (see Figure 6.1). Wonder flew with him to Boston, joining him on stage to play keyboards during the encore to the Boston concert.

Figure 6.1 Cocktail Pianists. Elton John and Stevie Wonder, on the *Starship* touring airplane, in 1973. (Photo credit: Bob Gruen.)

That would be the first of a series of guest appearances on stage and in the studio. When Taupin writes in his autobiography, "One day, Stevie Wonder turned up," one soon ceases to be surprised. Wonder soon became part of the larger support network of musicians that surrounded John—and vice versa.§ That role culminated (at least, so far) in "Finish Line," a John/Wonder duet on 2021's *The Lockdown Sessions*.

The song is enjoyable enough (featuring a classic John chord sequence, e.g., and a similarly classic Wonder harmonica solo), but the video for it is what matters. If the original appeal to Dwight/John and Taupin of African American music is explicable in terms of fantasies of difference, and I think that in part it certainly is, then that appeal evolved over the decades into a fantasy of racial harmony. And the "Finish Line" video is an unabashed, unambiguous—some might say saccharine—celebration of harmony and collaboration between people of difference. (It is also a guide to their collaborations, featuring every photograph of them together that can be found online, including the one that is Figure 6.1.)

The music industry has always attempted to pigeonhole artists—to create, label, and restrict genres, arguably often as a reflection of its racism and sexism, but also for commercial purposes (making it easier to program radio stations, market concerts and albums, promote bands on TV and in print media, and so on). It may give John too much credit to argue that he has bucked against that frequently, veering in and out of genres in ways that were sometimes subtle and successful, sometimes clumsy and disastrous; and that in doing so, he helped to break down those genre dividers (even if they remained in place to a large extent, and still do today, despite the open-access nature of the digital musical environment). Or perhaps the credit simply needs to be spread more broadly to include those Black American artists who saw—and then realized—the soul potential in his compositions, themselves inspired by (or appropriating) the deeper traditions of African American music.

---

§ For Wonder, that included having fun messing with people's perceptions of his abilities: for example, he'd drop a $20 bill at someone's feet without them knowing, and then casually say, "I think you dropped a Jackson"; and during the making of *Rock of the Westies* at Caribou Ranch, he offered Taupin a ride in a Jeep from his cabin to the studio, executing the drive perfectly—only after which did Taupin realize it was a well-practiced "party piece."

FANTASIES OF DIFFERENCE 99

A couple of decades after "Border Song (Holy Moses)" was a minor Aretha Franklin hit (and "Border Song" was a false start for Elton John), after both artists had experienced multiple career highs and lows, they performed the song together. They had recently collaborated, duetting on the title track for Franklin's 1989 album *Through the Storm*, a #16 US hit single (see Figure 6.2). The occasion for them reuniting over "Border Song" was a 1993 television special titled *Aretha Franklin: Duets*, given a one-hour prime-time slot.

The original show was actually a four-hour AIDS benefit concert in Broadway's Nederlander Theater, but Fox only broadcast forty-five minutes

Figure 6.2 A Different Storm. The cover of Elton and Aretha's 1989 single, "Through the Storm," which was a minor UK hit (#41), but a US hit (#16, Billboard Hot 100) that also succeeded on both the Adult Contemporary chart (#3) and the Hot R&B/Hip-Hop Songs chart (#17).

(plus ads), which "isn't enough," griped *Variety* magazine at the time. Still, the duet with John was included, sequenced near the start. John prefaced the performance with a small speech:

> "Of the many songs that Bernie Taupin and I have written, 'Border Song' has always had a special place for me. It was on my second album, and today that's twenty-three years ago, and it remains one of my favorite songs. When another artist records your song, especially when you're just startin' out, it's very exciting. When someone like Aretha Franklin records your song"—John smiled and shrugged—"there are no words to describe how excited I felt. So, um, this was one of the highlights of my early career, to have someone sing one of my songs, to have Aretha sing it, so, um, I think it was, she had eight top ten records, and she recorded this one and it didn't make it, so she still speaks to me after that."

John grimaced, smiled, the audience laughed, and then began a rousing four-minute rendition of "Border Song" (his and her studio versions were both 3′22″), complete with a gospel choir and two pianos, one for each of the two stars. As a plea for racial harmony, the song was no less apposite than it had been in 1970, a lamentable fact of which Franklin and John seemed well aware. Just a year earlier, the acquittal of four LAPD officers in the beating of motorist Rodney King had prompted six days of rioting in Los Angeles, in which sixty-three people died. King's plea on television during the riots, "Can we, can we all get along?" was so widely repeated and well known as to be an early 1990s equivalent of a meme.

King's words seemed to echo in the phrase that John had added to the original song, "He's my brother, let us live in peace." In the *Duets* concert, roughly halfway through "Border Song," when John sang "let us live in peace," Franklin interrupted him with a shout of "sing, Elton!" She then cut him off and took over the verse. He smiled and ceded to her a nice musical moment made poignant by the message of the lyrics. At the song's end, Franklin then added yet another two lines. "I want to know; can we live in peace? In 1993, can we live in peace?" she sang, looking across her piano at Elton, seated at his. He sang back, "Oh, yes, we can!" But the exchange seemed then, and now, more like a plea, an echo of King's plea, than a cheery affirmation of fact.

For the dream of living in peace in America seemed to move further out of reach, not closer, as the decades passed. Franklin and John remained connected, meanwhile, never forgetting to wish each other happy birthday (both were born on March 25), and regularly talking of possible collaborations. Sure enough, in 2017 Aretha performed a nine-song set at a benefit for the Elton John AIDS Foundation in New York's Cathedral of St. John the Divine. Despite being "really, really sick," John said, she "blew the roof off the cathedral" and brought the audience to tears.

It would prove to be the last performance of her life. Upon her death six months later, John paid tribute to "the greatest soul artist of all time." Five years later, at the final US concert of his Farewell Yellow Brick Road tour, he paid tribute again to her "lasting genius." As had become his habit, he recalled their shared history from 1970 to that final performance of hers. And then he sang the song that had become, and always would be, theirs: "Border Song."

7

Perfect Mistakes

Elton and Bennie

"Bennie and the Jets" (5:23, 1973)

The opening chord of "Bennie and the Jets" is—if you will forgive the music-writing cliché—iconic. John's sausage fingers (as he calls them) are on the piano keys for just a second, and then he pauses, but the sound of that fleeting chord is instantly recognizable. Listen to audience reactions on live recordings of the song or experience the reaction yourself at an Elton John concert: the crowd roars, taking collective delight in the recognition of a single, uniquely odd set of notes. Their noise fills the brief silence before the band comes in, four beats after that first chord, with Elton now playing the intended chord, the "right" one.

For that initial chord was never intended for the final version of the song. It was a mistake, a fleeting moment when John was finding the right notes in the studio, and producer Gus Dudgeon already had the tape rolling. It thus remained on the master tapes that Dudgeon and his engineer, David Hentschel, took from the Château d'Hérouville studio in northern France back to London, to make the final mixes in Trident Studios.[*]

There Hentschel noticed the initial chord. In one telling of the story, the chord reminded him of the sound a musician might make on stage to cue a band to start a song; he therefore decided not to delete the chord, but to take it as a production cue. In another telling, it is Dudgeon who spotted the mistaken chord and asked Hentschel, "What does that remind you of?" And Dudgeon thought, "Maybe we should fake-live this." Either way, they gave

---

[*] John had recorded his previous two albums at Château d'Hérouville, beginning with the album he named after the old house, *Honky Château*. Numerous albums, many now legendary, were recorded in the house; Bowie recorded *Pin Ups* there just a couple of months after the *Goodbye Yellow Brick Road* sessions, both albums being released that October 1973.

the track a slight slap or slap-back echo, and added applause taken from two sources: one of John's recent concerts at the Royal Festival Hall; and Jimi Hendrix's well-known 1970 Isle of Wight performance. Hentschel then recorded himself, Dudgeon, and a production assistant clapping, whistling, and stomping their feet, made to sound like a full concert hall through the use of a delay unit.

Dudgeon had thought the song a bit of an oddity, and John and Taupin seemed to have felt the same way. But as its subject matter was, according to lyricist Taupin, a sci-fi all-girl rock band, the faux live post-production not only worked but turned the track from a throwaway or a B-side into a Side One album track. Even John's stuttering "Buh-buh-buh-Bennie" delivery, which was "very much Elton's creation" (Taupin said) and a spontaneous reaction to being told that the fictional band were possibly automatons, matched the production—a fake mistake, if you like, that added to its perfection.

Dudgeon argued that the production treatment—complete with that accidental initial chord—should be retained. Elton was almost never involved in post-production and therefore had no idea what was being done in Trident until Dudgeon and Hentschel played him the final mix. He loved it, keeping that initial chord as his own opening cue, from the first (actually) live performances of the song later that year through to the final concerts of the Farewell Yellow Brick Road tour exactly a half-century later. Rightly so, as what was a spontaneous error became elemental to the song; that chord is a perfect mistake.

Mistakes and contradictions are at the heart of pop music. There are so many elements of pop music and its history that loosely fit the concept of "perfect mistakes"—the dyads of intended and perceived meanings; authenticity and the sellout; studio perfectionism and spontaneity; the weird and the normative; virtuoso and amateur; cool and uncool—that I have long contemplated writing a book on it. Perhaps I still will. Or perhaps you are reading it.

As David Hepworth has put it: "Making records is an art not a science and the things that make one work while another doesn't are often no more than minute differences of degree, infinitesimal increases in temperature, barely perceptible alterations in mood." Put more prosaically, "Making a record is a process of trial and error but also of chance happenings in the room." That's music historian Simon Morrison writing on *Avalon*, the 1982 pop tour de force by Roxy Music, whose Phil Manzanera had learned—since the band's avant-garde genesis a decade earlier—that mistakes in the studio were not only *not* to be feared but to be encouraged. "In the studio, you can head off into very strange territories by artificial means," he noted, "By accident, you can plug something into the wrong place on the desk and something amazing happens that you could never have dreamed of."

Phil Brown is something of an expert on the relationship between mistakes and perfectionism in the studio, having worked as sound engineer on the postpop masterpieces that are Talk Talk's later albums. He has confirmed stories told by the band's Mark Hollis—for example, of Hollis having Brown record a full brass section for *The Colour of Spring*'s "I Don't Believe in You," only to see Hollis throw out every note except a trumpet player blowing spit from his mouth (used 46 seconds into the track) and an accidental squeak (used at the 2′15″ mark). Much of Talk Talk's two subsequent albums would be created this way. When the English pop duo Go West asked Brown to record an album for them note by note, to eliminate all error, he refused and quit, arguing that "mistakes" are crucial to any album.

That is a perspective to which Elton John has always seemed open, an openness he has tended to express in what can seem like a strangely laissez-faire attitude toward recording. He is notoriously prone to fussiness over non-musical arrangements and details (as hilariously revealed by his husband in the 1997 documentary, *Tantrums and Tiaras*). But he is equally notoriously *not* a perfectionist in the recording studio.

There are numerous examples of him refusing to do further takes on a song, leaving the studio to the other musicians to continue recording, and letting the producer mix and sequence an album's tracks without his interference or even his input. This is not just casual disinterest (although the mature, sober John appears to have shown greater interest in the later stages of recording); it reflects a willingness to embrace "mistakes" as part of the creative process, as a technique for lending the music a more human quality.

As we saw in the previous chapter, "Bennie and the Jets" acquired its own history. John had been easily persuaded to keep the song, as mixed by Dudgeon and Hentschel, on *Goodbye Yellow Brick Road*, but he initially resisted plans by his American label, MCA, to issue it as a single ("I fought tooth and nail against it coming out," he later admitted).[†] Yet once he realized that his conviction in the song's weak commercial and radio appeal was wrong, he embraced its release. And even though it had been released

---

[†] John has also always been very open about his other erroneous judgments on what songs should be spared release as singles or even inclusion on the album just recorded. For example, after the sessions for *Sleeping with the Past* were complete, he was convinced that all tracks had turned out

PERFECT MISTAKES 105

Figure 7.1 Bendy. An example of the mistaken (and potentially gender-altering) spelling of "Bennie" on some 7″ single releases of the song.

as the B-side to "Candle in the Wind" in the UK and other markets, John did not oppose its re-release as an A-side in the UK in 1976 (as "Benny and the Jets"—another mistake that stuck, harmlessly adding to the song's quirky legend; see Figure 7.1).[‡]

---

well, save for "a five-minute-long ballad" titled "Sacrifice." "Demonstrating again the infallible commercial instincts that led me to announce I was going to strangle Gus Dudgeon if 'Don't Let the Sun Go Down on Me' was ever released, I said I didn't want it ["Sacrifice"] on the album." After giving in, John was appalled when it was then released as a single; "no one was going to play it." Not only was "Sacrifice" a global hit in 1989, as "Don't Let the Sun" was in 1974, but in 1990 "Sacrifice" became the first solo UK #1 single of his career.

[‡] I have previously detailed some of the sequencing "mistakes" made to Elton John albums in the 1970s and 1980s, when label employees shuffled songs around on pre-recorded cassettes and 8-tracks—ruining the order so carefully created by Dudgeon for the vinyl releases—in order to

Over the decades, he has also embraced the notion that there is no right or wrong way to perform it; live versions vary in length and style, and Elton has in the past inserted phrases from sources as disparate as Glenn Miller's "In the Mood" and the most recognizable notes from John Williams's *Close Encounters of the Third Kind* film score. Often included in lists with titles like "Greatest Songs of All Time" (in 2021, it was #371 on *Rolling Stone*'s list of 500, for example), the throwaway song with the mistake at the start is clearly perfect for the pop/rock canon.

The numerous John biographies and album guides are peppered with examples of studio hiccups, unfortunate moments of human error, that resulted in something creatively fortunate. For example, during the Toronto sessions for *Blue Moves*, a "technical breakdown" forced Elton to sit patiently at his piano while the problem was fixed, and it wasn't clear how long that would take. Never one to sit patiently for anything, he kept playing, exploring new chord sequences—and in fifteen minutes came up with the chords that would underpin "Idol."

A different type of example had occurred while "Someone Saved My Life Tonight" was being recorded. During that session, Dudgeon noticed that Nigel Olsson had developed a tic: "when he switched from the high hat to the ride cymbal, he could not stop hitting the high hat with his foot pedal, whereas any other drummer would have stopped to create a softer effect." That mattered, as the drums were central to the track's sound. But Dudgeon had played a—arguably *the*—key role in the invention on earlier John albums of the rock ballad. Underlying that inventiveness was an instinct to roughen up the soft edges of the ballads that John developed on the piano, to give them a hint of the punch inherent to rock. Therefore, what was technically a mistake by Olsson was not only retained, but it was made high in the mix by Dudgeon; that accidental "matte-sounding snare drum" is part of what makes the song perfect.

This is a rosy picture of human error in the creative process. But the full picture is complicated by other categories of mistake. For example, has John's willingness to experiment and take chances—to toss off songs or even whole

---

make each side as "perfectly" identical in length as possible. Such vandalization of the producer's art was designed to save labels (but presumably not consumers) paltry sums in tape costs. All of which I mention as preface to noting that I believe the earliest rendering of "Bennie" as "Benny"—the origin of the error, and of the re-gendering of the fictional band's singer as male, or at least more likely male, thus a possible "correcting" of their androgyny, by the same vandals—was on an early cassette issue of *Goodbye Yellow Brick Road*.

albums and then send them out into the world and walk away to move on to the next project—resulted in a flawed catalogue? Certainly, the albums vary greatly in quality, and it is not hard to find filler on many of them. Even the songs selected as singles vary. After all, the raw statistics on John's singles tend to emphasize the hits and records achieved: of his 140 singles, 57 of them went Top 40 in the US and 70 of them did in the UK, for example, and as of 2021 he was the only solo artist to have UK Top 10 singles across six decades. But that also means that dozens of singles lost momentum in the lower reaches of the charts or even failed to chart at all. In some cases, that is because they just weren't very good; or their release was poorly timed; or they weren't properly marketed.

On the other hand, regardless of who was to blame, one could argue that the sheer abundance of material—singles and albums—reflects a laudable willingness to let *us* choose. We, as listeners and buyers of tickets and albums (and holders of streaming accounts) are thereby granted the opportunity—the power, if you like—to decide what works for us and what does not. To baldly declare, as I just did, that John's albums vary in quality hides the fact that it is impossible to find two sets of rankings that are the same—and I've scoured magazines and websites, attempting to correlate rankings in search of a pattern, until realizing that the pattern is the point I'm making here. Indeed, my own rankings, presented in the Discography, differ from month to month (what you see there is the version of the month this book went to press).

Even John and Taupin disagree on their rankings or judgments of their own albums—both from year to year, and between each other. For example, John has often said he adores *Blue Moves* ("I just love it!") but Taupin dismisses it as "not great." Taupin has called *Jump Up!* "abysmal," but John only notes that it was "an improvement sales-wise" over its predecessor, with the co-writing of one of its songs with Andrew Lloyd Webber leading to "one of the most important musical partnerships of my career"; not much of a defense, but also not the damning criticism he makes of a few others ("I stuck any old crap on *Leather Jackets*").

Taupin took some of the blame for *Jump Up!* While asserting that "Elton, lost in a fog of drugs and holed up in Paris," undermined their tried-and-true writing method by "hammering out an endless stream of compositional ideas" with which he couldn't keep up, Bernie admitted that his lyrical contributions were "tragic"—that is, tragically bad, "nothing but blundering unimpressive schlock." And it should be said, but as a reflection of the importance of his role in the catalogue's making, that some of the catalogue's imperfections must be laid at Taupin's feet. As he himself admits, not all his lyrics stand the test of time or seem very poetic (you may remember the earlier Taupin quote on calling him a poet being "an insult to real poets").

He has said that a number of songs are obviously about specific people, from well-known or obvious examples like "Candle in the Wind" (the subject of the next chapter), "Empty Garden" (John Lennon), and "Roy Rogers," to more obscure ones like "Whitewash County" (white supremacist David Duke) and "I've Got Two Wings" (Black guitar-playing evangelist Rev. Utah Smith). But others were simply vague, obliging curious fans and unsatisfied critics to assign real subjects: Richard Nixon to "Madman across the Water," for example; Marc Bolan to "I'm Going to Be a Teenage Idol"; and Elvis to "Idol." Others still were, by Taupin's own admission, "simplistic" and "confusing"—"Daniel" being an example whose lyrical contradictions and non sequiturs Taupin has amusingly self-criticized ("If his eyes have died does that mean he's blind? If he is . . .," and so on). Taupin has heard the tale, but doesn't remember if it is true or not, of the missing final verse to "Daniel"; rather than clarifying the previous verses, it so nonsensically introduced "a ship's captain and a one-legged dog named Paul" that Elton tore it off and binned it while he composed the music.

The fact that for decades listeners have taken the line "Daniel, my brother, you are older than me" to refer to an actual older brother of Elton's or Bernie's is hardly Taupin's fault. Nor is he to blame for "Philadelphia Freedom" being misappropriated as a patriotic anthem any more than is Bruce Springsteen for the misuse of his "Born in the USA." (Taupin did not intend "Philadelphia Freedom" to be a gay pride anthem either, as we saw earlier, but that can be easily reconciled with the song's spirit and context.)

But, arguably, such mistakes of interpretation reflect the perfection of those songs. Such is "the eternal power of a hit song: it can mean what it says, and it can mean the exact opposite of what it says depending on the context in which it's heard. Amazing." That is one writer's response to hearing Joni Mitchell's "Help Me" played at a wedding, which is a context that has turned into classic love songs such bitter odes as U2's "One" (a divorce song) and the Police's "Every Breath You Take" (a "very sinister and ugly" song "about jealousy and possession," Sting, its writer, has insisted). Similarly, I've heard many John songs played at weddings, where the title refrain may work but not the song's clear meaning, conveyed in lyrics to which nobody is paying attention ("I Want Love"); where even the title's relevance is a stretch but clearly what is heard is simply a nice ballad not an adultery confession ("Sacrifice"); where the original context is same-sex love, and the wedding is not a same-sex one, but one hopes—yet doubts—the choice is a conscious statement that love is love ("Blue Eyes"). "Can You Feel the Love Tonight" is also a singalong wedding favorite, but again its context (animated animals) is often reversed for listeners (if they were children at the time of *Lion King*, repurposing the song to be about adult human love works to affirm in positive terms both their collective childhood and their collective joy at the wedding of a loved one). "Can You Feel the Love" is not one of my favorite John songs, but I cannot deny its eternal power as a hit song; I'm not going to choose to play it at home or in the car, but will I sing along to it, with tears in my eyes, at a wedding? Absolutely.

We have to stretch, and stretch hard, in a different direction to positively spin some of Taupin's early lyrics about women. He himself has defended how "filthy" the words are to some of the songs on *Goodbye Yellow Brick Road* and other John albums of those years, arguing that the subject matter of such songs required "more meat on the bone," while conceding that "there was an element of naivety to some of them." He also admits that "a couple may have been inappropriate (the less said about 'Island Girl' the better)." And he may be right that the misogyny in such lyrics is "Hallmark friendly ... compared with what gets said in hard-core rap today." Comparing or relativizing misogyny (or any form of bigotry) runs the risk of trying to defend something indefensible. Instead, I'll take the safer route of giving Taupin the excuse of naïveté, as that quality underpins some of his and John's more treasured songs ("Your Song" being the most obvious). And I will thereby adopt a different kind of relativist argument; if we have to have "Dirty Little Girl" in order to get "Your Song," so be it.

All this means, of course, that even John's top-selling and often highest-ranked album, *Goodbye Yellow Brick Road*, is not perfect. "Dirty Little Girl" was judged in a book by two serious John fans to be "the most repulsive and misogynistic song" on the album, and they're not wrong. "Your Sister Can't Twist (But She Can Rock 'n Roll)" isn't offensive, but as a more annoying sibling to "Crocodile Rock" (itself an "irresistible but sickly mousse," in Simon Reynolds's words) it could well have been put aside to serve as a B-side. The schoolboy pun of "Jamaica Jerk-Off" seems like an unnecessary and ill-advised way to take a jab at the island where John and the band tried to record the album (before decamping to France and returning to the honky Château d'Hérouville). It doesn't help that its cod-reggae anticipates "Island Girl"—a global hit and a million-selling US #1, but badly dated in terms of race and gender (apologies to Bernie; I said more). Like "Island Girl," a further couple of *Yellow Brick Road* tracks work well *musically*—even extremely well—but Taupin's lyrics have aged very badly: "Social Disease" is one example (an alcoholic tenant pays his landlady rent in the form of liquor and sex; really?); another is "All the Young Girls Love Alice," a great song (musically) that John has often performed, but those above-mentioned fans are right again about the "kind of gross" subject matter (a sixteen-year-old lesbian "yo-yo" turns tricks and ends up "in the subway dead").

The point is not to denigrate the album's reputation (the 1973 *Rolling Stone* verdict that it was "too fat to float, artistically doomed by pretention" seemed almost immediately to miss the mark, even more so as the decades have passed). There are too many superb rock/pop classics to whittle *Yellow* down to a single album. Even if it can be made perfect by trimming it to three vinyl sides, it is hardly the only double album in the history of doubles for which that is true. No, the point here is that three or five misfires have the effect of casting the rest of the eighteen tracks in an even brighter light. The mistakes make *Yellow* perfect, while preventing it from being perfect-perfect.

That effect also works on the John catalogue as a whole. "We are always subtly aware of his other albums as points of comparison and difference." The observation is Will Brooker's, writing on Bowie, whose adulation tends to permit his weak albums to be forgotten or rehabilitated as bold experiments. Our sense of each album (by any artist) is shaped by its contrast to others in the catalogue, so that no album stands alone, the lesser works buoyed up by the greater ones, all of value in their contribution to the whole. The posthumous generosity with which Bowie's experimentalism was judged might also be extended to others who are still with us, and who have likewise not shied away from trying something different, who have been unafraid to stumble—Paul McCartney, for example, Rod Stewart, and Elton John. Indeed, John's fearlessness with respect to making mistakes out of entire albums is crucial to appreciating the full extent of his catalogue.

He could so easily have buried *Victim of Love*, an album on which he plays no piano and composed no music, and whose dire commercial and critical fate was surely utterly predictable. Its release at the time—as opposed to a release many years later, arguably the safer, but perhaps cowardly option—meant a brave step into an unforgiving critical world. But it also ensured the album would serve as a gift to generations of future fans, free to scorn or defend the album, to dismiss or find some virtue in it, to appreciate how it fitted into John's musical development during that tricky 1970s-to-1980s transition period.

Part of that fearlessness is a willingness to recognize a mistake. John's musical bottom-of-the-barrel in the 1980s was *Leather Jackets*; he knew it, and titled the next album *Reg Strikes Back*. It was better, but not much. The title was mocked as wishful thinking. No matter, Elton moved on to create *Sleeping with the Past*, a stylistic concept album that in the US charted lower than *Reg* and was slow to catch on in the UK—but eventually became his first #1 album in his homeland in fifteen years, starting a run of six Top 5 albums. Its 1980s predecessors threw *Sleeping* and its 1990s successors into relief. One is reminded of Tom Petty's *Southern Accents*, cleverly interpreted by one writer as that artist's greatest mistake, but one that was necessary to Petty's finding himself and going on to make the best albums of his career.

It isn't simply that "bad" albums make "good" ones seem better, but that creative efforts that are relative failures help to illuminate those that succeed. To fully appreciate what makes *Made in England* the best Elton album of the 1990s (or *The One*; take your pick), we can revisit the 1985–1988 trio of *Ice on Fire*, *Jackets*, and *Reg* to hear similar but often lesser ingredients assembled in ways that just don't work as well. As a result, the weaker albums make the stronger ones more interesting. John has steadily presented us with a puzzle, and all its pieces are needed in order to appreciate the full picture.

"Among Angels" is the closing track on *50 Words for Snow*, Kate Bush's 2011 (and, to date, final) album, and one on which she sings a duet with Elton. "Among Angels" begins with "a false start, a wrong note and a stop before she starts it properly" (as one writer puts it). Confessed Bush, "I was going to take that out, but a couple of friends said to leave it, that it was drawing you into the song." She doesn't say if Elton was one of the friends, but it would make sense if he had been.

8

Queens

Elton and Diana

"Candle in the Wind" (3:50, 1973; 4:10, 1987; 4:11, 1997)

"Candle in the Wind" is a threnody—a memorial song or elegy—to Marilyn Monroe who, as a figure whose fame contributed to her life being cut short, fascinated the young Bernie Taupin. Supposedly. For his twenty-first birthday, in May 1971, Taupin received from Elton John a large glass-fronted case containing one of Monroe's dresses. Exactly two years later, Taupin's lyrics were put to music by John, sitting at the piano in Château d'Hérouville, where he and his band were recording John's seventh album, *Goodbye Yellow Brick Road*. The song's title was taken from a comment by Clive Davis, then president of CBS Records, that Janis Joplin had been a "candle in the wind"— a phrase used to title at least one magazine article on her life and premature demise (Joplin died in 1970, aged twenty-seven; Monroe had died in 1962, aged thirty-six).

Or was it? Decades later, after the song had taken on a life of its own, Taupin would complicate that narrative a little. The Monroe dress, "in a five-foot Lucite case adorned with flashing bulbs and a plaque of authenticity," was gifted by Elton in the wake of the song's success, Taupin would write, not two years earlier. As for the title, "I just, for some reason, kept hearing this term," he recalled. "I thought, what a great, great way of describing somebody's life," adding, "to be quite honest, I was not that enamored with Marilyn Monroe. What I was enamored with was the idea of fame, or youth, of somebody being cut short in the prime of their life." The song "could have been about" anybody in that category, and therefore about "how we glamourize death. How we immortalize people."

On another occasion Taupin remembered that the idea for the lyrics did indeed begin with the title (he has often said many of his lyrics begin thus), but that this one came specifically from Aleksandr Solzhenitsyn's 1960 play, *Candle in the Wind*. Later, John Huston's 1961 movie *The Misfits* and its star Montgomery Clift prompted the subject matter. Only later still did Taupin realize that not Clift, but his co-star Monroe, would be "more sympathetic in the minds of the masses, . . . inconsolably vulnerable, the perfect metaphor for the song's title."

Regardless of the title's origin, and whether or not the song's more expansive meaning was fully developed in Taupin's mind in 1973, the lyrics specifically identify Monroe, both with that stage name and her birth name of Norma Jeane (or Jean). The song was yet another Americana fable, of the kind John and Taupin would create on every one of their 1970s albums, but with the added resonance of being about a real person—someone whose life and death had elevated her into the pantheon of pop culture icons. Furthermore, John instantly connected to the theme: "I was a huge Marilyn Monroe fan," he declared, thinking at the time that she was "the most glamorous woman that's ever been." The dress given to a turning-twenty-one (or twenty-three or twenty-four) Bernie would have been right at home in Elton's collections, as anyone knows who has seen photographs of those collections over the decades.

The melody in E major that John composed for Taupin's lyrics perfectly matched the emotion of the topic, suitably sentimental but just shy of saccharine. An obvious single, it was released in February 1974, with "Bennie and the Jets" on the B-side. It went Top 10 in some markets, but not all, peaking at #11 in the UK. And its release in the US was scrapped—a seemingly odd decision that stemmed from the runaway success of "Bennie" as a US #1 in 1974 (as recounted in the previous chapter). John's breakneck creative pace meant that in May that year the single from the next album was already out ("Don't Let the Sun Go Down on Me," from *Caribou*, released in June). "Candle in the Wind" was therefore hardly a worldwide hit first time around.

But that catchy melody—both haunting and gently anthemic—gave it a long shelf life. It was sequenced by producer Gus Dudgeon on Side One of *Goodbye Yellow Brick Road*, between "Funeral for a Friend/Love Lies Bleeding" and "Bennie and the Jets"—one an FM radio favorite, the other a US smash single, and the two tracks that *Billboard* cited in 2017 as the most praised by critics. *Goodbye Yellow Brick Road* was a sales juggernaut, outselling its predecessors and successors, on the road to being John's biggest album. "Candle in the Wind" could therefore not easily be ignored.

By 1987, its status as a fan favorite was such that when John's record labels chose tracks as singles to promote his new album and DVD *Live in Australia with the Melbourne Symphony Orchestra*, "Candle" was one of them. The other two—"Your Song" was released first, "Take Me to the Pilot" third—flopped. The live "Candle in the Wind" (with the live "Sorry Seems to Be the Hardest Word" on the B-side) was a big hit. Reaching #5 and #6 in the UK and US, respectively, it was nominated for "Best Pop Vocal Performance" by a male artist at the 1988 Grammy Awards. The song lost to Sting. John had lost the same award in previous years to Ray Stevens, Stevie Wonder (twice), Paul Simon, and Lionel Ritchie. He would go on to be nominated for this particular Grammy another six times (to hold the record at twelve nominations), losing to Eric Clapton, Seal, James Taylor, and John Mayer, winning it in 1995 for "Can You Feel the Love Tonight" (from *The Lion King* soundtrack). But that Grammy's role in the "Candle" story was not over.

On August 31, 1997, Princess Diana died in a car accident in Paris. She was, like Monroe upon her sudden death, thirty-six years old. Between then and the funeral in London's Westminster Abbey six days later, John and Taupin decided to rewrite "Candle in the Wind" in honor of Diana. The opening line, "Goodbye Norma Jeane," was changed to "Goodbye England's rose," followed by "May you ever grow in our hearts" and other tweaks to the lyrics. The song's poetic quality was weakened a little, but the context swamped such considerations. As Taupin would later remark, "The quality of the melody has such a powerful character that it almost becomes a hymn. Never mind the words that go with it. People let themselves be carried by it, carried along by this sumptuous melody."

The hymnal potential of the song was fully realized on September 6, when John sang the new version as a threnody to Diana—at the piano, at her funeral. Broadcast live, the performance was watched by hundreds of millions of viewers around the world. John discreetly used a teleprompter, afraid that because "I'd performed 'Candle in the Wind' hundreds of times, it really wasn't beyond the realms of possibility that I might lose myself in the performance . . . and start singing the original lyrics." John pledged that he would never again sing that version live, lending the performance a kind of sacrality through its unique association with the funeral. That decision, combined with the nature of the song itself, contributed to the rapid sanctification of Diana.

But John did leave the Abbey that day and go straight to Townhouse Studios, where he sat at a piano and sang the Diana version of "Candle" one more time. Legendary Beatles producer Sir George Martin was there to capture the recording, after which he overdubbed a string quartet. A week later, it was released as a single. As it happened, John had just released a new single. "Something about the Way You Look Tonight" (from the otherwise disappointing *The Big Picture*) had been in the works since before Diana's death, and it had come out only two days after her funeral. "Candle in the Wind 1997" was therefore added to that single, which was re-released as a double A-side. All proceeds from the re-release were to go to the charities that Diana had created or supported. Nobody, John included, anticipated what that would mean in terms of donations to those organizations—including the Elton John AIDS Foundation—and how rapidly the single would begin to break sales records.

Immediately entering the UK charts at #1, it stayed there for five weeks, going on to sell five million copies in Britain—to this date, the country's best-selling single. Production struggled to keep up with demand, and record shops attempted to enforce purchasing limits after customers started buying copies of the CD single in batches of five or ten. The story was the same in the US, where the single sat for fourteen weeks in the #1 spot, selling over eleven million copies—also, to this date, that country's best-selling single. Inevitably, it was soon declared to be the best-selling single of all time, worldwide, with over 35 million units sold.*

As for that Grammy, "Candle in the Wind 1997" was nominated, and won, for "Best Male Pop Vocal Performance," taking the prize that a previous version of the song had been denied ten years earlier.

Elton John had not yet turned sixty when the British press—who had treated him with vile homophobia for much of his thirties and forties—began to call him the "Queen Mum of Pop." This grudging nickname of respect evoked similar musician nicknames—Michael Jackson's "King of Pop" moniker, Elvis Presley as "the King," Aretha Franklin as "the Queen of Soul," and so on—while also winking at his age and his sexual identity. But the label

---

* The claim is controversial, as Bing Crosby's 1942 recording of "White Christmas"—written by Irving Berlin for that year's musical film *Holiday Inn*—had long been touted as the world's best-seller at 50 million copies, a (suspiciously) round number due to the lack of reliable sales records in the decades before the 7″ single was invented, and before Billboard, the BBC, and other organizations started to maintain charts. So, one might argue either that "Candle in the Wind 1997" holds the record, period, or it holds it with the caveat "since US and UK singles charts began in the 1950s" (as the *Guinness Book of World Records* put it in 2009).

Figure 8.1 Jukebox John. Elton John and Princess Margaret, with her husband Lord Snowdon—who was, as this photograph captures, far less interested than the princess was in the palace's pop star. (Photo taken backstage at the Royal Festival Hall in 1972. Credit: Michael Putland.)

resonated for another reason. As one would expect of a boy growing up in a middle-class London suburb, Reg Dwight was a monarchist. John was thus quick to embrace a burgeoning friendship with Princess Margaret at the peak of his 1970s success (see Figure 8.1). Around the same time, he bought a house in Windsor, making his primary residence just down the road from the royal family's Windsor Castle home.

"No man's a jester, playing Shakespeare," John sang in "The King Must Die" from 1970's *Elton John*, "Round your throne room floor." If it stretches the simile too far to suggest that in the 1970s John was like a medieval jester at the British royal court, he certainly became one of the family's favored performers. From Taupin's perspective, John took very early to the satisfaction of charity and benefit concerts, but "his generosity was hijacked by the crown and channeled into securing his services as an in-house jukebox." Right at the moment when Elton became a global superstar, he also "became the musical brandy and cigars for a motley group of blue bloods and upper-crust insiders."

Taupin found "the privilege of royal request" somewhat "presumptuous," and seeing "satiated nobility reclining free of charge inches away from a pop megastar," he couldn't help but think of "the working stiff who had to fork out a fiver for a nosebleed seat." But, aside from suggesting that Elton not play "The King Must Die," he admitted that his job was to play the "inconsequential shadow masquerading as a genial factotum." Ever the observer and storyteller, Taupin absorbed such details as the Earl of Lichfield slipping from his chair "to the ground in an intoxicated stupor" while John sang "Your Song," and the Queen muttering as the final chords echoed through the room, "Lichfield's gorn again."

Elton appealed in particular to the frustrated party princess, Margaret, who saw him in concert, had him invited to the royal residences, and dined at his Windsor house (accounts vary as to the formality and frequency of such gatherings). They were friends and neighbors, of a sort. "It turned out," John later mused, "that Princess Margaret loved music and the company of musicians." Taupin tells amusing stories of meeting the princess at a dinner in Kensington Palace after one of Elton's charity concerts; and again, at a dinner held for her in Beverly Hills; and, at a gathering in Elton's Windsor house, Bernie being whisked off for a stroll in the gardens with the Queen Mother, who glanced through the trees at Windsor Castle, saw the Royal Standard raised, and remarked, "Oh look, Mr. Taupin, my daughter's home."

When Margaret was asked by a journalist what she thought of John's live shows, she said they were "louder than Concorde." In one version of this anecdote, the pianist is having tea with the princess in Windsor, and she tells him, "You play louder than Concorde!" John was so amused he named his 1976 tour The Louder Than Concorde Tour, which, in turn, delighted the princess. On at least one occasion, she called Elton up and "asked me to take her to the pictures" (they snuck undetected by fans or press into a cinema on Shaftesbury Avenue). On another occasion, when she was over at Elton's for lunch one day, his mynah bird—who had been taught by someone to tell people to "piss off"—delivered his signature phrase to the royal guest. John only notes that the bird "disgraced himself," not how the princess reacted. But one rather imagines that she was thoroughly amused.

John's discretion in not recounting many detailed anecdotes about the royal family says much (at least he tells ones that are amusing, not disloyal or indiscreet)—just as reading between the lines of Taupin's anecdotes one can detect the depth of John's appeal and connection to the royal women.

When John confesses that "I have always found them incredibly charming and funny people" he seems to have the female Windsors mostly or entirely in mind (even if he discreetly never says that). To the male Windsors and related aristocrats he has been, perhaps, a court jester and in-house jukebox. To the women, he seems to have been more—a happy and harmless dancing partner to queens and princesses, a confidant, a partial insider with outsider appeal. Some might sniff at the whiff of elitism and social climbing. But I think that behind such appearances is evidence of the solidarity between gay men and women necessitated by the deep-rooted homophobia and sexism of society at large—manifested not just despite the context of extreme privilege, but in a way because of it.

Not long after Diana Spencer joined the royal family, she and Elton became friends. Given his relationship to the Windsors, it was not surprising that Elton would be asked to attend and briefly perform at Prince Andrew's twenty-first birthday party in 1981 (around the time that Diana became engaged to Prince Charles). Diana apparently insisted that an initially reluctant Elton dance the Charleston with her (having shuffled around the makeshift dance floor with Princess Anne to "Hound Dog," and with the Queen to "Rock Around the Clock"—"a completely surreal evening," recalled John). "I was completely bowled over by Diana," John writes, and his reaction was "nothing compared to the impact she could have on straight men. They seemed to completely lose their minds in her presence."

No wonder she enjoyed Elton's company. Their friendship lasted through years that were especially turbulent for him and then for her (see Figure 8.2). The British press constantly poked around for drama and dispute, largely in vain; John has described how "she was a very dear friend for years," reconciling after their one falling-out over the foreword Diana had written but then at the last minute withdrawn, under palace pressure, for a book assembled by his friend Gianni Versace of photographs by the likes of Herb Ritts and Robert Mapplethorpe (which, as we shall see later, John was collecting). Images and video footage of Diana comforting a distraught John during the funeral in Milan for Versace—in July 1997, just a month before her own accidental death—became well known.

Their bond's survival of the royal marriage's collapse inspired John and Taupin to turn "Candle in the Wind" into that funeral eulogy to Diana, making John's prominence at the funeral both appropriate and problematic; initial objections from the Palace may have reflected the mid-1990s tension between Diana and the royal family, although Palace sources insisted their

Figure 8.2 Very Versace. This 2022 Sierra Leone postage stamp is an example of the widespread use of images from this photo shoot of Elton John and Princess Diana, both Versace-clad, at a 1993 awards ceremony. It also reflects their persisting global celebrity. Their friendship, dating from 1981, was facilitated by John's prior relationship with his royal neighbors in Windsor. (Photo credit: Peregrine / Alamy Stock Photo.)

concern was entirely about the perceived disconnect between the somber nature of the occasion and John's image as a flamboyant pop star. But if there are three versions of every Elton story, there are six of every Diana tale, so who knows? John merely mentioned in his autobiography that he found support for the idea of his performance from all quarters. Unlike "Gianni's memorial service," when Italian "church officials hadn't thought it appropriate for me to perform . . . the Archbishop of Canterbury was incredibly nice and hugely supportive." That makes sense: in Italy, John is too foreign and too flamboyant (even more than was Versace); in Britain, he is pop royalty, *the* court jester and jukebox.

There was nothing flamboyant about the only live performance of "Candle in the Wind 1997," of course, and its success brought its own reward. John's service to the family went unmentioned, according to tradition and as one might expect, when John's knighthood "for services to music and charitable services" was announced in the New Year's Eve honor list later that year. But the timing could not be ignored. At the time of the announcement, "Candle in the Wind 1997" was still in the UK Top 10 (as a former #1 having already spent four months in the charts), bringing what would end up as tens of millions of dollars into Diana's charitable trust. Two months later, Reginald Kenneth Dwight became Sir Elton Hercules John, CBE. His future husband was with him, as was his mother and stepfather Fred ("Derf").

"You must be terribly busy," the Queen told Sir Elton. It was one of her standard lines, but in this case, she knew what she was talking about; after all, she'd known him for a quarter of a century. "They don't come much bigger than this," enthused new-Sir Elton outside the Palace. "I love my country, and to be recognized in such a way—I can't think of anything better."

John's pride contrasted strongly with David Bowie's reaction to the same award five years later. Having turned down a CBE (Commander of the Order of the British Empire) in 2000 (an award John had accepted in 1995), Bowie then rejected a knighthood in 2003. "I'd never have any intention of accepting anything like that," he remarked. "I seriously don't know what it's for. It's not what I spent my life working for." Fair enough; John *did* know what his was for. Bowie was not asked about Sir Elton, but he was asked about Sir Mick—knighted the same year Bowie declined to be. "It's not my place to make a judgment on Jagger. It's his decision. But it's just not for me." A few years later, Paul Weller declined a CBE with a similar comment, made through a spokeswoman (he was "flattered, but it wasn't really for him").

Two cultural phenomena were lurking behind these reactions to being offered membership into the Order of the British Empire:[†] class and cool. Bowie and Weller, always deemed cool, coolly declined the honor. Bowie had long affected a kind of expat classlessness, underscored by his permanent move to New York. Weller's attitude toward the class system was to embrace an anti-establishment working-class pride. In contrast, the reaction of Rod Stewart, who accepted a knighthood in 2018, was telling. Asked how

---

[†] There are five classes of appointment to the Order. In ascending order, they are MBE (Member), OBE (Officer), CBE (Commander), KBE (Knight), and GBE (Knight Grand Cross). No musicians hold GBEs.

his parents (long deceased) might have reacted, Stewart said, leaning into his working-class London accent, "Oof, our Roddy, a knight! From a council house [government housing] to Buckingham Palace!" And Sir Elton? "He was the first to congratulate me," said Sir Rod, adding that Elton marveled that "a couple of old tarts from London have become knights!" In the fine-grained British class system, Stewart's London origins are a tad more working-class than John's, as reflected in their accents—even after their accents have been smoothed out by decades of non-British travel, residence, and romantic partners. But for both, music made them mobile—in an upward social sense—and knighthoods, as the ultimate recognition of that upward mobility, were "for them."

The relationship between Sir Elton and the royals has continued to be marked by performances, tributes, and awards, as it has since early in his career. When John and Furnish married in 2014, they chose the same location—Windsor Guildhall—where Prince Charles had married Duchess Camilla just months earlier. The parallel between the two 2014 weddings was covered repeatedly in the press, still being considered a story of note years later. In 2021, Prince Charles made John a member of the Order of the Companions of Honour in a Windsor Castle ceremony; the award, dating from 1917, recognizes a recipient's "major contribution to the arts, science, medicine, or government over a long period of time." "I got this for music and for work for charity," said John. "So, this is just a reminder that there's more to do. More work to do for music, more work to do for charity and life is great. I'm so lucky."

The earnest, heartfelt, and committedly uncool royalist was performing in Toronto when news reached him of the September 8, 2022, death of "Her Majesty Queen Elizabeth." He alluded to his role at court—"I've been around her and she's fantastic"—going on to say, with a portrait of the smiling monarch on the giant screens, that "I'm 75 and she's been with me all my life and I feel very sad that she won't be with me anymore. But I'm glad she's at peace, and I'm glad she's at rest and she deserves it. She worked bloody hard." He then went on to play—to "celebrate her life"—"Don't Let the Sun Go Down on Me."

If calling Sir Elton the "Queen Mum of Pop" was a nod to other musicians (Jackson, Presley, Franklin), those references are generic in the US (obviously not a monarchy). Whereas there really was a Queen Mother in Britain, much beloved; she died, aged 101, just before John's "Queen Mum" nickname started appearing in the UK press. In a sense, there are now two deceased Queen Mums and one still living. The notion, therefore, of John as royalty resonates in multiple ways. Not least of those is the way that his rise from commoner obscurity to royal levels of wealth and celebrity seems to be a parable about class mobility in Britain. But it is, in fact, a tale of mobility that *reinforces* the class system. There can only be one living Queen Mother and one living Queen Mum of Pop.

9

Poppermost

Elton and Dua

"Cold Heart" (3:22, 2021)

"Cold Heart" helped Elton John break yet more records. In addition to thereby being the first solo artist to reach the UK Top 10 in six consecutive decades, the song also made him the oldest artist (aged seventy-four) to hit #1 on the Australian singles chart. A Top 10 hit in more than forty countries, "Cold Heart" also made him the oldest artist ever with a hit that big and that global. And it gave him the longest span (fifty years and ten months) of appearances in the US Top 40. All of which matters not only because it is more data to add to Elton's superlativeness; it also matters because it matters to John himself, the consummate chart-watcher, the ultimate collector.

More specifically, "Cold Heart" is not just the latest, but one of the best songs to introduce this topic, due to the way in which it reflects Elton's career. First, it is a mashup of samples and re-recorded components from four John/Taupin songs, primarily the old hits "Rocket Man" (1972) and "Sacrifice" (1989), with snippets from old hit "Kiss the Bride" (1983) and *Blue Moves* obscurity "Where's the Shoorah?" (1976). Go back to those original songs and their parent albums, and you've given yourself a quick but effective tour of his catalogue. Second, the track was created by young Australian trio Pnau, whose mashups of old John tracks gave Elton his previous #1 album (in 2012). Listen to *Good Morning to the Night*, then dive into the catalogue to hear the forty or so original songs that Pnau's Littlemore and Mayes used to create the album, and you've qualified yourself to answer Elton questions on trivia night.[*]

---

[*] The dance music group Pnau were a duo when they made *Good Morning to the Night*, with Sam Littlemore joining his brother Nick and Peter Mayes in 2016; all born in the late 1970s, they are roughly thirty years younger than John.

Third, it is significant that Elton did not simply re-record his own old songs—a twenty-first-century trend that, for my tastes, has seldom seemed anything other than pointless. I applaud Taylor Swift's motives—to regain control over her own catalogue—but the re-recordings by Sting, U2, and so many others only sent me back to the originals or, irritated, to another artist. Acoustic re-recordings, or new versions with full orchestras, may work in a live context. After all, it is the differences between studio recordings and live performances that highlight the personal nature of the concert experience. If I want to hear John playing with an orchestra, I'll put on 1987's superb *Live in Australia with the Melbourne Symphony Orchestra* and imagine I am in the audience enraptured and applauding; I don't want him to re-record his old songs with an orchestra in a studio.

Perhaps I am splitting hairs. My point here is that John gave permission for Pnau to do the reworking and reimagining, giving them full creative freedom while also engaging with them in what amounted to a highly original collaboration—and an extremely successful one. "Cold Heart" took that process a step further by bringing in the magnetic young British pop star Dua Lipa to re-record some of Elton's old vocals (see Figure 9.1). In other words, the nature of the collaboration is classic John: a duet that is also a sharing and also a kind of collecting.

Dua Lipa is just one of two dozen collaborators on the "Cold Heart" parent album, *The Lockdown Sessions*. Sure, numerous artists turned the COVID pandemic's lockdown into a "rockdown" (as Paul McCartney dubbed it; or he was the most famous person to call it that); from their virus-free home studios they remotely recorded collaborations. But John's relationship to the concept runs far deeper than that. For he has always been a collector not just of records, but of artists themselves. Those artists have sometimes helped him to stay close to a place he has always cherished—the charts—but they also allow him to remain connected to something more visceral: his living musical collection.

Size matters, sometimes. And how do we quantify and evaluate size? Collection and measurement. Elton has always been obsessed with the size of his record collection. He began collecting when he was still Reg Dwight. Psychoanalytic studies of the collecting impulse show that it is strongest in the preteen years of seven to thirteen; for Reg, that was the late 1950s, when his collection began. Taupin has said that in 1970 John—still more Reg than

Figure 9.1 Warm Heart. One of the several versions of the cover art to Elton John and Dua Lipa's "Cold Heart." Australia's Pnau produced the single and album version, also being given co-writing credit.

Elton at this pre-fame stage—was very reluctant to travel to the US to perform, only agreeing to the trip when he realized it would give them access to the massive Tower Records store in Los Angeles ("Kids in a candy store is putting it mildly.")

The impulse typically fades, a little or a lot, during the subsequent sexually active decades, often returning in mid-life—when a completist impulse can emerge, and the intent to listen to every record (or read every book or wear every shoe or item of clothing) ceases to matter, as the act of hunting and gathering takes on its own death-defying logic. If the impulse faded for Elton in his twenties, it would be explicable in terms of the relentless labor of music-making and touring during his imperial 1970s; yet if it did, it barely showed, and the acquisition of great wealth facilitated the transition to a vast and sweeping collecting obsession.

It is believed that John now has one of the largest private record collections in the world, housed in multiple locations, amounting to hundreds of thousands of seven-, ten-, and twelve-inch platters, discs, and tapes (see Figure 9.2). On at least one occasion, he has sold portions of his collection (as many as tens of thousands of items) and then started over again. His acquisition, curation, and display of physical copies of albums and singles in various formats reflects two historical trends, one rooted in the deep past, the other a development in his lifetime. The royal and aristocratic impulse to collect goes back many centuries, manifested in Aztec Mexico, Ming China, and early modern Europe. As rock royalty, with universal acclaim and longevity of rule, Sir Elton is a modern heir to that tradition.

His collection also anticipated, and was further propelled by, a far more recent development: the compact disc boom. Philips, the corporate inventor of the CD, promoted the new format in the 1980s for its archival—as well as sonic—superiority. If, as Derrida claimed, "the structure of the archive is spectral," easy-to-read labels on durable jewel boxes made curation and display more transparent, encouraging the acquisition of albums already owned in tattered-spined record sleeves. In the CD era of the 1980s and 1990s, the weird logic of collection and accumulation, completion and display, went mainstream. Even after digital file-sharing and streaming gutted CD sales in the twenty-first century, the resurgent popularity of vinyl, CDs, and cassettes among a minority of music fans serves only to reinforce the rationale behind John's collection.

As the monarch of the musos, he is simply doing what those fans are doing, what he has been doing all along, but on a scale befitting his status. The French philosopher Jean Baudrillard (1929–2007) wrote that "it is invariably *oneself* that one collects," and that is patently relevant to the symmetry of one of the world's greatest creators of recorded music being one of its greatest collectors. That mentality, moreover—that obsessive desire to quantify and measure, to *know*—also extends to Elton's lifelong passion for chart-watching. That likewise began in childhood. And as Elton himself became a regular presence on the charts, his compulsive chart-watching came to center on his own position—both on the weekly charts and on the larger rankings and records of veteran rock stars. As we've seen, thanks to "Cold Heart," #1 in a dozen countries in 2021, Britain included,

Figure 9.2 Want Wax? Elton John at home with his record collection in Windsor, in the mid-1970s. (Photo credit: Terry O'Neill / Iconic.)

"Elton is the first act to score a UK Top 10 single in six different decades"—a statistic that matters a great deal to him (he has always taken great pride in being at "the toppermost of the poppermost," to borrow John Lennon's phrase).

For Reg/Elton, however, the act of collection was not just about the music or the objects on which it was captured. The musician and filmmaker Questlove, whose own collections include "more than 200,000 records," has noted that "the collector's impulse becomes a connecting impulse." Collecting is personal, it connects the collector to other people, and prompts "a personal question" that Questlove says he asks all the time: "Am I only the sum of all the things that I have collected?"

John's record collecting, like his chart obsession, may seem to be about him (about *Me*, as his autobiography proclaims), an exercise in self-collection. But I see it as far more about Questlove's connecting impulse. Music writer and editor Chris Charlesworth interviewed John very early in both their careers. He was struck by their common passion for record-collecting, and especially by young Elton's intense interest in knowing as much about as many artists as possible. Other collectors seldom knew about the artists, "but Elton *did* know all that history of pop."

John's impulse to collect, quantify, and measure extends beyond the acquisition of records—of both the vinyl and statistical kind—to include other musicians. His obsessive passion is for other artists as well as their music, and his collecting is manifested in his mentoring. This is related to the relationships he has developed with other musicians, such as those in the various iterations of his band (bassist Dee Murray and drummer Nigel Olsson were the only musicians with him for the breakout 1970 US shows; both were mainstays of the classic Elton John Band, Murray until his early death in 1992, Olsson until today). But those relationships are adjacent, rather than on point, to my argument that a career-long pattern of idol-recognition and mentoring is an expression of John's collecting impulse.

In 2022, Elton approached Britney Spears with a duet idea. The template was the previous year's collaboration with Dua Lipa, and the idea was to use that now-classic chorus line from "Tiny Dancer" as the new song's hook and title: "Hold Me Closer." Spears was coming out of a period in her life that by all accounts (especially her own) seemed deeply harrowing, one made very public by her legal battle to escape the court-ordered conservatorship that permitted her father total control over her life. She had not recorded for years, and she had no plans to do so. The press wondered "if Spears would ever perform again." But she changed her mind about going into the studio for two reasons that are commonly heard by those who have collaborated with or been mentored by Elton John: he is "an artist I've admired all my life" (in Britney's words); and he reached out with "the sweetest video message," following it up with what seemed to her kindness and "incredible compassion."

For many years, between the late 1970s and early 1990s, the press had been vile to John, and he was well aware of the cruelty that Spears had endured from critics, on social media, even from family members. "Britney was broken. I was broken when I got sober. I was in a terrible place. I've been through that broken feeling and it's horrible," John said when "Hold Me Closer" was released. "Now I've got the experience to be able to advise people and help them because I don't want to see any artists in a dark place." Here we see Elton's collecting impulse from childhood, evolved into a mentoring impulse as a young man, enhanced in middle age by a post-rehab empathy (with a dab of survivor's guilt), fully developed in old age by the experience of philanthropic and paternal satisfaction.

Two other factors helped make "Hold Me Closer" happen, making it a comfortable and "fantastic experience" for Spears, ensuring that once it was released, to her "it felt *great.*" First, the core of the recording, that old opening track from *Madman*, was a song that happened to be particularly "meaningful" to her: "as a child, I listened to 'Tiny Dancer' in the car in Louisiana as I rode to and from my dance and gymnastics classes." In other words, the old ambiguity in the John/Taupin songwriting dynamic permitted yet another personal interpretation and appropriation of the song: Elton was singing to Britney as a child, literally a tiny dancer (see Figure 9.3). ("The song meant so much to her," said its producer, Andrew Watt, "and you can hear it in her vocal performance.")

And second, Elton was not creepy, neither then nor now, especially not to young women—for whom the music industry was, for many decades, the dangerous stalking ground of predators (and to some extent, still is). Sympathetic to the plight of young musicians ("there's a lot of pressure," says John), especially to those who have suffered ("Britney was broken"). John works hard to be welcoming: "I'm Uncle Elton. They can phone me." John's sexual identity may be secondary to the empathy behind his mentoring impulse, but they are clearly connected, and it thus matters that Sir Elton is also gay Uncle Elton. Britney has characterized her "special relationship with the gay community" as being based on safety and support; whether she was out

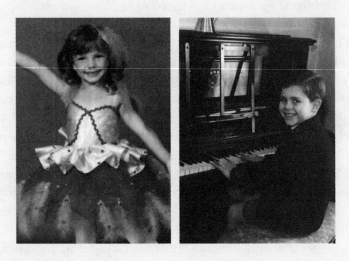

Figure 9.3 Beauty and the Beat. Britney Spears and Elton John as children on the cover of 2022's "Hold Me Closer" single.

on the town or performing on stage, she could count on the "supportive role" played by "the gay guys around me." To her, safe Uncle Elton is, in that tradition, "a beautiful man on all levels."

John's infinite collecting/mentoring impulse means that the list of musicians that he admires never runs out. It can include someone like Spears, thirty-four years his junior, whom he thought from the start of her career "just put out incredibly brilliant records." Or it can include someone like Neil Sedaka, who had his first big hit when Elton was twelve-year-old Reg. Sedaka was one of the artists whom John admired, and who became—along with Cliff Richard, Kiki Dee, and others—"comeback" successes thanks to Rocket Records, which served from the very start as a vehicle to help other artists, especially those in career doldrums. Elton in his twenties couldn't play the role of uncle to Neil in his thirties, but this is the beginning of the phenomenon that would lead to Britney's Uncle Elton.

John had been a fan of Sedaka's early-1960s hits, of his songwriting chops, and of his "Laughter in the Rain"—a 1974 UK hit around the time the two musicians met in England. John was shocked to learn that the song would not see a US release, as Sedaka no longer had an American label ("Over there, they think I'm a ghost!"). Seeing a golden opportunity to close an idol/mentor loop, John offered to help. "I can make you a record star again," he told Sedaka. Pulling the best tracks from Sedaka's most recent three British albums, John had Rocket Records release *Sedaka's Back* (as they called it) in America, with liner notes by John himself. Within a few months, "Laughter in the Rain" was #1—Rocket's first chart topper. Two other singles were hits, the album reached #23, Sedaka's comeback in the US was underway, and a lasting friendship was forged.

Elton's instinct for mentoring other artists sprang from his deep desire to connect with them, to extend his record collection into a personal collection of friends and colleagues in music-making. There is no sign that this instinct was a controlling one; it was more about connectivity. Even before the example of Sedaka and Rocket Records, there was the case—detailed in an earlier chapter—of his and Rod Stewart's attempt to pay back in kind the mentoring they had received in the 1960s from Long John Baldry.

And even before that was the example of his friendship with Lesley Duncan (1943–2010). They had met in London during his laboring days as a session player, when they were hired for vocal work in the same studio. A few years older than John, Duncan was a talented singer-songwriter whose shyness and fear of the stage would route her career into singing backing vocals on other people's albums (from John's early albums to Pink Floyd's *Dark Side of the Moon*), and into writing songs that others would record (her own five solo albums of the 1970s did not sell well).

From his earliest records and throughout his career, John has seldom covered the songs of others on his albums. But considering himself a friend and admirer of Duncan's, he wanted to strengthen that connection by recording one of her songs. "Love Song," with Duncan playing acoustic guitar and singing backing vocals, stands out on *Tumbleweed Connection*. It is a beautiful recording, a gem. It is, as one writer gently put it, "perhaps slightly out-of-place." But it thus "speaks volumes for Elton as a fan of, and mentor for, other artists." Duncan would record her own version of "Love Song" for her debut album the next year—Elton, of course, played piano on the album—but it was the John recording that made the song famous, and prompted other covers, starting with Olivia Newton-John's that same year. It has now been covered over 150 times.[†]

For John, being successful offered opportunities to complete circles of idolization and mentorship. A standout example of this is John's thrill at seeing Leon Russell "in the second row" of the audience while he was singing "Burn Down the Mission" during his breakthrough 1970 week at the Troubadour. "I practically froze," confessed John. "He was my idol, without question. He changed the way I played the piano. Or tried to play the piano." Afraid that Russell would chastise him for being a second-rate hack, John found Russell to be "a southern sweetheart who embraced me and was very complimentary," which was "a huge boost for me, to have that approval from someone who was your idol." The two toured together soon after that, allowing John to hone his performing skills "on the road with Leon."

But then, for decades, John rode the rollercoaster of unprecedented stardom while Russell slipped into obscurity. Still prominent in the pop pantheon in his early sixties, John started to reflect more deeply on his past and to recall something he'd forgotten—"how nice" Russell had been to him, "how encouraging he was to me." Calling Russell up to thank him was hardly enough for John; the circle needed to be completed. So, into the studio the two elderly musicians went—armed with fresh lyrics from Taupin, naturally—and an album emerged, 2010's *The Union*. "It's not often in your life that you get to, as a professional, as an artist, you get to work with your idol," commented John that year.

Of course, giving that experience is as important to him as having it. If the John-Russell story is a circle, the Lennon-John-Michael story is a chain. "The only person in this business that I've ever looked up to," said John in 1974, "who is one-hundred percent sacred to me, the *only* person," was John Lennon. That uniqueness was not quite true, as this chapter is arguing, but as an ex-Beatle just a few years after that band's dissolution, Lennon's star was extremely high in the firmament, making his budding friendship with Elton a dizzying experience even for the world's biggest rock star at that moment.

[†] "Love Song" offers another connection between David Bowie and Elton John. Bowie had also met Duncan during their early London years: around 1966, according to him in a 2003 interview, he had "an on-again, off-again thing with a wonderful singer-songwriter who had previously been a girlfriend of Scott Walker." That was Duncan. Bowie's trio Feathers performed "Love Song" live, and he recorded a demo of it in 1969; he would have beaten Elton to the punch had it been included in 1969's *David Bowie*, where it would have fit nicely.

That year, Elton coaxed Lennon onto the Madison Square Garden stage to perform a few songs with him—an appearance that is now legendary, as it proved to be Lennon's last (he only did it with great reluctance, because he lost a bet to Elton when "Whatever Gets You Thru the Night," on which Elton played piano, hit #1).

"It's our great privilege, and *your* great privilege, to see and hear," Elton told the Garden audience, pausing for effect, "Mr. John Lennon." The arena "detonated" (as one journalist put it), giving Lennon a standing ovation of ten full minutes. After their three-song set, Elton launched into "Don't Let the Sun Go Down on Me"—eyes closed, tears rolling down his face. That song helps link the chain of idols and influences, of "Misters." For just as Elton as young Reg had idolized Lennon, playing his records over and over in his childhood bedroom, so had young George Michael, still Georgios Panayiotou, bonded with future Wham! partner Andrew Ridgeley over *Goodbye Yellow Brick Road* and "Don't Let the Sun Go Down on Me."

Elton and George first crossed paths at the Château de Miraval studio in Provence in 1984. Just as Elton had forged a collaborative friendship with his idol Lennon, so did George forge one with his idol Elton. Wham! manager Simon Napier-Bell later argued that John then "took over the role in George's life previously played by Andrew." Ridgley "had given George the courage to stand up and be a pop star—to be onstage, to be in the public eye." But George was now eager to move on, and Elton "provided the perfect model" for Michael as a solo artist: "in charge of his own business and his own life—able to make every decision for himself, good or bad."

Elton played on the last Wham! album, while George sang on the global smash "Nikita," as well as on its campy follow-up, "Wrap Her Up." As a George biographer noted, "Michael began to view John as a gay surrogate father." There was a competitive edge to the relationship, both being equally obsessed with their chart numbers. In David Geffen's rather uncharitable take on it, "Elton wanted to be friends with all the biggest stars. He admired them until they surpassed him, making him only human. George had replaced Elton at that moment in time." But John and Stewart's friendship not only survived but thrived on rivalry, and John's with Michael likewise endured.

During 1985's Live Aid in Wembley, John had played piano to Michael's rendition of "Don't Let the Sun Go Down on Me." Six years later, during a Wembley Arena concert—the final UK gig of his Cover-to-Cover tour—Michael performed that song, investing Taupin's words with as much emotion as John ever had. At the three-minute point, Michael shouted out to the audience, "Ladies and Gentlemen . . . Mr. Elton John!" The audience, as surprised as the Garden crowd of seventeen years earlier, likewise detonated, their cheering spiking as John started to sing and as the two sang the remaining chorus together. Their perfect pairing made the performance electrifying. Well aware of the chemistry of the collaboration, they repeated it in Chicago, this time filming it for a video to go with the release of the live duet as a single. Quickly going to #1 both in the UK and then the US, and nominated for a Grammy, the single gave both men's careers—neither of which was at a low point—a further boost.

One of Michael's biographers saw competitiveness afoot in the body language of the video (at the end they "embrace, but Michael had won"), while conceding that it was also "one of the great gay summits in nineties pop." And for John, there was more at stake than just sharing, or competing for, the stage limelight and the top of the charts; his rehab had worked, and he was now unequivocally out as a gay man. He could see that Michael was as conflicted and miserable as he himself had been, and his instinct to save those in his loops-and-chain sequences of mentorship and admiration meant that he would repeatedly urge George to come out too. But "George thought it was too soon, and it wasn't anybody's business."

When Michael finally did come out, in a famously indirect but resounding manner (cruising public restrooms until he was arrested in a Beverly Hills park in 1998), his career in the US was all but destroyed—an echo of John's career dive in the US in the wake of his 1976 "bisexuality" interview. American radio stations refused to play "Outside," Michael's brilliant celebration of the incident, and it failed to chart—as did all fifteen of the singles he would release in the US during the remaining sixteen years of his life. The story was different in the UK, where "Outside" reached #2, and was prominent on the *Ladies & Gentlemen* hits compilation, which went to #1. John was happy that his friend was out, whatever the circumstances and career consequences, but he remained anguished by the ongoing drug use that he feared would prove fatal. Michael refused to let John save him, even grousing about his meddling in a 2009 *Guardian* interview: Elton "will not be happy until I bang on his door saying, 'Please, please help me, Elton. Take me to rehab.' It's not going to happen."

In September 2016, John performed sixteen songs in London's Hyde Park. "I want to dedicate this song to one of the greatest talents that I have ever met out of Great Britain," he told the massive crowd near the end of the set, "this is for you, George Michael. I love you. I think you're amazing" (a reference to the chorus of one of Michael's hits). Launching into the song of his that Michael had made theirs, "Don't Let the Sun Go Down on Me," John was still trying to save and mentor his mentee. Three months later, Michael was dead. Performing in Las Vegas a few days later, John paid an emotional tribute to that chain of idols, of which he was the only surviving link, singing "Empty Garden" (his and Taupin's homage to Lennon and that legendary 1974 night at Madison Square Garden) and "Don't Let the Sun Go Down on Me." Before picking out the opening chords, he said "I only wish George was here to sing it with me." He barely made it through the song, turning his back to the audience after the last note, his head down and shoulders shaking.

Salvation: the theme runs through the John story, with him in later years being very frank about wishing he could have saved those lost to addiction—he writes of trying to reach Whitney Houston, for example, and of course George Michael, whom "I loved." The successes are thus savored all the more. And if you are tempted to see too much credit given to John, consider what makes his otherwise unlikely friendship with Eminem possible: "When I first wanted to get sober, I called Elton," admitted the rapper in 2009. Needing help from someone who understands "the business . . . the pressures . . . the drugs," he called Uncle Elton (not that he calls him that; he calls him "cunt," a partially successful effort to grasp the complex way in which the English use that term, including as a term of endearment, and which, John says, "I guess is very Eminem"). "Your sobriety day is in my diary," John told Eminem in a published phone exchange, "I'm just so proud of you." Responds Eminem, "I love you too."

Salvation—always part of John's own origin and career mythology, a strong link to his collecting of mentees and musical friends—has for long gone both ways. For example, because John's piano playing on his early records was the primary inspiration for a teenage Kate (then Cathy) Bush to compose and play pop songs on the same instrument, it has been "utterly surreal" to her to see John become a collaborator and friend. But for him, the relationship is not just about welcoming a fan as a peer but recognizing her role in his salvation. "This was one record that saved my life," John said of "Don't Give Up," Bush's 1986 duet with Peter Gabriel. "That record helped me get sober. So, she played a big part in my rebirth."

Delightfully surprised that Bush showed up to his and Furnish's 2005 civil partnership ceremony, John was also delighted at how much everybody "wanted to meet Kate Bush," despite the fact that "there were a lot of very famous people" at the event. "She's kind of an enigma. I mean, when has the next Kate Bush come along, after Kate Bush? There hasn't been one." That's one musician showing appreciation for another; but it is also, in less obvious psychological terms, an expression of joy by a collector and a completist. If and when "the next Kate Bush" does come along, John will want to meet her, befriend her, and play her songs on his Rocket Hour podcast.

In 2024, John and Furman decided to sell the property in Atlanta that had been one of their homes for thirty-one years, and which had given the *Peachtree Road* album its name. As one might expect of Elton, he had filled the place with several of his collections, which were consequently auctioned off through Christie's. This was far from the first time John had auctioned off collections; he has periodically purged them in order to raise funds for charitable organizations, including his own AIDS Foundation (the EJAF), in order to renovate or sell a property (as in the 2024 case), and—even if he denies this and it may not be conscious—to start collecting all over again. I mentioned above a massive sale in the 1980s of his record collection (which was immediately restarted), and in 1988 he raised over $8 million for charity by auctioning off some 2,000 items of clothing and concert costumes, artwork and jewelry, and memorabilia. Millions more were raised for his new AIDS Foundation in mid-1990s wardrobe auctions—one in London was called "'Out' of the Closet," and one in Atlanta called "Elton's Closet." Twenty exotic British and Italian cars were sold in the UK in 2001 for several million dollars, as John said he was abroad too often to enjoy driving them (in addition to the Atlanta house, there were homes in Los Angeles, Nice, Venice, and elsewhere). A few years later the entire contents of his and Furnish's Holland Park (London) house were auctioned off for charity, in order to make room for their growing art collection.

The Atlanta auction was similar in content, but greater in scale and value. Among the jewelry and watches, furniture and paintings, a grand piano, and a convertible Bentley were some unique collections. One of them comprised hundreds of hand-stitched, elaborately printed silk shirts and other clothes designed by Elton's old friend, Gianni Versace (1946–1997)—so many that they essentially enjoyed their own walk-in closet, and too many to all be worn. ("I just love them," confessed Elton. "I never wore half of them, I just wanted to hang them. It was like an art installation with shirts, and they look *so* beautiful.")

Another collection—of particular interest to us here—comprised some 7,000 photographic prints, enough to justify their own curator. Newell Harbin, the director of the Sir Elton John and David Furnish Photography Collection, assumed the task in 2010, overseeing an acquisition of "about 1.5 pieces a week" (she said in 2024). How did this collection echo Elton's record-collector mentality? In two ways.

First, it began the way a record collection begins, with a genre or a few favorite artists. Elton had for long been interested in the medium of photography but had tended to buy either celebrity portraits or dramatic figurative images (to put it prosaically: striking photographs of naked men). The appeal of artful images of beautiful male bodies to a man obliged by the homophobia of the 1970s and 1980s to remain officially closeted is palpable; we might see it as a cultured act of private resistance (Bruce Weber pieces, e.g., became a core portion of Elton's collection). As for celebrity portraits, since 1970, Elton had himself been almost constantly photographed, including as a celebrity by collectible photographers, and such images were thus the equivalent to a record-maker collecting the records of his peers.

"I'd had my photograph taken by so many famous photographers," said John, "but I never considered it an art form until I got sober. And then I changed my appetite for photography and for contemporary art." In the early 1990s, echoed Furnish, "through clean and sober eyes, he very much looked at the world differently, and new things spoke to him in ways they hadn't spoken to him before." With characteristic completist zeal, he turned to educating himself about, and acquiring, photographs.

That does not mean Elton was indiscriminate, but his collection steadily came to comprise a virtual guide to the art form from 1910 into the 2020s (Avedon, Arbus, Lange, Newton, Ray, Ritts, Sherman, and so on). He took to collecting "at the masterpiece level and was behind a lot of interest and collecting power during the '90s and the 2000s," recalled Christie's International Head of Photographs Darius Himes. In 1993, for example, Elton broke the record for the purchase at auction of a single photograph, paying $193,895 for Man Ray's *Glass Tears*. But the completist mentality did drive a kind of omnivorous-ness; encountering a photographer new to him, Elton wanted not only to ensure they were represented in his collection, but "to know everything about that artist," said Harbin, "what books they've published, what exhibitions they've been in and so on." And within the acquisition of each artist's work, a completism operated; for example, "there is not a series by [Irving] Penn that we do not have in this collection," noted Harbin.

Second, just as records are to be curated, displayed, and occasionally moved in order to be played, so were the photographs of the John/Furnish Collection curated (by the couple themselves, and by Harbin), displayed, and occasionally shuffled, both in the 13,500-square-foot Peachtree Road residence and between there and a studio space in nearby Park Place purchased for this specific purpose. In order to maximize display, they were largely hung salon style, often juxtaposed in ways more available to a private collector than a public museum. Noted Harbin, "It's amazing what Elton can put on the wall and get away with versus what other people can" (which really means, of course, we would expect excess of Elton and a certain getting-away-with-it). There were also exhibits at public museums—the Tate Modern (in 2016–2017) and Victoria & Albert Museums in London (in 2024), and the High Museum of Art in Atlanta (in 2000).

The collections are more than a mere hobby or distraction. As "one of the most famous people in the world," said his husband, Elton "tends to spend more time in his homes," where the "objects that speak to him and inspire him are a big part of what motivates him, the creator, the soul that gets fed, that turns into the beautiful notes that come out on the piano."

His house isn't large enough for him to devote a whole room to Elton John, but Antonio González Román does have an Elton gallery in his home in Avilés, in the Spanish province of Asturias—a corridor displaying posters, magazine covers, records, and books. "I do know there are well-known fans who have entire big rooms dedicated to him," González told *Record Collector*, but his collection is only "650–800 items." He's "not into stuff like clothes, shoes, dolls, and other Elton-related stuff," but is focused on printed materials and of course "CDs, tapes, LPs, singles, CD singles," and so on. As a child in the 1980s, his uncle introduced him to the hits of John's earlier imperial phase, planting the seed of a lifelong obsession. Not that he would consider himself obsessed. He's only seen John live four times. And he's not worried that he can't afford some of the items most prized by collectors—such as the brown vinyl edition of *Captain Fantastic and the Brown Dirt Cowboy*, signed by the Captain and the Cowboy themselves. You can't have it all.

Andrea Grasso's collection is larger: "I'd say more than 1,000 items." Most of those are music in all formats, but some are books, magazines, and other memorabilia. A native of Catania, on the Italian island of Sicily, where he still lives with his collection, Grasso became a fan as he became a teenager at the turn of the 1990s. Like González, despite missing John's imperial phase in real time, he has "a soft spot for the albums in the first half of the '70s." González's favorite album is *Captain Fantastic*; Grasso's is *Goodbye Yellow Brick Road*. Hardly original choices, but they don't care, and nor should they.

Their most prized possessions are vinyl releases whose sleeves John has signed for them. Grasso, who has seen Elton live seventeen times, all in Italy, brought to a concert in Venice a copy of the South American release of *The Fox* (titled *El Zorro*). After the show, John signed it for him. González carried two 7" singles to his first John concert, in Madrid in 2010: a copy of "Philadelphia Freedom" and a rarer 1970s release of "Lady Samantha" paired with "Skyline Pigeon" (these details matter to collectors). On stage, Elton signed both of them for his fan from Avilés. The value of those signed records—not monetary value, but personal—is obvious. Those particular objects are alive. They trigger the memory of that moment of artist-fan contact. They connect the collection of an ordinary fan to its source, personalizing the connection, linking the collection to the mother-ship collection that is Elton's own.

That connection is not a solitary one, any more than John's relationship to collecting is secluded. On the contrary, it is a social one. Certainly, the start of the process is an isolated one: just as Elton began collecting as Reg, alone in his room, so did the hundreds of Elton collectors around the world start with a few records stacked on a shelf. But before Reg became Elton, his collecting in his bedroom turned into a parallel process, with Bernie's budding collection on the other side of the tiny bedroom. Similarly, Elton collectors are connected to a global online network. David Bodoh may be one of the "well-known fans" that González had in mind; he estimates that his records, tapes, and CDs "probably exceed 5,000 Elton John items," plus "another 2,000 items" of "paper goods" (posters, tour programs, books, magazines, and the like). His collection isn't public, but Bodoh maintains a website, Eltonography.com, with some 2,000 followers, and he enthuses that "the biggest thrill has been meeting new friends through our mutual interest in being fans."

Another superfan, Patrick Andrey of Lausanne, Switzerland, has a particular fondness for John's 1980s (as does Bodoh), the era when he began to assemble a collection that now fills his "beautifully curated Elton room" (as *Record Collector* hailed it). In the 2010s, Andrey met John backstage before a show in Majorca ("he was very friendly, you can tell that was a dream come true!"). A decade later, in Paris, Andrey attended his 150th concert, holding up a sign that read "PATRICK / 150th Show / Elton & The Band / I'll Miss You" (with a heart emoji at the end). Elton saw the sign "and acknowledged me by saying my name."

That shout-out added a sonic thread between the arch-collector/collection subject and one of his collector-fans, heard by tens of thousands of fellow fans. No wonder Andrey remembers the moment so fondly. It highlighted the fact that Andrey himself is part of Elton's collection, a member of the collected/collective community woven into existence through object and sound and shared experience.

John is hardly alone in having inspired superfans and devoted collectors; the phenomenon is expansive, explained not only by the appeal of an artist's music but by the way in which celebrity culture has evolved in quasi-religious ways in the modern era. As noted earlier, stars attract fans to their orbit. But in Elton's case, I suggest that of particular significance is the fact that, as the ultimate collector—the collector's collector—John has attracted like-minded fans. Those innumerable fans have been drawn, consciously or not, into a mutual relationship of collection. As you collect him, so does he collect you.

10

No Jexit

Elton and Jesus

"This Train Don't Stop There Anymore" (4:37, 2001)

The closing track on late-career masterpiece *Songs from the West Coast* is "This Train Don't Stop There Anymore." Depending on your perspective, the album was either Elton's last great studio album or the record that kicked off his late-middle-aged renaissance—a fifteen-year run (2001–2016) of six new studio albums whose critical reception, average chart showing, and overall quality bested his 1980s and 1990s. The albums did not generate sales to compare to his imperial years, nor did they produce hit singles to rival those of the previous decades; likewise, the musical theater and film soundtracks of John's twenty-first-century renaissance did not raise his profile and sales figures the way that *The Lion King* had.[*] But for an old pop/rock star, aged between fifty-four and sixty-nine, the level of sustained creativity across those six albums was extraordinary.

The first three of the six are, to my mind, the best—*West Coast*, *Peachtree Road*, and *The Captain & the Kid* (the autobiographical sequel to *Captain Fantastic*)—representing a five-year roll of songs that are recognizable John/Taupin compositions yet at the same time do not sound like retreads or hollow echoes of older hits. That is a tough trick to pull off. But they do it—save for much of *Wonderful Crazy Night*, the last and least successful of the

---

[*] The sales comparison is of course based on the false premise of a static market: John's fifteen-year renaissance coincided exactly with the decline in sales of physical product; in the US, 95 percent was in CD format in 2001 (900 million CDs sold, producing $22 billion in revenue), collapsing to 19 percent for CDs and vinyl combined in 2016 (110 million CDs and vinyl records, giving $800 million in revenue) (2024 numbers are roughly half those of 2016). In view of that dramatic shift to downloads and then streaming, John's sales of CDs and LPs actually increased during his renaissance period *relative to the larger trend.*

six, an exception therefore that proves the rule (but, of course, your opinion may differ).

All of which very much runs against the grain of "This Train Don't Stop There Anymore." Because the song is all about endings, not about a new lease on life or about treating the transition from middle age into old age as a renaissance of productivity. The song is a languidly melancholic ballad, built around Elton on piano and vocals. There is no guitar, just bass and drums, underpinning strings arranged by Paul Buckmaster (1946–2017), who had worked with Elton on and off since 1969. Elton John Band veterans Davey Johnstone and Nigel Olsson don't play, but they do sing backing vocals (along with Take That's Gary Barlow). Released as a single in various markets, including the UK (#24) and US (#10 on the Adult Contemporary chart), the aforementioned video featuring Justin Timberlake as a young Elton helped to invoke the theme of aging both amusingly and poignantly.

The words are one of Taupin's later contributions to his long run of bitter-heartbreak lyrics. He's the train that was once full of "steam and whistles," get-up and go ("I used to be the main express"). And where does this train no longer stop? Love, of which "I'm dried-up and sick to death." John leans deftly into the theme, giving it his classic melodic piano treatment, making the song a wry and poignant reflection on the disillusionment of old age and lost love. The pair have written other ruminations on these intertwined topics since 2001, and no doubt they will create more. But they have yet to match "This Train Don't Stop There Anymore" as a postscript to their lives and careers, to the history of popular music since the two first met in a late-1960s London—so full of promise and possibility, ready to be "riding on the storyline, furnace burning overtime."

"This Train Don't Stop" would have made a great career coda, the final song to a great final album. But there's a twist, beyond the facts that John and Taupin never intended *Songs from the West Coast* to be a swansong, and that they've continued to write songs together for decades. The twist is that John has repeatedly come to an end, or tried to do so, for almost his whole adult life and career—be it angst-driven moments of attempted suicide, overly self-medicating periods of deep addiction, exhausted declarations of quitting, or happier and celebratory retirements. And, as we saw earlier, for every brush with the end there have been comebacks and rebirths. Musically and personally, Reg just keeps on striking back.

For John, like Jesus, there is no real exit: no Jexit.

Rock stars were not supposed to get old and die. They were supposed to remain "forever young on our behalf." Or they were supposed to flame out like shooting stars, to achieve some sort of immortality by being sacrificial lambs, dying for their art before they became geriatric—before they became us. Back in rock's genesis years, "it was a funny idea that musicians would have careers after their twenties, like rock music was *Logan's Run* and Mick Jagger would be shot on his 30th birthday." The expectation that young musicians in the 1960s would not get old making the new music was combined with an assumption that "what was going on in the music business" at the time "was a sudden bright flash in the sky which was destined to fade and fall just as fast as it rose," as Rod Stewart later reminisced. "We thought it was a fad—a big crush that everyone would get over eventually."

As early as the late 1960s, rock stardom was proving to be remarkably dangerous, with the demise of the likes of Hendrix and Joplin setting a pattern that would persist for decades. In time, the high risk of premature death from lifestyle-related causes ceased to be restricted to rock figures like Kurt Cobain, as R&B and pop artists like Whitney Houston, Prince, and George Michael succumbed before their "natural" time. And yet, as tragic as those deaths seemed, they remained in a different category of tragedy from deaths among the rest of us. After all, when was the natural time for the supernatural to die?

As the twentieth century moved through its closing decades, musicians in their thirties and forties struggled to seem relevant. But those who clung on into their fifties started to be "lauded for longevity"—and then in their sixties started to release albums built upon the rock-geriatric identity of their creators. Johnny Cash's four *American Recordings* albums come to mind (released when he was between sixty-two and seventy), as do Bowie's pair of comeback/swansong albums (put out when he was sixty-six and sixty-nine). Cash and Bowie are, of course, far from being the only musicians born in the 1930s, 1940s, and 1950s who are no longer with us. Yet those who still are, now in their seventies and eighties, "are neither clapped out as we assumed, nor too old to rock 'n' roll, but instead, in many cases, making brilliant music."

In the twenty-first century, the annual roll call of famous musicians soldiering on into senility or moving on to the Heavenly Hall of Fame is longer than the list of those admitted into Cleveland's Rock & Roll Hall of Fame. By the 2020s, artists who in the past would have been told to retire were being applauded for their stamina. Not everyone gets "a late flourish"— as Neil Finn recently put it, promoting a new Crowded House album (thirty-nine years after he formed that band, forty-seven after he joined Split Enz)—because "fame destroys the soul that some people have for it." But the late flourish is becoming so common that Finn's interviewer wondered if it wasn't "time to retire that old saw about pop stars doing all their best work in their early years"; after all, surely "you're going to write some of your finest songs when you've actually lived a life?"

Reviews of the 2023 Rolling Stones album were threaded with comments on age, but the ageism was muted. A commercial success and mostly well received by critics (at least initially), *Hackney Diamonds* was generally seen not just as an "impressive feat" for "an octogenarian rock band," but their best in decades (in forty-eight years, a hyperbolic—and unconvincing—*Variety* review proclaimed); even if few critics could not resist noting that, after six decades, it "could be the last" Stones record.

"Weirdly, music has ceased to be ageist," mused Neil Tennant, publicizing the 2024 release of the fifteenth Pet Shop Boys album in four decades. Aware that the cause was technological change, he remarked that "you could have a fond memory of seeing the video for 'Strawberry Fields Forever' on *Top of the Pops* in 1967, and then you never saw it again." Today, however, thanks to streaming services and YouTube, all songs and videos exist "at the same time." Exclaiming that "young people are listening to their parents' records," Tennant almost misses the point; surely, they aren't so much listening to those records as their *parents'* records, or even as *records*, but as song collections de-coupled from a particular moment or passing fashion. As Tennant adds, "It's all up for grabs."

During that conversation with Tennant, the interviewer remarked that "Madonna, 65, is no longer lambasted for ageing, but triumphantly touring her Celebration retrospective." That may be too sanguine, however, and there is surely a gender counterpoint here. "*Even* Madonna" and "*less* lambasted than in earlier decades" would be more accurate, as the press—especially the tabloids—brutalized her in the 1980s as much as they did Elton John, hunting her long after they had eased up on Elton, persecuting her for her sex—that is, her gender and her sexuality. As early as the year she turned thirty, ageism was added to sexism, and the two have been wielded as a pair of weapons ever since. As one scholar of music marketing has explained, female pop stars were tolerated only as "short-term person brands," meaning that for almost her whole career Madonna has been subjected to pervasive and cruel snipes "about her having passed her use-by date."

When Kim Gordon released a well-received new album at the age of seventy, discussion centered on whether to celebrate her advanced age or ignore it. "What Kim's doing is totally, absolutely normal," Bikini Kill and Le Tigre's Kathleen Hanna said. "We're not witnessing a miracle, we're witnessing what happens when the thing that is supposed to happen is just allowed to happen." That hint of defensiveness reflects a persisting double standard. Furthermore, Gordon's defiance of sexist expectations regarding women's roles in popular music was always more subtle than Madonna's, whose megastar profile and unflinching refusal to back down have always made her a prime target. A better comparison would be Kate Bush, as a rule-proving exception: in the wake of 2022's "Running Up That Hill" phenomenon, Bush, also in her sixties, was scolded for apparently *being* retired rather than failing to do so (her last album was in 2011); but Bush, traumatized by the objectifying sexism of the press upon her initial rise to stardom, has not toured since 1979, taking the opposite tack to Madonna's, settling (as the lesser of two evils) for press accusations that she is a "weirdo recluse."

As frustrating as Bush finds British press "concerns" about her "mental health," simply because she chooses to live her life privately, she has understandably preferred them to the decades of vindictive commentary on her body that Madonna has endured. For while she has also suffered accusations that her music is no longer "relevant," it is the malevolent critique of her body that exposes how sexism is woven into her increasingly ageist treatment. Speculation in the 2020s over Elton's possible facelift and surgeries was minimal and—like most press and online chatter regarding male musicians—it tended to focus on questions of health. But equivalent commentary on Madonna's plastic surgery was about denigration, not health concerns; "what is wrong with Madonna's face?" is a continuation of accusations as far back as 1987 (she was twenty-nine) of hair loss, wrinkles, and "ugly sagging." Calling Madonna "Grandma" and "Grand Madge"—nicknames usually accompanied by suggestions that she is over-the-hill and overdue for retirement—carries a malice that the "Queen Mum of Pop" label lacks.

Thus, while the "Queen Mum of Pop" nickname remains homophobic, regardless of any intentions of endearment, Sir Elton's male identity has helped him survive in the public eye. And, among the growing throng of aged pop and rock stars, he is apparently hell-bent on outlasting all of them. He has become the poster septuagenarian not simply for longevity (for that, he's up against McCartney and Jagger), but for defying the path that mere mortals must take—retirement, senescence, and the ultimate fadeout.

As John sang in 2006's "The Bridge," old rock stars must decide whether "to cross the bridge or fade away." The reference to the Rolling Stones hit "Not Fade Away" cannot have been far from Taupin's mind when he penned that line, especially as Jagger and Richards seem almost as determined as John not to fade away. (Indeed, John played piano on two of the songs on *Hackney Diamonds*.)

It may not, therefore, be overly rhetorical to characterize John as a postmodern Christ, a redemption figure who has retired and returned multiple times, defied actual death while his career has burned to the ground and risen repeatedly from its own ashes. In *Rocketman* and in *Me*, John is a flawed Jesus, a son of the deity Music, sacrificed and redeemed for our sakes. His Farewell Yellow Brick Road tour, begun in 2018 and prolonged into 2023 by the global pandemic—but also by John's insistence on adding dates—was seemingly designed to be a kind of infinite goodbye, despite his insistence that "Jexit really does mean Jexit" (as the *NME* put it in 2021). Sir Elton's performance in the 2010s and 2020s as a high-profile resurrected rock star, a new kind of Jesus Christ Superstar, points the way to a new normative narrative for musical artists in the post-rock twenty-first century.

Elton's recent retirement statements, the ones surrounding the protracted Jexit or faux-Jexit that climaxed in 2023, focused on his desire to "spend more time with my sons"—a poignant motivation, considering that when he turned seventy-five, they were only aged eleven and nine. He has also often added another positive rationale, "to be able to dedicate more of my time to other projects, like the Elton John AIDS Foundation." This contrasts with the earlier retirement statements, which reflected in turn the context of his life during his less-settled younger decades.

Let's revisit those decades for a moment. Audiences for John's 1972 world tour were flummoxed by the dark humor of his performance of "I Think I'm Going to Kill Myself," a track from his recent *Honky Château* album. Larry "Legs" Smith had contributed the tap-dancing solo on the record, reprising his act for the tour's US leg, as well as for the Royal Command Performance at the London Palladium (wearing, confoundingly, a wedding dress). A parody on "teenage blues," the song captured something of the farcical and performative nature of John's actual suicide attempts—details of which would emerge a few years later. The first, mentioned earlier, was the pre-fame cry-for-help over his impending marriage, complete with an open window and a pillow for his head in the oven, causing Taupin more amusement than concern. The second attempt, in Los Angeles in 1975, was more dramatic—suitably reconstructed in *Rocketman*—and even more obviously a desperate plea for understanding. Having swallowed a bottle of sleeping pills, he jumped off a swimming pool diving board—announcing his impending demise in front of his family. "Well, I guess we can all go home now," his mother, visiting from England, allegedly remarked.

John's attempted suicides remind me of Angie Bowie's reflection on her own such attempt (made in 1978 when her soon-to-be-ex-husband denied her access to their son, and likewise using a bottle of sleeping pills). "My heart wasn't in it," she admitted. "I'm very competent. If I really wanted to kill myself, I think I would have succeeded." John was similarly "very competent." But he was facing a killer combination of relentless pressure, impending burnout, and the psychological distress of being a closeted celebrity.

In the six and a half years leading up to the release of *Blue Moves* in 1976, John gave over 530 concerts. Having broken records with his run of sold-out Dodger Stadium shows in 1975, he broke records again in 1976, selling out Madison Square Garden seven straight nights. Profoundly exhausted, he tried to quit. "I just can't do this anymore," he told a New York audience. "I love you all, and this is the greatest, but I have to take some time off." For seven months he gave no concerts at all, performing only thirteen times in all of 1977 and 1978.

"It came to the point where I sang 'Yellow Brick Road' and I thought, 'I don't have to sing this anymore,' and it made me quite happy inside," John told Jahr in the 1976 interview that so rocked the boat of his early career. Having completed his summer tour with a Madison Square Garden concert, he sighed that it might have been "the last gig forever. I'm definitely not *retiring* but I want to put my energies elsewhere for a while." In other words, Jexit/no Jexit. Of course, it is conceivable for an artist to retire from performing while still making records—Kate Bush is the most famous example of that (at least in Britain). But nobody believed in 1976 that such an option could be reconciled with John's personality, nor does anyone believe that today.

Asked in 2018 if he was surprised that he'd never managed to tour with his old friend John, Stewart said he was. But "it's too late now," he added, with a little smirk. "She's retiring." The smirk meant, of course, that Sir Rod didn't believe for a minute that "she" was really going to retire. After all, Stewart saw his friend repeatedly retire and return beginning with those difficult late-1970s years. He loved playing, yet it was killing him. "I've made a decision tonight," he told the crowd in London's Wembley Empire Pool arena in 1977, after he had come out of retirement, "this is going to be the last show! All right?" "No!" roared the audience. "This is the last one I'm going to do," he repeated.

It wasn't, of course, and the cycle of album recording and promoting, fueled by cocaine and alcohol, continued. Taupin has described the harrowing experience of seeing his creative soulmate "deep in the stranglehold of addiction" throughout the 1980s. It was hard enough having to pair lyrics with "unremarkable melodies" that John could crank out by the hundreds—most of them utterly "forgettable" yet "to someone as high as he was, they were brilliant." Witnessing a man "talented beyond belief and one of the finest musicians and melodists in the musical firmament in the thrall of crash and burn" was deeply depressing. Even worse, seeing his "best friend so disconnected and raw to the bone was heartbreaking."

One way to understand the Elton John story is to see it as one of bullying—various forms of bullying over decades, prompting various responses to the suffering of it, culminating in triumph over it. Considering Sir Elton's status today, that may seem hyperbolic. But when, as his star was rising rapidly, John referred to himself as "this overweight, bespectacled thing," he was internalizing how he had been treated by schoolyard bullies and then by hecklers at Reg Dwight's earliest solo gigs and some of the less felicitous Bluesology concerts. Later, the relentless prodding and mocking of his sexual identity and love life—the homophobic chanting by football fans at the club over which he presided (and had invested enormous amounts of time and money), the burning of his records in the US and his banning from radio stations and teen magazines because of his confession of "deviance," the hounding and taunting by the UK press—comprised decades of public bullying.

For John, the experience of being alternately deified and persecuted must have felt like the school bully helping him to his feet and applauding him as a hero, before knocking him back down to spit insults and kick him in the face. I'm using a Christ metaphor in this chapter for the sake of rhetorical drama, but John surely did not see his experience that way. For him, he wasn't being crucified so much as being teased, again and again. It doesn't take a psychiatrist to see the connection between that perception of relentless bullying and the downward spiral into substance abuse and multiple addictions.

Put that way, the resurrection does seem miraculous. The turning point was a successful six-week stint in rehab in the summer of 1990 (at a Chicago clinic). But if one round of rehab was always enough to do the trick, addiction would not be the modern crisis that it is. It is thus noteworthy that in his case it was enough. Why? His support network is only part of the answer (Taupin describes the emotional impact of his old friend "drained of the poisons that" had been "eating him alive," and John reading him his farewell love letter to cocaine, later included in John's autobiography). But along with rehab also came the impact of seeing the damage done by the AIDS epidemic and—crucially—how poorly AIDS sufferers were treated; in a way, bullied. AIDS saved Elton. That is, his reaction to it catalyzed a reaction to his own distress. And that in turn allowed him to accept help from his support network, and to be open to its expansion—including the all-important addition of the man who would become his husband. Free to be himself, he was also free to make the music he wanted to make—including composing for musical theater.

In the wake of rehab, then, came Elton's pop cultural rehabilitation, the foundation for which was laid during the 1990s. There were various landmark elements to that process, their significance varying from country to country, and among different demographic sectors of John's fanbase—the success of the family-oriented *Lion King* movie and soundtrack, his knighthood, the success of the AIDS Foundation, the publicity surrounding family life. But behind these and many other factors was the simple fact of resurrection. None of it would have mattered as much, or even at all, if Elton had not suffered multiple downfalls. As one writer recently put it, "Elton's ability to bounce back from addiction, illness, and personal turmoil—and his willingness to use his fame and fortune for the benefit of others—is a testament to this much-loved entertainer." A testament, sure, but more importantly an explanation for how Elton the punching bag became Sir Elton, Uncle Elton, the national treasure, the international treasure. For years, he was crucified by critics and journalists and fans of whoever was deemed cool at the time. But he came back, he rose again, for us.

At the end of 2023, John was once again in the UK Top 20. "Step into Christmas," which had been a modest seasonal hit in 1973 (reaching #24), charted thirteen more times in the very different chart environment of the twenty-first century—every year since 2014, and in the Top 20 every year since 2017. This is not surprising in the context of the success of John's most recent compilation album, *Diamonds*. Released late in 2017, *Diamonds* not only never left the charts in multiple countries, by 2023 topping the 1.2 million mark in the UK and 2 million in the US, but it racked up *increasing* sales

Figure 10.1 Leaving Already? Sir Elton at Glastonbury, Britain's biggest annual music festival, on June 15, 2023, the final performance in his home country of his five-year Farewell tour. (Photo credit: Matt Crossick / Empics / Alamy Live News.)

and streams; having been the 36th and 62nd best-seller of 2018 in the UK and US respectively, it was the 4th and 18th best-seller in those markets in 2023. In the summer of that year, *Diamonds* bounced to #2 in Britain, in the wake of John's June 25 performance at the Glastonbury Festival—the nation's premier popular music festival. John drew one of the largest crowds in the half-century history of the festival, and 7.6 million watched him on BBC TV—another record broken by Elton (see Figure 10.1).

The "Glasto" performance was the final concert in John's home country of his five-year retirement tour. Having begun in Pennsylvania in 2018, the tour wrapped up in Stockholm on July 8, 2023. Its extraordinary length was partly due to dates being postponed and rescheduled as a result of the Covid-19 pandemic. But that wasn't the only reason. It also sold extremely well, breaking a global record by grossing $800 million by January 2023 (that figure reached $940 million by the tour's end, by which time Taylor Swift's The Eras Tour had broken John's record by grossing over $1 billion). Many dates sold out, prompting John to add more. In the end, over

6.25 million people in North America, the UK, Europe, and Australasia bought tickets.

In his speeches to the crowds at Glastonbury and the other closing concerts of the tour, as well as the message posted to his Rocket Club fans, John expressed his gratitude for "your unwavering love and support," for "52 years of amazing love and loyalty," for "every show you've attended, song you've sung and feather boa and sparkling outfit you've worn." But his emphasis was on "the next fabulous chapter," on "the next adventure with all of you by my side." "While this tour may mark the closing of one chapter," he conceded, "it signals the beginning of a new one."

The year 2023 was therefore an end point in ways, but it hardly seemed like the end. As his official eltonjohn.com website exclaimed, it was "a year of lasts and firsts." "Elton may have retired from touring," conceded the website (note the use of "may"), but don't forget "that this is a man who continues to share his love of entertaining!" Within months, word was out that a new studio album was imminent, as well as details of a future concert residency of some kind—possibly in Las Vegas.

"Who wants to be a 45-year-old entertainer in Las Vegas like Elvis?" John was twenty-nine when he blurted out this rhetorical question (during the 1976 Jahr interview). A year later, aged forty-two, Elvis was dead. Decades later, as Elton turned seventy, he approached the end of a pair of residencies in Las Vegas, where across fourteen years he played some 450 Caesars Palace concerts. As his Farewell tour wound down in 2022 and 2023, Furnish assured interviewers that John would no longer "be touring in any capacity." But would he stop performing completely? Of course not, Furnish conceded; "it's in his blood." Long before the last shows of the last tour, Furnish speculated on "the possibility of a special one-off or a small residency in one venue." Probably not in Las Vegas, as "Elton feels he's done the best he can" there; but anything's possible.

In November 2023, Bernie Taupin was finally inducted into the Rock & Roll Hall of Fame. Kate Bush was also inducted. It surprised nobody that Bush opted not to perform, not even to appear in person, but instead sent a message of thanks that devoted more words to congratulating Taupin than to referencing her own career. Bernie is "an incredible lyricist who inspired me to keep writing songs," enthused Bush; and even though John wasn't the one being honored (he was inducted in 1994), she added that "when I was growing up my hero was Elton John. I pored over his music, longed to be able to play the piano like him and to write songs that could move people in the way his work moved me."

Part of Bush's legend is that she is generous and self-effacing, to a fault, and that she loathes touring as much as John loves it. As noted above, she toured once, in 1979, and never again—not even giving another full concert until a one-time London residency in the autumn of 2014. John, on the other hand, has given over 4,600 concerts in over eighty countries since 1970. It therefore also surprised nobody that John not only showed up to induct Taupin at the ceremony in Brooklyn, but that he performed too—singing "Tiny Dancer" in honor of Bernie, and later joining Sheryl Crow, Chris Stapleton, and Brittany Howard to perform "The Weight" in honor of Robbie Robertson (1943–2023).

It is difficult to imagine a pop culture and pop music landscape without Elton John in it. And, of course, we don't need to try. As I write, he's in his late seventies, and it would be foolish to pretend that he will still be pulling off another phoenix act two decades from now. Sure, the Queen Mother lived to 101 and Queen Elizabeth to ninety-six, so why shouldn't the Queen Mum of Pop live into his nineties? Different genes and very different lifestyles in their twenties and thirties, that's why. In blunt terms, the train has to stop before too long. But it is Reginald Dwight who will pass on, not Elton John. In terms of the music—the 500 recorded songs and everything that goes with them and is prompted by them—the train need never stop.

Source Notes

Epigraph

"Quit": *The Record Mirror* (February 20, 1971), in Spignesi and Lewis, *Fifty Years On*, 7.
"Liable": Taupin, *Scattershot*, xii.

Preface

"Musical legend": Bego, *Elton John*, 178. Also see Doyle, *Captain Fantastic*, 194; Restall, *Blue Moves*, 4.
"The biggest star in the world": quoted in Taupin, *Scattershot*, 209.
Brooker's immersive Bowie-fan project: Brooker, *Why Bowie Matters*, esp. 2–13.
On the cool/uncool divide maintained by critics, see Reynolds, *Blissed Out*, 10; Quantick, "Latter-day landmarks"; Warner, *Tago Mago*, 22.
The *Top of the Pops* era: Glass, *Tapestry*, 84; Shumway, *Rock Star*; Hepworth, *Uncommon People*; Bromley, "Back in the Day"; Barry, *Compact Disc*; Morrison, *Avalon*; Humphries and Blacknell, *Top of the Pops*.

Chapter 1—Half and Half

The Nation's Favorite Song: quotes reported variously online; for example, www.smoothradio.com/news/music/nations-favourite-elton-john-song/.
Vote prior to a 2002 concert special in New York City: "I'm Still Standing" came sixth in the 2002 New York vote, likewise, reported variously online; see, for example, www.irishexaminer.com/lifestyle/arid-30043333.html.
Quotes and details on the "I'm Still Standing" video: John, *Me*, 179–84; Ollivier and Roubin, *All the Songs*, 370–71.
"I didn't like the look of any of it": Ollivier and Roubin, *All the Songs*, 370; David Geffen founded the label in 1980 (en.wikipedia.org/wiki/Geffen_Records_).
Blue Moves: Restall, *Blue Moves*.
"Well-oiled machine": John, *Me*, 180.
"Got milk?" advertising campaign: Ollivier and Roubin, *All the Songs*, 484, reproduces one of the "got milk?" advertisements.
"When you listen to Elton John": quoted in Podolsky, *Rock 'n' Roll Survivor*, 194; Gambaccini goes on to cite Neil Sedaka and Howie Greenfield as a similarly exceptional case (Sedaka makes an appearance in Chapter 9 of this book).
Difford and Tilbrook details and quotes: Earls, "Squeeze, Song by Song."

London advertisement; "fantastic codswallop"; "incredibly close," "sixth sense," and "mutual observation": Taupin, *Scattershot*, 18, 342–43; Gibson, *Elton John FAQ*, xii, 17, 20.

"Odd, dark, depressing songs" and Depeche Mode details: Spence, *Just Can't Get Enough*, quote on 258. Dutch interview: Vandromme, "Blijven Gahan" (original quotes: "Voor twee autisten die muziek maken, is communicatie niet gemakkelijk.... Die spanningen, en de manier waarop ze uiteindelijk zijn opgelost, hebben een betere plaat opgeleve").

"Americanism... in my soul": Taupin, *Scattershot*, 223.

"Like an American road trip" and "Some of Bernie's lyrics": booklet accompanying 2022 50th anniversary multidisc reissue of *Madman across the Water*; John, *Me*, 91.

"Absolutely fantastic": Doyle, *Running Up That Hill*, 27–28.

"Slow-burn sleeper": Roberts, "Still Crazy."

Taupin's 1971 wedding (and subsequent marriages): Heatley and Hopkinson, *The Girl in the Song*, 130–31.

"Fragments of a handful of LA females": Taupin, *Scattershot*, 257.

Story behind "Blues Never Fade Away"; and "love songs in the traditional sense": Taupin, *Scattershot*, 199, 211.

"I wanted to write stories" and "Like writing a story": Taupin, *Scattershot*, 10, 15; Gibson, *Elton John FAQ*, 21.

"Three good songs": Taupin, *Scattershot*, 255–58.

"Declarations of love" and "admissions of adultery": Taupin, *Scattershot*, 290.

"These free spirits" and "bookend": Spignesi and Lewis, *Fifty Years On*, 31, 23.

"Sacrifice" and *Sleeping*: Taupin, *Scattershot*, 293; John, *Me*, 219–20.

"I Want Love": Taupin, *Scattershot*, 349–50; John, *Me*, 295, 352; Spignesi and Lewis, *Fifty Years On*, 133.

Elton has contributed lyrics/"Border Song": John revealed this rare moment as a lyricist in a 1975 interview with Paul Gambaccini (and perhaps earlier, too); the original manuscript of the lyrics, sold at auction in 2019, seems to support the story too. Ollivier and Roubin, *All the Songs*, 48, 68–69.

"Nikita": Bernardin and Stanton, *Elton John from A–Z*, 186.

On "Sorry Seems to Be the Hardest Word": Eames, "The Story of... 'Sorry'"; Spignesi and Lewis, *Fifty Years On*, 69; Kearns, *Elton John*, 100; Taupin, *Scattershot*, 212; John, *Me*, 140.

"Song for a Gay" (footnote): John, *Me*, 165–66.

"I cry when I sing this song": Interview in *Rolling Stone*, quoted in Spignesi and Lewis, *Fifty Years On*, 60–61.

"He is an eternal love": Taupin, *Scattershot*, 393.

Chapter 2—Once Upon a Time

"A lasting contribution to rock": Landau, "Captain Fantastic."

"Someone Saved My Life Tonight": chart numbers and other details: Ollivier and Roubin, *All the Songs*, 232–34, 240–41.

"He's talking about attempting suicide!": Gambaccini, "Captain Fantastic"; Ollivier and Roubin, *All the Songs*, 241; Kearns, *Elton John*, 77.

"Old-fashioned chivalry" and "to kill a wasp": John, *Me*, 50–52.

"You're gay": John, *Me*, 53; Ollivier and Roubin, *All the Songs*, 240.

The performativity of identity: the theorist ("Identity as a 'production'") is Stuart Hall ("Cultural Identity and Diaspora," 222), the communications scholar is Leslie Meier (*Popular Music as Promotion*); both quoted and discussed by Sloan and Harding, *Switched on Pop*, 108–12.

Green Belt: on its relevance to Bowie, John, and music history; see Restall, *Ghosts*, Chapter 3.
On Bowie's origins: Brooker, *Why Bowie Matters*, 18–68, 173–75.
Nepantla: For the sake of my Bibliography's thematic coherence, I have not included in it works on the Aztecs; but a trio of hefty starting points would be Susan Kellogg, *A Concise History of the Aztecs* (Cambridge: Cambridge University Press, 2024); Matthew Restall, *When Montezuma Met Cortés: The True Story of the Meeting That Changed History* (New York: Ecco, 2018); and Camilla Townsend, *Fifth Sun: A New History of the Aztecs* (New York: Oxford University Press, 2019).
Shaar Murray: quoted in Spitz, *Bowie*, 291.
Charlesworth: quoted in Gibson, *Elton John FAQ*, 156. On glam, see Philo, *Glam Rock* (for whom Bolan is foundational, Bowie central, and John marginal); Hoskyns, *Glam!*; Reynolds, *Shock and Awe*; "The Rift of Retro"; Thompson, *Children of the Revolution*; and the essays in the Tate Liverpool catalogue, *Glam!*
"Conflict and anxieties," etc., including John quotes: Gibson, *Elton John FAQ*, 1–11; also see the feature film *Rocketman*, and the documentaries *Madman across the Water: The Making of Elton John* and *Tantrums and Tiaras*. Also see Restall, *Blue Moves*, 27–32.
"Bespectacled thing" and "like an old couple": Flynn, *Elton John*, 11, 13.
Name change: Gibson, *Elton John FAQ*, 82, 271; Spitz, *Led Zeppelin*, 442–43. Atkinson interview on YouTube and other sites, including sunnyskyz.com/happy-videos/12194.
"Sense of the absurd" and "really pursued his craft": August 27, 1970, Hilburn review quoted in Spignesi and Lewis, *Fifty Years On*, 30; Quaye quoted in Gibson, *Elton John FAQ*, xii (also see Quaye, *A Voice Louder than Rock & Roll*; Quaye had a religious epiphany in 1979 and has since been a minister in Southern California).
"Tubby little singer": easily found online, but also in St. Michael, *Elton John*, 7 and Restall, *Blue Moves*, 31.
"A joke," etc. (John and Charlesworth): Gibson, *Elton John FAQ*, 147, 149, 152.
"How did I get here?" etc.: Jeffrey, *Once Upon a Time*, 39.

Chapter 3—Starmen

On "Rocket Man": Ollivier and Roubin, *All the Songs*, 140–43; Higgins, "Rocket Man." Website and fan club: eltonjohn.com/rocket-club.
"Novelty record" and other quotes and details on "Space Oddity": Trynka, *Starman*, 104; Pegg, *The Complete David Bowie*, 335; Wiederhorn, "David Bowie Producer"; Spitz, *Bowie*, 223; Brooker, *Why Bowie Matters*, 59.
"The Laughing Gnome": Spitz, *Bowie*, 79.
"Low-grade photocopy": all quotes in this paragraph, and likewise Bush's "sacred space" and John's "Judy Garland," quoted by John or by Doyle in *Running Up That Hill*, 41; save for "silly boy" (Jahr, "Elton's Frank Talk," 17) and "a cunty thing to say" (Hagan, *Sticky Fingers*, 322).
Space Law (footnote): law.unl.edu/songsforspace/.
"An otherworldly being" and "comforting image"; "a single positive": Brooker, *Why Bowie Matters*, 15–17, 246; also see 47, 96, 204–9, 222–36. Also, on *Blackstar*, see Kardos, *Blackstar Theory*.
The Man Who Fell to Earth: see my Filmography; and Compo, *Earthbound*.
"Starmaker machinery": Joni Mitchell, "Free Man in Paris," on *Court and Spark* (Asylum, 1974). Also see Nelson, *Court and Spark*, 51–58, 111; Shumway, *Rock Star*; Hepworth, *Uncommon People*.
Hollywood Bowl: I here paraphrase Reynolds, *Shock and Awe*, 153.
LaBelle: Bertei, *Why Labelle Matters*, 113–18.

Farthingale: Heatley and Hopkinson, *The Girl in the Song*, 58–60; Pegg, *The Complete David Bowie*, 162–63; Spitz, *Bowie*, 158.

Bush and Shatner: The *Wogan* appearance was on December 16, 1991, accessible at www.youtube.com/watch?v=ZM5MM8Q6FqI; also see Thomas, *Kate Bush*, 75–76; Doyle, *Running Up That Hill*, 34. Taupin, *Scattershot*, 288.

Chapter 4—Pride

"Force of nature": Taupin, *Scattershot*, 160.

Musicians' Union rules (in footnote): For example, Heatley and Hopkinson, *The Girl in the Song*, 90.

"A pride anthem": McCabe, "Philadelphia Freedom," 19.

"We talked and talked" and "I couldn't refuse" and sources differ (note): Ollivier and Roubin, *All the Songs*, 248; *The Tonight Show* (September 20, 1993); John, *Me*, 121; Heatley and Hopkinson, *The Girl in the Song*, 88–89.

"It's got a good beat": Heatley and Hopkinson, *The Girl in the Song*, 89–90.

Philly Soul and "I don't like it, Elton": Higgins, "Billie Jean King"; Ollivier and Roubin, *All the Songs*, 248–49.

"Most famous": Segal, *And Then I Danced*, 241; Bego, *Elton*, 345; Restall, *Blue Moves*, 124.

"The slightest bit camp": Taupin, *Scattershot*, 33–34.

The words of Madonna's recent biographer: Gabriel, *Madonna*, 22.

"Open about their lesbianism": Gaar, *She's a Rebel*, 379.

Dee and Quatro: Barber, "I've still got the music in me"; Norman, "Suzi Quatro"; Gaar, *She's a Rebel*, 218–21.

"Toying with personae": Gaar, *She's a Rebel*, 219–20.

Bowie: Spitz, *Bowie*, 180–86, 205, 326; Brooker, *Why Bowie Matters*, 136–86.

"Angry and unhappy inside": Taupin, *Scattershot*, 188.

Swift (in footnote): Marks, "Look What We Made Taylor Swift Do."

Rolling Stone interview and reactions: Jahr, "Elton's Frank Talk," 17; Restall, *Blue Moves*, 100–4; DeCouto, *Captain Fantastic*, 627–28; Hagan, *Sticky Fingers*, 322–23; Hoskyns, *Glam!*, 73; Parker, "Funny," 110; Clarke, *Elton, My Elton*, 13–14.

"Flamboyance and kinkiness": quotes by Reynolds, *Shock and Awe*, 461.

"Elton's Song," etc.: John, *Me*, 163, 206; Spignesi and Lewis, *Fifty Years On*, 84–85.

Blauel: John, *Me*, 187–92, 209–10; Taupin, *Scattershot*, 283–84; Stewart, *Rod*, 282–83.

Boyfriend Gary: his full name was Gary Clarke, and he told the story from his viewpoint in Clarke, *Elton, My Elton*.

The UK tabloids and "I'll see you in court": John, *Me*, 200–9.

Smash Hits: The event's full name is Mylan WTT Smash Hits (WTT is World Tennis Team, an organization cofounded in 1973 by King's then-husband, of which she eventually became majority stakeholder until 2017); see numerous online sources, such as wtt.com/tag/smash-hits/, and pages within www.itatennis.co/; also mentioned in Heatley and Hopkinson, *The Girl in the Song*, 91; John, *Me*, 245.

Biden ceremony: youtu.be/AkR2XUNJ7-k.

"Your Song": See the hilarious spoof on the song's lyrics in Smyth, "I'm the Person 'Your Song' by Elton John Was Written For."

"The reason I started the" EJAF: www.youtube.com/watch?v=uUdKLFWe-gQ (speech of November 30, 2023); also see www.eltonjohnaidsfoundation.org.

"Rock 'n' roll's most heroic pansexual": Spitz, *Bowie*, 350.

Chapter 5—For All Seasons

Billy Elliot score: John only recorded three of the soundtrack's songs himself, all three added to the 2005 extended edition of his *Peachtree Road*: "Electricity"; "The Letter"; and "Merry Christmas Maggie Thatcher." The trio comprised Side Four of the vinyl version of the 2005 release, which was an hour-long double-LP. The *Peachtree Road* and *Billy Elliot* albums are briefly covered in Ollivier and Roubin, *All the Songs*, 495–507.

"Overcoming obstacles": paraphrasing Ollivier and Roubin, *All the Songs*, 506. *Billy Elliot the Musical* was still running when, on April 8, 2013, Margaret Thatcher died; the audience for the next performance were polled as to whether they thought the song "Merry Christmas Maggie Thatcher" should still be performed, as the final line of its chorus runs "we all celebrate today, because it's one day closer to your death." The vote was overwhelming: sing the song.

"Clive Davis's dog": Interview with Hall of August 20, 2007, available on pitchfork.com/features/interview/6673-daryl-hall/.

It Ain't Easy: for a contrary opinion to mine, arguing that Stewart does a better job than John, whose side "lacks the fireworks" of Stewart's, see Little, "Graded on a Curve."

"He discovered me": Stewart, *Rod*, 44.

"A dandy and a gentleman": Myers, *It Ain't Easy*, 251–52.

"Phyllis" and "Sharon": Stewart, *Rod*, 57, 178. "Football in common": Stewart, *Rod*, 178. Vulgarian personas (in footnote): Seabrook, *Bowie in Berlin*, 169. Also "Elton John. The Only. Interviews" (listed in "Other Media" below).

"Repeats the formula": Little, "Graded on a Curve."

"A traitor": Stewart, *Rod*, 196–97.

"Quirky breed of Englishmen": Taupin, *Scattershot*, 223.

"Da Ya Think I'm Sexy?" and other rock-disco: Thompson, *I Feel Love*, 63, 257; Stewart, *Rod*, 223–27, 269, 281; an example of fans' perspectives is on reelnerdspodcast.com (see Ryan's "Foolish Behaviour," July 30, 221).

Songbook and Stewart's own account: Stewart, *Rod*, 348–54.

On *Blue Moves*: Restall, *Blue Moves*, 3–11, 57, 110; Swartley, "Blue Moves"; Sheffield, "Essential Albums"; Bego, *Elton John*, 195–96.

"Not to everyone's taste": Taupin, *Scattershot*, 185.

"Old fart" and "fat cunt": Stewart, *Rod*, 208; Restall, *Blue Moves*, 64; Black, *In His Own Words*, 63, 112; Norman, *Elton John*, 345; John, *Me*, 159–60. Also "Elton John. The Only. Interviews" (listed in "Other Media" below).

"Glam Liberace": Hoskyns, *Glam!*, 51, 88.

"Annus mirabilis": Hepworth, *Fabulous Creation*, 64–65; *Never a Dull Moment*.

"Phallic substitutes": Gabriel, *Madonna*, 22.

"Annus mirabilis": Philo, *Glam Rock*, 1, 133; also see Hoskyns, *Glam!*; Reynolds, *Shock and Awe*; Thompson, *Children of the Revolution*.

"Moose Droppings, Ohio": Hepworth, *Fabulous Creation*, 165 (referring to UK punk bands of the late 1970s, but the point applies more broadly). On the dovetailing of the 1970s US/UK difference in music culture and the pop/rock divide, see Reynolds, *Bring the Noise*, 152–56. For examples of English acts unwilling to "break" the US (such as the band Japan, Kate Bush, Talk Talk, and Wham!), see Restall, *Ghosts*.

Singer-songwriter movement (including note): Gioia, *Love Songs*, 238–39.

Hot streak and "horrified": Wilkinson, "The Wonderful World," 12; www.orlandoweekly.com/news/how-gay-day-pushed-disney-out-of-the-closet-2262655.

Scholar of musical theater: Barrios, *Dangerous Rhythm*, 198.

For a brief guide to John's soundtracks, from *Friends* (1971) to *Gnomeo and Juliet* (2011), see Gibson, *Elton John FAQ*, 248–56.

"Shrewd referencing": Roberts, *Rocket Man*, 202.

Genres have collapsed; "a strange simultaneity": Fisher, *Ghosts of My Life*, 8–9; Restall, *Ghosts*, Chapter 2.

Chapter 6—Fantasies of Difference

Details behind "Border Song": Ollivier and Roubin, *All the Songs*, 48, 68–69, 82, 91, 252; Kearns, *Elton John*, 19–20.
Top of the Pops (including note): John, *Me*, 69; Ollivier and Roubin, *All the Songs*, 69; Humphries and Blacknell, *Top of the Pops*; Restall, *Ghosts*, Chapter 1; totparchive.co.uk/artist?id=454.
"An affinity for Black music": a *Rolling Stone* interview, quoted in Gibson, *Elton John FAQ*, 137. Also see "Elton John. The Only. Interviews" (in "Other Media" listed below); and Bertei, *Why Labelle Matters*, 54–55, 136.
"A fantasy of difference": John, *Me*, 65–66; Morrison, *Avalon*, 76. Also see Thompson, *I Feel Love*, 63. On Troy: Nathan, *The Soulful Divas*, 129.
Details on "Bennie and the Jets": Spignesi and Lewis, *Fifty Years On*, 46–47; Ollivier and Roubin, *All the Songs*, 186–87; Kearns, *Elton John*, 58–59; Taupin, *Scattershot*, 67 ("tenacious"); Spitz, *Bowie*, 240 ("fluke crossover hit"); www.allmusic.com/song/bennie-the-jets-mt0009263845.
"Such panache" and "an unreal thing": John, *Me*, 39, 122.
Questlove: from his *Soul Train* book, quoted in Gibson, *Elton John FAQ*, 141. Bowie/*Soul Train* quote: Thompson, *I Feel Love*, 63.
"I love Black music": Gibson, *Elton John FAQ*, 138.
On *Thom Bell Sessions* and *Victim of Love*: Rosenthal, *His Song*, 152–54, 172–74.
"Rip-offs": Gibson, *Elton John FAQ*, 144.
"An intensely urgent, horn-fueled beast": Silverman discusses all three covers mentioned here, in "Soul in the Middle of the Road."
On Black American women collaborators: John, *Me*, 218; Nathan, *The Soulful Divas*, 36, 129, 222, 259; Rosenthal, *His Song*, 119, 255, 258, 266, 365; Gibson, *Elton John FAQ*, 52, 58, 137–38.
On LaBelle and Wickham (footnote): Bertei, *Why Labelle Matters*, 66.
On Wonder: Rosenthal, *His Song*, 75–76, 224, 365, 430, 432.
"People's perceptions of his abilities": Taupin, *Scattershot*, 186–87.
"Finish Line" video at youtube.com/watch?v=bDnwBeRSJag.
John speech starting "Of the many songs": A one-hour edit of the concert is at www.youtube.com/watch?v=OZKpDdTjikI&t=2523s, and the *Variety* review (May 7, 1993) is at variety.com/1993/tv/reviews/aretha-franklin-duets-1200432289/.
Final concert: coverage of various websites, e.g., wxyz.com/news/elton-john-honors-the-lasting-genius-of-aretha-franklin-during-his-final-show.

Chapter 7—Perfect Mistakes

Details and quotes on "Bennie and the Jets": Spignesi and Lewis, *Fifty Years On*, 46–47; Ollivier and Roubin, *All the Songs*, 186–87; Kearns, *Elton John*, 58–59.
"Making records": Hepworth, *Fabulous Creation*, 61.
Morrison and Manzanera: Morrison, *Avalon*, 21–22.

Talk Talk and Go West: Restall, *Ghosts*, Chapter 11; Brown, *Are We Still Rolling?*, 275–76.
"Infallible commercial instincts" (in footnote): John, *Me*, 220.
"Bennie" as "Benny" (in footnote): Restall, *Blue Moves*, 112–14.
"Technical breakdown": Rosenthal, *His Song*, 132.
Dudgeon noticed: Here I quote (both times) Ollivier and Roubin, *All the Songs*, 241, not Dudgeon directly.
Jump Up! etc.: John, *Me*, 163, 181, 195; Taupin, *Scattershot*, 285 ("abysmal"), 277 ("schlock").
Amusingly self-criticized: Taupin, *Scattershot*, 232–34.
Songs at weddings: Catanzarite, *Achtung Baby*, 18–19; Nelson, *Court and Spark*, 50; Heatley and Hopkinson, *The Girl in the Song*, 24–26.
"An element of naivety" and other quotes in that paragraph: Taupin, *Scattershot*, 196.
Two serious John fans: Spignesi and Lewis, *Fifty Years On*, 44–51.
"Sickly mousse": Reynolds, *Shock and Awe*, 418.
"Points of comparison and difference": Brooker, *Why Bowie Matters*, 231–32. My "Our sense of" paraphrases Brooker.
Petty: Washburn, *Southern Accents*.
"A couple of friends" and "Among Angels": Thomas, *Kate Bush*, 116.
Chapter 8—Queens
"I was not that enamored with Marilyn Monroe" and other Taupin quotes on "Candle in the Wind" lyrics: Ollivier and Roubin, *All the Songs*, 184; Taupin, *Scattershot*, 200–2 (including "the perfect metaphor"). On Monroe herself, see Barrios, *On Marilyn Monroe*.
"The most glamorous woman": Ollivier and Roubin, *All the Songs*, 184.
That Grammy's role: NARAS ran the competition for the "Best Pop Vocal Performance" from 1959 to 2011, with its specific name changing slightly eight times; see the Wikipedia page for Grammy_Award_for_Best_Male_Pop_Vocal_Performance#Recipients.
"The quality of the melody" (Taupin): Ollivier and Roubin, *All the Songs*, 184; Taupin, *Scattershot*, 343–45.
"And start singing the original lyrics" (John): John, *Me*, 279.
"The Queen Mum of Pop": Restall, *Blue Moves*, 125–26; Buckley, "A Life Less Ordinary."
Elton, Margaret, and Diana: Taupin, *Scattershot*, 175–80; John, *Me*, 97, 141, 271–82; Gibson, *Elton John FAQ*, 202–4; Restall, *Blue Moves*, 77–78; Rosenthal, *His Song*, 139–40 (who cites Norman, *Elton John*; and Toberman, *Elton John*). Also "Elton John. The Only. Interviews" (listed in "Other Media" below).
Musician knighthoods: numerous websites reporting quotes and details; all quotes corroborated on multiple sites.
"The parallel between the two 2014 weddings": e.g., Murphy, "Sweet Wedding Connection."

Chapter 9—Poppermost

"Cold Heart" details: Ollivier and Roubin, *All the Songs*, 582, and from numerous websites and online reports. Lipa: Arnold, "Elton John's Manager."
On John and Taupin's earliest collections: Taupin, *Scattershot*, 50, 56 ("Kids in a candy store").
"Weird logic": I am paraphrasing Barry, *Compact Disc*, 119: "A weird logic of collection and accumulation started to go mainstream during the CD era."
"Invariably *oneself* that one collects": quoted in Reynolds, *Retromania*, 95.
A statistic that matters; "poppermost": www.nme.com/big-reads/elton-john-cover-interview-2021-the-lockdown-sessions-3075718. Lennon's phrase was a play on the expression "top of the pops," first used in the 1950s (e.g., in *The Melody Maker*) and made famous by the British TV program of that name.

160 SOURCE NOTES

Questlove and Charlesworth quotes: Questlove Thompson, "Collecting Things"; Gibson, *Elton John FAQ*, 29.
"Uncle Elton": Snapes, "'Britney was broken.'"
"An artist I've admired" to "a beautiful man": Spears, *The Woman in Me*, 262–64, 271.
Neil Sedaka: Podolsky, *Rock 'n' Roll Survivor*, 125–64 (quote on 145), 205–8; Bego, *Rocket Man*, 144.
Duncan and "Love Song": Kearns, *Elton John*, 27; bowiebible.com/songs/love-song/; Duncan's obituary in *The Independent*: independent.co.uk/news/obituaries/lesley-duncan-singer-and-songwriter-who-worked-with-elton-john-and-pink-floyd-1942138.
Leon Russell: John quotes from the 2010 BBC documentary *Madman across the Water* (see Filmography); also see Gibson, *Elton John FAQ*, 71, 167–68, 180; Taupin, *Scattershot*, 90.
George Michael: Napier-Bell, *I'm Coming to Take You to Lunch*, 143–44; Restall, *Blue Moves*, 91–108; Gavin, *George Michael*, 59, 182, 275, 356; Herbert, *George Michael*, 232–33.
Salvation: John, *Me*, 242; Roberts, *Rocket Man*, 213.
"She played a big part in my rebirth": quoted in Doyle, *Running Up That Hill*, 354.
1988 auction: *Classic Pop* (Sept/Oct 2023), 106. Exotic cars and Holland Park: Roberts, *Rocket Man*, 212.
Photography: details and quotes at www.christies.com/stories/elton-john-photography-collection and www.christies.com/en/stories/elton-john-atlanta-collection.
European fans Bodoh, Andrey, Grasso, and González are profiled in Flynn, *Record Collector Presents Elton John*, 28–29, 56–57, 88–89, 102–3.

Chapter 10—No Jexit

Details on "This Train Don't Stop There Anymore": Ollivier and Roubin, *All the Songs*, 492.
John's relative sales (footnote): see RIAA websites, e.g., www.riaa.com/u-s-sales-database/.
"Forever young": Hepworth, *Uncommon People*, xviii.
"Mick Jagger would be shot": Quantick, "Latter-day Landmarks."
"We thought it was a fad": Stewart, *Rod*, 62.
Hendrix and Joplin: Gioia, *Music*, 400–1.
"Making brilliant music": Quantick, "Latter-day Landmarks."
Finn: Kirkley, "Defying Gravity," 40.
"Octogenarian rock band": variety.com/2023/music/reviews/rolling-stones-hackney-diamonds-album-review.
"Lambasted" (Madonna) and "all up for grabs": Snapes, "'Music has ceased to be ageist.'"
"Short-term person brands": Scholar is Kristin Lieb; Gabriel, *Madonna*, 556 ("use-by date"), 559.
"Absolutely normal" (Gordon): Zoladz, "Never Conventional."
"Weirdo recluse" and "mental health": Whelan, "Kate Bush's frustration."
"Ugly sagging," etc.: Gabriel, *Madonna*, 240, 530, 556, 626, 649, 696, 725, 781.
"Jexit really does mean Jexit": www.nme.com/big-reads/elton-john-cover-interview-2021-the-lockdown-sessions-3075718.
"Spend more time": numerous interviews, but e.g., in *People* magazine (a 2023 story updated January 11, 2024), at people.com/elton-john-celebrates-son-elijahs-11th-birthday-842 5511#.
Suicide attempts: Gibson, *Elton John FAQ*, 207; Spitz, *Bowie*, 293 ("very competent"). For an example of a possibly ambivalent suicide attempt that did not fail, see Barrios, *On Marilyn Monroe*, 225.
"I just can't do this anymore": Black, *In His Own Words*, 45; Doyle, *Captain Fantastic*, 209–10; Restall, *Blue Moves*, 78.
"The last gig forever": Jahr, "Elton's Frank Talk," 11.

"She's retiring": interview with Stewart on *60 Minutes Australia*, September 26, 2018, found on YouTube and various other websites.

"The stranglehold of addiction" and "Drained of the poisons": Taupin, *Scattershot*, 119, 304–5.

"Elton's ability to bounce back": Matthew White in Roberts, *Rock Chronicles*, 255.

"A year of lasts and firsts": eltonjohn.com/stories/2023the-year-in-review.

"It's in his blood": Arnold, "Elton John's manager."

"In Las Vegas like Elvis?": Jahr, "Elton's Frank Talk," 11.

Kate Bush: variety.com/2023/music/news/kate-bush-not-attending-rock-hall-induction-ceremony-1235779770/; Doyle, *Running Up That Hill*, 28, 34; Restall, *Ghosts*.

"The 500 songs": in 2023, Vulture ranked "all 378 Elton John songs" (Krochmal, "All 378"), while Wikipedia listed 464 recorded by him (wikipedia.org/wiki/List_of_songs_recorded_by_Elton_John); as of early 2024, a new album was in the works, due for release late in 2024, so I am assuming he will easily surpass the 500 mark.

Discography

The lists below offer two different ways to view the Elton John catalogue of studio albums. See the Index for other albums and songs, by John and by other artists, mentioned in the chapters but not listed here.

1. Elton John's Studio Albums

Listed by year and chart peak position (UK and US only). All years (1968–2021) are listed in order to convey the highly intense pace of production of new material in the early years (26 vinyl sides in eight years, 1969–1976), the less intense pace of the middle years (23 vinyl sides in twelve years, 1978–1989), and the reasonable pace of the later years (22 vinyl sides in thirty years, 1992–2021). The chart positions underpin my argument regarding the correlation, across decades, between Elton's rock-vs.-pop, closeted-vs.-out image and his US-vs.-UK popularity.

YEAR	ALBUM	UK	US
[1968]	Regimental Sgt. Zippo	—	—*
1969	Empty Sky	—	—†
1970	Elton John	5	4
	and Tumbleweed Connection	2	5
1971	Madman across the Water	41	8
1972	Honky Château	2	1
1973	Don't Shoot Me I'm Only the Piano Player	1	1
	and Goodbye Yellow Brick Road	1	1

  * *Regimental Sgt. Zippo* was the first album Elton John recorded (in 1968), but it was shelved for over half a century—until most of the tracks were released in the *Jewel Box* compilation (2020) and then the whole album was released in 2021. It did not chart in any market, save for a brief 2021 appearance at #197 in the US Billboard 200. Because *Regimental Sgt. Zippo* was not released in 1968, *Empty Sky* is considered in this book and others (and by John himself) as his first album.
  † *Empty Sky* was released in 1969 only in the UK, where it did not chart; it was not released in the US until 1975, at the peak of Elton's imperial phase, when it reached #6.

DISCOGRAPHY

YEAR	ALBUM	UK	US
1974	Caribou	1	1
1975	Captain Fantastic and the Brown Dirt	2	1
	Cowboy *and* Rock of the Westies	5	1
1976	Blue Moves	3	3
1977			
1978	A Single Man	8	15
1979	The Thom Bell Sessions [EP]	—	—[‡]
	and Victim of Love	41	35
1980	21 at 33	12	13
1981	The Fox	12	21
1982	Jump Up!	13	17
1983	Too Low for Zero	7	25
1984	Breaking Hearts	2	20
1985	Ice on Fire	3	48
1986	Leather Jackets	24	91
1987			
1988	Reg Strikes Back	18	16
1989	Sleeping with the Past	1	23
1990			
1991			
1992	The One	2	8
1993	Duets	5	25
1994			
1995	Made in England	3	13
1996			
1997	The Big Picture	3	9
1998			

[‡] Recorded in 1977, three of the Thom Bell–produced tracks were remixed by John and Clive Frank and released as an EP in 1979 (as *The Thom Bell Sessions '77*, with the '77 dropped in the US). All six tracks, in original Bell-produced versions, came out as a thirty-five-minute album in 1989 (as *The Complete Thom Bell Sessions*).

YEAR	ALBUM	UK	US
1999			
2000			
2001	Songs from the West Coast	2	15
2002			
2003			
2004	Peachtree Road	21	17
2005			
2006	The Captain & the Kid	6	18
2007			
2008			
2009			
2010	The Union (with Leon Russell)	12	3
2011			
2012	Good Morning to the Night (vs. Pnau)	1	—§
2013	The Diving Board	3	4
2014			
2015			
2016	Wonderful Crazy Night	6	8
2017			
2018			
2019			
2020			
2121	The Lockdown Sessions	1	10
2022			
2023			
2024	[new studio album]		

§ Although this brilliant remix album debuted at #1 in the UK (and reached #9 in France), it only peaked at #40 in Pnau's home country of Australia, and in the US reached #20 in the "Top Electronic Albums" chart while failing to crack the Billboard 200.

2. Six Sixes

A discographic dialogue with Hope Silverman over my opinionated grouping of the studio albums. The groupings of albums in sixes reflect my personal opinions, rather than an authoritative claim to what is better or worse—as this is, after all, an "Opinionated Guide"—so your opinion on the relative artistic success of each album will surely be different. Comments on specific albums are in most cases truncated versions of my evaluations in the chapters above.

Hope Silverman is a lifelong veteran of the music business, having done everything from managing a record shop to running a record label. She is a regular contributor to websites like *Cover Me*, and her own *Picking Up Rocks* is read by many thousands of music fans. Included among her many blog appraisals of artist catalogues on *PuR* are some dialogues with me, similar to the one below, in which we rate, rank, and bicker over the albums of Kate Bush, ABBA, Dire Straits, Paul McCartney, and others.

1–6: The Imperial Six

MR: I think this continuous run of six albums in four years (1970–1973) represents one of the greatest creative and commercial streaks in the history of popular music. By borrowing and reinterpreting glam and country, by inventing the rock ballad, by redirecting pop music and reaching global audiences, these albums delivered Elton John his imperial phase. While few album-rankers would claim these were his best six, none would deny that most or all of these are to be found at or near the top. Or would they?

They are **Elton John** (1970), **Tumbleweed Connection** (1970), **Madman across the Water** (1971), **Honky Château** (1972), **Don't Shoot Me I'm Only the Piano Player** (1973), and **Goodbye Yellow Brick Road** (1973). The best-selling of these is *Yellow Brick Road*, while either it or *Tumbleweed Connection* is most commonly rated as his all-time best album. *Elton John* and *Honky Château* also have their advocates for his all-time best, but not *Don't Shoot Me*, which tends to be damned with the faint praise that it is a great pop album. I have no argument with such opinions, but my personal favorite here is *Madman across the Water*.

HS: I have to start this with a hot take, but I swear it's a considered one! By any measure that run of LPs is exceptional in terms of overall quality. But EJ's singles are so unimpeachably brilliant and memorable that on many of his albums they overshadow the deep cuts to the point of invisibility (or listener indifference, otherwise known as "don't bore us, get to the chorus"). As the years have passed, I've come to think of EJ as a singles artist in the vein of ABBA, *but better*. His first two greatest hits albums—1974's *Greatest Hits* and its follow-up, 1977's *Greatest Hits, Volume II*—are impeccable ("Grow Some Funk of Your Own" aside!).

This concept wasn't part of my childhood consciousness, as I bought each new album full of hope, and of course listened to them unquestioningly front to back. But the seeds were planted. If I'd possessed more sophisticated analytical skills, I probably would have noticed that my most played Elton album as a kid was not *Goodbye Yellow Brick Road*—the first one I ever owned—but the aforementioned *Greatest Hits* LP, with its iconic sleeve, the man white-suited and bow-tied at his piano. The singles are what define his discography, and their quality and ubiquity are what seal the deal as far as Elton being, unquestionably, one of the greatest pop artists of all time.

MR: Interesting perspective, and one I've not emphasized much in the book above, even though I suspect most people would agree with you. And sales statistics support your view: (1) the success of the 1970s *Greatest Hits* volumes (with combined sales of 24–37 million, depending on the source, comparable to the 31 million sales of John's best-selling studio album, *Goodbye Yellow Brick Road*); (2) the fact that after *Yellow*, the next seven (!) best-selling John albums are all compilations (1974's *Greatest Hits* is second, its 1977 sequel sixth); (3) the success of 2017's *Diamonds* (which just passed 2007's *Rocket Man: Number Ones* to be John's seventh best-seller); and (4) the record-breaking success of the 2018–2023 Farewell tour (whose set list leans heavily on the era of the 1970s *Hits* volumes). However, to be argumentative, half the best-selling Beatles albums are hits compilations; were *they* a singles band? I know the counterargument: they were both. How about this point, then? To include *Tumbleweed Connection* in this top six isn't controversial or eccentric, and yet that album produced no singles and remains unrepresented on those old *Hits* volumes as well as on later compilations like *Diamonds*. But that's probably the exception that proves you are, generally speaking, right!

HS: Funny you should say that. Because, of the six LPs you list here, the only ones I would play all the way through without skipping tracks are

Goodbye Yellow Brick Road and *Tumbleweed Connection*. They just offer a higher ratio of fabulous songs than you'll find on the remaining four (which are cherry-picking affairs).

I admit my top six EJ albums, the ones I believe are the most straight-up enjoyable, are all over the chronological and critical map. I still believe 2004's *Peachtree Road*—a glorious throwback to the 1970s radio stylings with a twenty-first-century production flavor—is one of the most criminally underrated LPs in the whole discography; it would definitely be in my top six. But I confess that my preferred way of listening to Elton is via a self-curated custom playlist of favorite songs.

7–12: Another Six of the Best

MR: A half-dozen selection of brilliant and varied albums, these are my top picks from the subsequent two decades (1975–1995). None may be perfect, but they all hold up as coherent and compelling song collections, as good as the day they were released. They are **Captain Fantastic and the Brown Dirt Cowboy** (1975), **Blue Moves** (1976), **A Single Man** (1978), **Too Low for Zero** (1983), **The One** (1992), and **Made in England** (1995). Surely the least controversial selection here is *Captain Fantastic*, which is typically ranked in the top three (so, if anything, I am placing it lower than most would). My choice for the high points in a relatively weak pair of decades (1980s and 1990s) are not everybody's, but there was plenty of love for *Too Low for Zero* at the time of its release—when it was a huge hit, a sales high point for that decade. Nor is my appreciation for *The One* and *Made in England* unusual; John's early 1990s, when he was newly sober and newly in love (he met his husband in 1993), and when he made those two albums as well as the *Lion King* hits, was a creative peak he had not experienced for a decade, and he would not do so again until the century turned.

I might add that after I drafted these rankings, I came across Taupin expressing fondness for two in this group, *Too Low for Zero* and *Made in England*, as well as for *Sleeping with the Past*—which I've ranked further down, but I recognize that others agree with Bernie. He also judged *Caribou*, *Rock of the Westies*, and *Blue Moves* as "not great albums" but each containing "a couple of legitimate perennials" (*Scattershot*, 368). That echoes your comments, Hope, on John as a singles artist, and Taupin's take on *Caribou* and *Westies* matches ours, as shown below. But

I'll stick to my opinion on *Blue Moves*, while understanding that for its lyricist, considering the blue emotions he therein expressed, it is "not a great album."

HS: *Blue Moves* is an album within your "Another Six" that I'd actually rank as one of the "Imperials." It is crazy-ambitious and relentlessly demanding (and your book on it only enhanced my love of it). I think of it the same way I do Fleetwood Mac's polarizing, latter-day critical darling *Tusk*, another album thought to be a disappointment upon release that was rightfully lauded decades later.

That said, the realization that Elton was more of a "songs guy" than an album one is really driven home with this second-tier of six. Apart from the superior *Blue Moves*, all of the LPs you mention are home to small but perfectly formed clusters of tunes that are outnumbered by a whole lotta "just okay" stuff.

MR: It is always good to hear *Blue Moves* being appreciated. I really hope the EJ team put together an amazing 50th anniversary deluxe re-release (if only they'd ask us to write the liner notes!). The late 1970s are generally viewed as a weak and troubled period for John, a career trough in strong contrast to the preceding imperial years. Even with *Blue Moves* slowly growing in esteem, my selection requires some explanation. You kindly claim my book for the 33⅓ series had a persuasive impact on you, but it did on me too: that is, I always liked *Blue*, but as a result of writing that book, I grew to adore the album and deeply value its complex and varied musicality, as well as the tension between Bernie's bleak lyrics and Elton's experimental pop compositions. As for *A Single Man*, I could not make the same case for its enduring quality, but I was fourteen when it came out and was given to me by an aunt of whom I was very fond; I played it a lot, thereby incorporating its sounds into my synapses. Objectivity is impossible. Still, personal factors aside, I do think it is greatly underrated.

HS: The thing about EJ is that every album, even the most heinous 1980s releases, which invariably land at the bottom of these rankings, have at least one irredeemably good song on them (or at least the framework of one). I agree that when it comes to the 1980s/1990s output there isn't a real consensus as far as what's best. But I definitely rank frothy, poppy *Jump Up!* (1982), and alternately fun and forlorn *The Fox* (1981) higher than *A Single Man* or *Too Low for Zero*, as to my ears they simply have more memorable songs.

13–18: The Great Late-Middle-Aged Renaissance

MR: Between the ages of fifty-four and sixty-nine, John enjoyed an extraordinary renaissance, inspired by Taupin as his perennial lyricist and by various other collaborators in the studio. These six albums in those fifteen years comprised a sustained late-career peak: *Songs from the West Coast* (2001), *Peachtree Road* (2004), *The Captain & the Kid* (2006), *The Union* (with Leon Russell, 2010), *The Diving Board* (2013), and *Wonderful Crazy Night* (2016). In fact, we can narrow the creative burst down even more, as the best of these are the first three, representing a five-year streak of quality not seen since the early 1970s. These cannot match that early imperial phase in terms of quantity, critical acclaim, and sales, but they nonetheless broke the uneven patterns of the 1980s and 1990s. I'd actually rank *Songs from the West Coast*, and possibly *The Captain & the Kid* too, up in the top third of all John studio albums, whereas the weakest of these (to my mind, *Wonderful Crazy Night*, although *The Diving Board* has its critics) might go in the bottom third, but I've grouped them together to highlight this comeback pattern.

HS: I totally agree that these LPs were a somewhat reassuring return to form after the inconsistency of the 1980s and 1990s. As "I Want Love" from *West Coast* made perfectly clear, John and Taupin still had it in them to kick out an immaculate anthem. But, as already mentioned, I believe *Peachtree Road* is the standout gem that rates higher than the rest of these generally high-quality twenty-first-century offerings. I have to add that in terms of pure melody, I think *The Diving Board* crushes the more acclaimed *The Captain & the Kid*.

MR: A theme of our conversations—here and on your *PuR* website—is that the listening experience, and our resulting opinions of an album, are seldom fixed and static; as we change, so does our perception of a particular album. I was totally underwhelmed by *The Captain & the Kid* when it came out. I think I expected it to sound more like *Captain Fantastic*, as it was billed as the sequel autobiographical concept album—an expectation on my part that, in retrospect, was a little absurd. On the other hand, *The Diving Board* struck me immediately as just the kind of mature album John should be making—complete with miniature piano instrumentals. So, my initial reactions to both albums matched yours. But over time, I found *The Captain & the Kid* grew on me, emerging to my ears as a coherent collection of catchy pop songs, whereas *The Diving Board* didn't grow in the same way. I would not be surprised if five years from now, I'm raving instead about *The Union*—which many people, including Elton himself—rate very highly.

Incidentally, when Taupin mused on these six albums, he judged *West Coast*, *The Union*, and *The Diving Board* ("a very grown-up record" on which "Elton's playing is inventive, subtle, and compelling") to be "the best of the bunch" (*Scattershot*, 369). So, there's that.

HS: Having one's existing opinions about albums and songs validated is fine, but I love being "wrong" about albums and songs. Revisiting an album or song that had never resonated with me before—and then having one of those classic "damn this *is* so good!" epiphanies—is the freakin' best! Which is why I am now anxious to revisit *The Captain & the Kid*. Just talking about it here has triggered that eternally hopeful 'n' nerdy curiosity.

19–24: A Mixed Six

MR: The top of the bottom half of the catalogue is a controversial place to be. All six of these albums will have their champions, insisting they should be ranked higher, as well as their detractors: **Empty Sky** (1969), **Rock of the Westies** (1975), **21 at 33** (1980), **Breaking Hearts** (1984), **Sleeping with the Past** (1989), and **Good Morning to the Night** (2012). But while I concede that every one of these has at least one great or stone-cold classic John song, none of them is consistently great *as albums* (save for *Good Morning*, to which I'll return).

HS: I concur. None of these are great albums, but each is home to at least one brilliant tune ("I Feel Like a Bullet" on *Rock of the Westies*, for example, "Sad Songs" and "Burning Buildings" on *Breaking Hearts*, and "Sacrifice" on *Sleeping with the Past*, to name a handful). Again, this feeds my feeling that John was an unimpeachable singles artist, and that his albums weren't and aren't really the point.

MR: Would it be nitpicking to try to argue that he starts as an album artist (1969–1971), that *Honky Château* begins a three-decade run as a singles artist (1972–1997), and then he returns to his album roots (since 2001)?

Of course, the varied nature of John's output since the 1990s—such as the soundtrack work, which we've ignored in this conversation—does complicate that pattern. And another example of that variety is *Good Morning to the Night*, billed as Elton John vs. Pnau. Within this "Mixed Six" group, it is very much an exception to our mixed-bag judgment, being superb from start to finish. It is an oddball in terms of genre, as an original studio album but of remixed earlier tracks. But I think it is a stunning success, creatively speaking (and it was commercially successful in a few markets too, most notably the UK, where it hit #1). I'd have ranked it higher were it not for that genre issue.

HS: Yes, I love *Good Morning* and all of its gorgeous and lush reimaginings—so much that I wish they'd done a Volume 2.

25–30: A Very Mixed Six

MR: The bottom dozen albums do not slot well into two groups of six, as they all contain at least one redeeming song as well as at least a few clunkers. And few fans would agree on which songs are thus judged. Furthermore, if you are like me, your opinion is always changing, so that one month these albums might seem to deserve a higher ranking, and another month their relegation here or below might seem well justified: ***Caribou*** (1974), ***The Thom Bell Sessions*** (1979/1989), ***The Fox*** (1981), ***Jump Up!*** (1982), ***Ice on Fire*** (1985), and ***The Big Picture*** (1997).

HS: Yes, there are redeeming tracks on almost every one of these, and thus a few of them are a bit slippery in terms of characterization. It does seem cruel to cast 1970s mega-hit *Caribou* aside, but apart from classics "The Bitch Is Back," "Don't Let the Sun Go Down on Me," and sleeper "Pinky," it is rife with filler. I think *Ice on Fire is* unequivocally rubbish, including its megahit "Nikita" (although that video is ludicrously fabulous). But I have to reiterate that the overall vibes of both *The Fox* and *Jump Up!* resonate with me and I rank them way higher than here. And sometimes I find the exuberant, shiny, and sweetly soulful *Thom Bell Sessions* to be pretty damn listenable (and quietly underrated).

MR: I understand that placing *Caribou* this low is problematic, mostly because "Don't Let the Sun Go Down on Me" is to my mind one of the best half-dozen songs in the entire John/Taupin catalogue. Sometimes, when asked to name just one Elton song as his best or my favorite (an annoyingly impossible task), I cite the live version with George Michael—as it illustrates the genius of the songcraft, the energy of John's live performances, and the importance of his complex connection to pop music history during his lifetime. But there's the rub: a song that good and significant only makes the rest of *Caribou* deeply disappointing.

As for your affection for that 1981–1982 sibling pair (*The Fox* and *Jump Up!*), all I can say is that I shall give them another chance. And

I agree about the *Thom Bell Sessions*, often excluded from rankings of the John catalogue because they were technically an EP. That three-track EP has a smooth soul charm that makes one wish John and Bell had stuck it out until they'd created a whole album of that quality. Unfortunately, the additional three tracks not released in 1979, but included in the *Complete Thom Bell Sessions* release of 1989, are not nearly as good (the re-recording of "Shine On Through," for example, is far superior on *A Single Man*). For those reasons, the EP/LP is included here, but ranked low.

31–36: The Bottom of the Bag

MR: Six albums had to be at the bottom, and I gave the honors to ***Victim of Love*** (1979), ***Leather Jackets*** (1986), ***Reg Strikes Back*** (1988), ***Duets*** (1993), ***The Lockdown Sessions*** (2021), and ***Regimental Sgt. Zippo*** (2022). Three of these were not hard to pick, as *Victim of Love* and *Leather Jackets* are routinely cited as John's biggest clunkers—including by Sir Elton himself. When I first heard *Victim* and was told it was Elton's "disco album," I honestly thought it was a spoof—and a weak one, as there was nobody pretending to play piano. But it did mean that when he dropped another resounding dud seven years later (*Leather Jackets*), it was easy to dismiss and wait for better albums, because you knew they were coming; the rollercoaster pattern had been well established. The title of the *Leather Jackets* sequel, *Reg Strikes Back*, was a tacit recognition that its predecessor had been a forgettable flop, but it failed to match its billing (if album titles could be swapped to match their impact, I'd swap *Too Low for Zero* and *Reg Strikes Back*).

HS: I am 100 percent aligned with your choices for the dregs of the discography. What's weird (and sad) is that every couple of years I'll revisit *Victim*, *Leather*, and *Reg Strikes* to see if they've gotten any better; if maybe, just maybe, there was a diamond I hadn't noticed. There never is.

MR: Yes, I know, I have done the same, especially during the course of writing this book. I actually came to appreciate the "Victim of Love" title track, which I do think deserves to be included in the longer list of hit singles and other classics (it is on *Diamonds*, but only on the extra disc of the 3-CD version). As for *Duets* and *The Lockdown Sessions* (which could have been called *Duets 2*), they are the very definition of mixed bags, and thus predictably juxtapose successful collaborations with some that fail to inspire multiple listens. That means that two of my absolute favorite versions of John songs are down here at the bottom of the bag: the above-praised live duet with Michael of "Don't Let the Sun Go Down on Me" (on *Duets*); and the Pnau-produced "Cold Heart" duet with Dua Lipa (on *Lockdown*). The later album is stronger than *Duets*, perhaps because half of it features new songs co-written by John, whereas *Duets* is mostly covers. Nonetheless, these collections cannot compete as *albums*.

HS: Yes, these are curios, and not remotely essential! But I agree about the diamonds in the rough here. The live version of "Don't Let the Sun Go Down on Me" still gives me chills every time I hear George Michael shout, "Ladies and Gentlemen, Mr. Elton John!" Glorious forever. And "Cold Heart"? A low-key banger, y'all.

At this point EJ could keep making these duet albums, even if the results are inevitably mixed; he doesn't need to make a new studio album (although he will), as his legacy is oh-so-sealed. And the existing stuff remains a gift no matter how many years have passed. Even after hearing it hundreds (maybe thousands!) of times, "Someone Saved My Life Tonight" still has the ability to transport me to the backseat of my mom's car, where the AM radio was blasting every time that we went anywhere.

MR: And that is a perfect place to leave it. Because in the end, none of the details I have assembled from interviews and biographies, and none of my opinions and arguments and efforts to persuade you that Elton offers us unique insight into the history of popular music and culture—none of that matters as much as the sweet, simple fact that his songs transport us and soundtrack our lives. Now turn up the volume....

Bibliography

Arnold, Chuck. "Elton John's Manager Is Already Saying He'll Play More Concerts." *New York Post*, November 21, 2022. nypost.com/2022/11/21/elton-johns-manager-is-already-saying-hell-play-more-concerts/.

Barber, Richard. "I've Still Got the Music in Me, Says Elton's Old Pal Kiki Dee." *Daily Mirror*, August 21, 2008. www.dailymail.co.uk/tvshowbiz/article-1047929.

Barrios, Richard. *Dangerous Rhythm: Why Movie Musicals Matter*. New York: Oxford University Press, 2014.

Barrios, Richard. *On Marilyn Monroe: An Opinionated Guide*. New York: Oxford University Press, 2023.

Barry, Robert. *Compact Disc*. Object Lessons series. New York: Bloomsbury, 2020.

Bego, Mark. *Elton John: The Bitch Is Back*. Beverly Hills, CA: Phoenix Books, 2009.

Bernardin, Claude, and Tom Stanton. *Elton John from A–Z*. Westport, CT: Praeger, 1996.

Bertei, Adele. *Why Labelle Matters*. Austin: University of Texas Press, 2021.

Black, Susan. *Elton John: In His Own Words*. London: Omnibus, 1993.

Bromley, Tom. "Back in the Day." *Classic Pop*, November/December 2012, 94–99.

Brooker, Will. *Why Bowie Matters*. London: William Collins, 2019.

Brown, Phill. *Are We Still Rolling? Studios, Drugs and Rock 'n' Roll: One Man's Journey Recording Classic Albums*. Portland, OR: Tape Op Books, 2010.

Buckley, David. *Elton: The Biography*. Chicago: Chicago Review Press, 2008.

Buckley, David. "A Life Less Ordinary: The Continued Comeback of the Queen Mum of Pop." *Mojo*, October 12, 2006.

Catanzarite, Stephen. *Achtung Baby*. 33⅓ series, 49. London: Bloomsbury, 2007.

Clarke, Gary. *Elton, My Elton*. London: Smith Gryphon, 1995.

Compo, Susan. *Earth Bound: David Bowie and the Man Who Fell to Earth*. London: Jawbone, 2017.

DeCouto, David John. *Captain Fantastic: Elton John in the '70s*. Chandler, AZ: Triple Wood Press, 2016.

Doyle, Tom. *Captain Fantastic: Elton John's Stellar Trip through the '70s*. New York: Ballantine, 2017.

Doyle, Tom. *Running Up That Hill: 50 Visions of Kate Bush*. Lanham, MD: Rowman & Littlefield, 2023.

Eames, Tom. "The Story of... 'Sorry Seems to Be the Hardest Word.'" *Smooth Radio*, September 16, 2018. www.smoothradio.com/features/sorry-seems-to-be-the-hardest-word-meaning-lyrics/.

Earls, John. "Squeeze, Song by Song." *Classic Pop* #51, April 2019, 39–43.

Fisher, Mark. *Ghosts of My Life: Writings on Depression, Hauntology, and Lost Futures*. Winchester, UK: Zero Books, 2014.

Flynn, Rik, ed. *Elton John, The Rocket Man: 50 Years and Still Standing*. *Classic Pop* special ed. London: Anthem, 2016.

Flynn, Rik, ed. *Record Collector Presents Elton John*. Special ed. London: Diamond, 2023.

Gaar, Gillian G. *She's a Rebel: The History of Women in Rock & Roll*. New York: Seal Press, 2002 (1st ed., 1992).

Gabriel, Mary. *Madonna: A Rebel Life*. New York: Little, Brown, 2023.

Gambaccini, Paul. "Captain Fantastic and the Brown Dirt Cowboy." Liner notes in booklet to album's Deluxe Edition re-release, 2005.

Gavin, James. *George Michael: A Life*. New York: Abrams, 2022.
Gibson, Donald. *Elton John FAQ: All That's Left to Know about the Rocket Man*. Guilford, CT: Backbeat Books, 2019.
Gioia, Ted. *Love Songs: The Hidden History*. New York: Oxford University Press, 2015.
Gioia, Ted. *Music: A Subversive History*. New York: Basic Books, 2019.
Glam! The Performance of Style. Exhibition catalogue. Liverpool: Tate, 2013.
Glass, Loren. *Tapestry*. 33⅓ series, 40. New York: Bloomsbury, 2021.
Hadju, David. *Love for Sale: Pop Music in America*. New York: Farrar, Straus & Giroux, 2016.
Hagan, Joe. *Sticky Fingers: The Life and Times of Jann Wenner and Rolling Stone*. New York: Knopf, 2017.
Hall, Stuart. "Cultural Identity and Diaspora." In *Identity: Community, Culture, Difference*, edited by Jonathan Rutherford, 222–37. London: Lawrence & Wishart, 1990.
Heatley, Michael, and Frank Hopkinson. *The Girl in the Song: The True Stories behind 50 Rock Classics*. Chicago: Chicago Review Press, 2010.
Hepworth, David. *1971. Never a Dull Moment: Rock's Golden Year*. London: Bantam, 2016.
Hepworth, David. *A Fabulous Creation: How the LP Saved Our Lives*. London: Black Swan, 2020.
Hepworth, David. *Uncommon People: The Rise and Fall of the Rock Stars*. London: Penguin, 2017.
Herbert, Emily. *George Michael: The Life, 1963–2016*. New York: Lesser Gods, 2017.
Higgins, John F. "Billie Jean King Talks about 'Philadelphia Freedom.'" *Eltonjohn.com*, September 10, 2018. www.eltonjohn.com/stories/billie-jean-king-talks-about-philadelphia-freedom.
Higgins, John F. "Rocket Man: The Lifetime of a Song." *Eltonjohn.com*, March 21, 2023. www.eltonjohn.com/stories/rocket-man-the-lifetime-of-a-song.
Hilburn, Robert. "The Man with the Words: Bernie Taupin Offers a Rare Look into his Collaborations with Elton John." *Los Angeles Times*, September 30, 2001, F5.
Hoskyns, Barney. *Glam! Bowie, Bolan and the Glitter Rock Revolution*. New York: Pocket Books, 1998.
Humphries, Patrick. *The Elton John Story*. London: Aurum Press, 1998.
Humphries, Patrick, and Steve Blacknell. *Top of the Pops: 50th Anniversary*. London: McNidder & Grace, 2014.
Jahr, Cliff. "Elton's Frank Talk: The Lonely Love Life of a Superstar" (cover title); "Elton John: It's Lonely at the Top" (interview title). *Rolling Stone*, October 7, 1976, 11, 16–17.
Jeffrey, Alex. *Once Upon a Time*. 33⅓ series, 157. New York: Bloomsbury, 2021.
John, Elton. *Me*. New York: Henry Holt, 2019.
Kardos, Leah. *Blackstar Theory: The Last Works of David Bowie*. New York: Bloomsbury, 2022.
Kearns, Peter. *Elton John: Every Album, Every Song, 1969 to 1979*. On Track series. Tewkesbury, UK: Sonicbond, 2019.
Kirkley, Paul. "Defying Gravity." *Classic Pop*, May/June 2024, 38–42.
Landau, Jon. "Captain Fantastic and the Brown Dirt Cowboy [Review]." *Rolling Stone*, July 17, 1975.
Little, Michael H. "Graded on a Curve: Long John Baldry, *It Ain't Easy*." *The Vinyl District*, December 8, 2017. www.thevinyldistrict.com/storefront/2017/12/graded-on-a-curve-long-john-baldry-it-aint-easy/.
Marks, Anna. "Look What We Made Taylor Swift Do." *New York Times*, January 7, 2024, Opinion, 8.
McCabe, Allyson. "Philadelphia Freedom." *New York Times Magazine*, January 9, 2022, 18–19.
Meier, Leslie. *Popular Music as Promotion*. Cambridge: Polity, 2017.
Miller, M. H. "A Brilliant, Tortured Life." *New York Times Magazine*, March 27, 2022, 80–81.
Moorefield, Virgil. *The Producer as Composer: Shaping the Sounds of Popular Music*. Cambridge, MA: MIT Press, 2005.
Morrison, Simon. *Avalon*. 33⅓ series, 155. New York: Bloomsbury, 2021.

Murphy, Nichola. "Elton John and David Furnish's Sweet Wedding Connection to Prince Charles and Duchess Camilla." *Hello!*, December 21, 2021. www.hellomagazine.com/brides/2021122 1129417/elton-john-david-furnish-wedding-connection-prince-charles-duchess-camilla/.

Myers, Paul. *It Ain't Easy: Long John Baldry and the Birth of the British Blues*. Vancouver: Greystone Books, 2007.

Napier-Bell, Simon. *I'm Coming to Take You to Lunch*. New York: Wenner Books, 2005.

Nathan, David. *The Soulful Divas*. New York: Billboard Books, 1999.

Nelson, Sean. *Court and Spark*. 33⅓ series, 40. New York: Bloomsbury, 2007.

Norman, Philip. "Suzi Quatro: The Girl in the Gang." *Sunday Times*, 1974. rocksbackpages.com/Library/Article/suzi-quatro-the-girl-in-the-gang.

Norman, Philip. *Elton John*. New York: Harmony Books, 1991 [updated as *Sir Elton*, 2001].

Ollivier, Romuald, and Olivier Roubin. *Elton John: All the Songs. The Story behind Every Track*. New York: Black Dog & Leventhal, 2023 [Hachette (in French), 2022].

Pappademas, Alex. "Even the Rock Gods Sing His Praises." *New York Times*, December 17, 2023, Arts, 20–21.

Parker, Ian. "He's a Little Bit Funny." *New Yorker*, August 26, 1996, 110.

Pegg, Nicholas. *The Complete David Bowie*. London: Titan Books, 2000 (rev. ed., 2016).

Petrusich, Amanda. "Domestic Arts: Bill Callahan on Home and Its Comforts." *New Yorker*, June 10 and 17, 2019, 88–89.

Petrusich, Amanda. "Merging Lanes: The Notion of Genre Is Disappearing." *New Yorker*, March 15, 2021, 68–72.

Philo, Simon. *Glam Rock: Music in Sound and Vision*. Lanham, MD: Rowman & Littlefield, 2018.

Podolsky, Rich. *Rock 'n' Roll Survivor: Neil Sedaka. The Inside Story of His Incredible Comeback*. London: Jawbone, 2013.

Quantick, David. "Latter-day Landmarks." *Record Collector*, no. 547 (August 2023): 42.

Quaye, Caleb. *A Voice Louder than Rock & Roll*. Carson, CA: Vision, 2006.

Questlove Thompson, Ahmir. "Collecting Things Is an Act of Devotion." *New York Times*, March 27, 2022, Arts, 10.

Restall, Matthew. *Blue Moves*. 33⅓ series, 146. New York: Bloomsbury, 2020.

Restall, Matthew. *Ghosts: Journeys to Post-Pop. How David Sylvian, Mark Hollis, and Kate Bush Reinvented Pop Music*. Tewkesbury, UK: Sonicbond, 2024.

Reynolds, Simon. *Blissed Out: The Raptures of Rock*. London: Serpent's Tail, 1990.

Reynolds, Simon. *Bring the Noise: 20 Years of Writing about Hip Rock and Hip-Hop*. Berkeley, CA: Soft Skull, 2011 [London, 2009].

Reynolds, Simon. *Retromania: Pop Culture's Addiction to Its Own Past*. New York: Faber & Faber, 2011.

Reynolds, Simon. "The Rift of Retro: 1962? Or Twenty Years On?" In *Glam! The Performance of Style*, 63–73. Exhibition catalogue. Liverpool: Tate, 2013.

Reynolds, Simon. *Shock and Awe: Glam Rock and Its Legacy from the Seventies to the Twenty-first Century*. New York: Dey St. [London: Faber & Faber], 2016.

Roberts, Chris. *Elton John: Rocket Man*. New York: Sterling, 2019.

Roberts, Chris. "Still Crazy." *Record Collector*, no. 533 (July 2022): 92–93.

Roberts, David, ed. *Rock Chronicles: Every Legend, Every Line-up, Every Look*. New York: Firefly, 2019.

Rosenthal, Elizabeth J. *His Song: The Musical Journey of Elton John*. New York: Billboard Books, 2001.

St. Michael, Mick. *Elton John*. New York: Smithmark, 1994.

Seabrook, Thomas Jerome. *Bowie in Berlin: A New Career in a New Town*. London: Jawbone, 2008.

Segal, Mark. *And Then I Danced: Traveling the Road to LGBT Equality*. Brooklyn: Open Lens/Akashic Books, 2015.

Sheffield, Rob. "Elton John's Essential Albums." *Rolling Stone*, March 24, 2017.

Shumway, David. *Rock Star: The Making of Musical Icons from Elvis to Springsteen*. Baltimore: Johns Hopkins University Press, 2014.

Silverman, Hope. "Cover Genres: Soul in the Middle of the Road." *Cover Me*, January 14, 2022. covermesongs.com/2022/01/my-cover-story-soul-in-the-middle-of-the-road.html.

Sloan, Nate, and Charlie Harding. *Switched On Pop: How Popular Music Works, and Why It Matters*. New York: Oxford University Press, 2020.

Smyth, Tom. "I'm the Person 'Your Song' by Elton John Was Written For, and I Would Like a Real Gift Instead." *New Yorker*, August 17, 2022. newyorker.com/humor/daily-shouts/im-the-person-your-song-by-elton-john-was-written-for-and-i-would-like-a-real-gift-instead.

Snapes, Laura. "'Britney Was Broken. I've Been Broken and It's Horrible': Elton John on Helping Britney Spears Sing Again." *The Guardian*, August 25, 2022. theguardian.com/music/2022/aug/26/britney-was-broken-ive-been-broken-and-its-horrible-elton-john-on-helping-britney-spears-sing-again.

Snapes, Laura. "'Music Has Ceased to Be Ageist': Pet Shop Boys on 40 Years of Pop Genius." *The Guardian*, February 3, 2024. theguardian.com/music/2024/feb/03/pet-shop-boys-nonetheless-interview.

Spears, Britney. *The Woman in Me*. New York: Gallery Books, 2023.

Spelman, Nicola. *Popular Music and the Myths of Madness*. Farnham, UK: Ashgate, 2012.

Spence, Simon, *Just Can't Get Enough: The Making of Depeche Mode*. London: Jawbone, 2011.

Spignesi, Stephen, and Michael Lewis. *Elton John: Fifty Years On*. New York: Post Hill Press, 2019.

Spitz, Bob. *Led Zeppelin: The Biography*. New York: Penguin, 2021.

Spitz, Marc. *Bowie: A Biography*. New York: Crown, 2009.

Stanley, Bob. *Yeah! Yeah! Yeah! The Story of Pop Music from Bill Haley to Beyoncé*. New York: W. W. Norton, 2014.

Stewart, Rod. *Rod: The Autobiography*. New York: Crown Archetype, 2012.

Stone, Alison. "Feminism, Gender and Popular Music." In *The Bloomsbury Handbook of Religion and Popular Music*, edited by Christopher Partridge and Marcus Moberg, 54–64. London: Bloomsbury Academic, 2017.

Swartley, Ariel. "Blue Moves [Review]." *Rolling Stone*, December 30, 1976.

Taupin, Bernie. *Scattershot: Life, Music, Elton, and Me*. New York: Hachette, 2023.

Thomas, Bill. *Kate Bush: Every Album, Every Song*. On Track series. Tewkesbury, UK: Sonicbond, 2021.

Thompson, Dave. *Children of the Revolution: The Glam Rock Story, 1970–1975*. London: Cherry Red, 2010.

Thompson, Dave. *I Feel Love: Donna Summer, Giorgio Moroder, and How They Reinvented Music*. Lanham, MD: Backbeat Books, 2021.

Thompson, Derek. *Hit Makers: How Things Become Popular*. London: Penguin, 2017.

Toberman, Barry. *Elton John: A Biography*. London: Weidenfeld & Nicolson, 1988.

Tobler, John. *Elton John: 25 Years in the Charts*. London: Hamlyn, 1995.

Trynka, Paul. *David Bowie. Starman: The Definitive Biography*. New York: Crown, 2009.

Vandromme, Frederick. "Blijven Gahan: Depeche Mode." *Humo*, March 20, 2017. humo.be/nieuws/blijven-gahan-depeche-mode~b7bcfd20/.

Warner, Alan. *Tago Mago*. 33⅓ series, 101. London: Bloomsbury, 2015.

Washburn, Michael. *Southern Accents*. 33⅓ series, 139. London: Bloomsbury, 2019.

Whelan, Luke. "Kate Bush's Frustration at Being Called 'Weirdo Recluse'—Mental Health History Explained." *Express*, July 30, 2022. express.co.uk/life-style/health/1648328/kate-bush-health-ocd-mother-death-mental-health-running-up-that-hill.

White, Katherine. *Rock & Roll Hall of Famers: Elton John*. New York: Rosen Central, 2003.

Wiederhorn, Jon. "David Bowie Producer Tony Visconti Recalls 'Holy' Career Highlights." *Yahoo! Entertainment*, April 16, 2016. web.archive.org/web/20210916204213.

Wilkinson, Alissa. "The Wonderful World of Disney?" *New York Times*, December 17, 2023, Arts, 12–14.

Zoladz, Lindsay. "Never Conventional, Always Creative." *New York Times*, March 3, 2024, Arts & Leisure, 14.

Filmography

Far from a comprehensive list, this comprises films used and cited in the Source Notes.

"The Boy and the Piano," television commercial, 2 mins, for British retailer John Lewis and Partners, 2018.
Madman across the Water: The Making of Elton John. Andrew Dunn, producer. 59 mins. BBC, 2010.
The Man Who Fell to Earth. Nicolas Roeg, director. 2 hours, 19 mins. Lion International, 1976.
Rocketman. Dexter Fletcher, director; Lee Hall, writer. Rocket Pictures, 2019.
Soundbreaking: Stories from the Cutting Edge of Recorded Music. Jeff Dupre and Maro Chermayeff, directors. 8 episodes. Higher Ground. 2016.
Tantrums and Tiaras. David Furnish, director. 2 hours. Rocket Pictures, 1997.

Other Media

There are hundreds of websites devoted to Elton John, as well as countless interviews on YouTube. Some I have cited where specifically relevant, but the following were of general and frequent use.

"Elton John. The Only. Interviews." MVD Audio (on CD), 2016. (Although not identified as such, this is clearly the Elton voice track, with interviewer voice deleted, from a long 1983 interview.)

Eltonjohn.com. Official artist (Rocket Club) website. The EJAF also has its own website: eltonjohnaidsfoundation.org.

Fan websites of particular use: Eltonjohn.world; eltonfan.net; eltonlinks.com; eltonography.com; and the Crazy Water Forum message board at tapatalk.com/groups/thecrazywaterezboard/. The @EltonJohn YouTube channel is youtube.com/channel/UCcd0tBtip8YzdTCUw3OVv_Q.

Index

For the benefit of digital users, indexed terms that span two pages (e.g., 52–53) may, on occasion, appear on only one of those pages.

Figures are indicated by an italic *f*

Note that references to David Bowie, Elton John, and Bernie Taupin are too ubiquitous to be usefully included.

addiction 4, 7–9, 22–23, 60, 61–62, 72, 134, 135, 148
aging 143–44, 145
AIDS 30–31, 56, 60–61, 62, 99–100, 148–49. *See also* EJAF
Americana 9, 43, 89, 113
Atkinson, R 30
awards xv, 30, 48, 60–61, 63–64, 89, 96–97, 114, 115, 119, 120

Baez, J xviii–xix
Baldry, LJ 21–22, 29, 69–73, 77
Baudrillard, J 126–28
Beatles and ex-Beatles xvi–xvii, xviii–xix, 5, 7, 114–15, 167
Bell, T 52, 93–95
Bentley (car) 2, 136
Biden, J 63–64
Blauel, R 61–62
Bluesology 20, 28–29, 70–71, 73, 89, 148
Bolan, M 25–26, 81, 108
Bowie, A 38, 41, 147
Bradbury, R 39–40
Bromley 24, 25
bullying 148–49
Bush, K 10, 39, 47–48, 54, 111, 135–36, 145, 147, 151–52

Cannes 2*f*, 2
Charles, R 89–90, 95
collecting practices xx–xxi, 124–28, 127*f*, 130–31, 135, 137–38
collaboration and creative process 7, 8, 9, 10, 16, 40, 50–52, 92, 95, 96–97, 104, 113, 124, 142
costumes 44, 45*f*, 86*f*. *See also* stage persona and presence
country music 12–13, 26–28, 66, 67–68, 69, 79–80, 82, 89

cover songs 10, 47–48, 70, 73, 74, 88–89, 90, 95–97, 99–101, 131–32

Davis, C 70, 73–74, 76, 86, 112
Dean, E 29, 71
death 8, 12, 26, 36–37, 41–42, 60–61, 100–1, 112, 114, 118–19, 134–35, 143
Dee, K 36, 54, 130–31
Depeche Mode 7–9
Diamond, N 3
Diana, Princess xx–xxi, 1, 114–15, 118–19, 119*f*
Difford, C 6–7
disco music 49, 52, 68–69, 73–76, 78–79, 82, 93–95
Disney 83–85. *See also* soundtracks
Dodger Stadium xvi–xvii, xvii*f*, 147
Dudgeon, G 20, 21, 36, 38, 40, 52, 93, 102–3, 104–5, 106, 113
Duncan, L 70, 131–32

Eagles xvi–xvii
EJAF (Elton John AIDS Foundation) 4, 36, 62, 64–65, 100–1, 114–15, 136. *See also* AIDS
Eminem 135

Farthingale, H 37, 46–47
Franklin, A xx–xxi, 52, 88–89, 95–96, 99–101, 99*f*, 115–16, 121–22
Furnish, D xx–xxi, 62–63, 64, 121, 135–38, 151

Gahan, D 7–9
Gambaccini, P 5
Gamble, K 52, 93
Geffen, D and record label 3, 43, 133
George, B 56, 63
glam rock 25–26, 44, 54, 79, 81, 91–92
Glastonbury 34–35, 149–50, 150*f*, 151
Gore, M 7–9

gospel music 88–89, 92, 93, 96, 100

Hall, D 70
Hall, L 66–67
Hepworth, D 79–80, 81, 103–4
Hentschel, D 102–3
homosexuality and homophobia xviii, 5, 21–22, 50, 52–65, 72, 78–79, 83–84, 117–18, 129–30, 134, 137
Houston, W 135, 143
Huff, L 52, 93–94

Jackson, M xv n.[†], 115–16, 133
Jesus Christ, xx–xxi, 142, 146, 148
Joel, B 68–69, 87
Johnstone, D 3–4, 13 n.[*], 21, 40, 54, 142
journalists 4–5, 38, 93, 117, 133, 149. *See also* tabloid press

King, BJ 49–52, 51*f*, 53–54, 64–65
Knight, G 96–97
knighthood xvi, 79, 119–21

Labelle, P 44, 90, 96
lawsuits 62, 83–84
Lewis, JL 28, 79, 89–90
Lennon, J 21–22, 108, 132–33, 134–35. *See also* Beatles and ex-Beatles
Lennox, A 1
Liberace, 38, 44, 68–69, 79, 89–90
Liberty Records 6–7, 29
Lincolnshire 6–7, 11–12, 29, 40
Lipa, D xx–xxi, 66 n.[*], 124, 125*f*, 128–29, 173
Little Richard, 28, 68–69, 89–90
love songs 10, 12–17, 41, 54, 60–61, 63, 84, 108–9, 131–32, 142
Lulu 1

Madison Square Garden 87, 132–33, 134–35, 147
Madonna 53, 144–45
Mapplethorpe, R 118
Margaret, Princess 115–16, 116*f*, 117
Martin, G 3–4, 114–15
Marx, G 30, 31*f*
McCartney, P 5, 73–74, 89, 110, 124, 145–46, 166. *See also* Beatles and ex-Beatles
mental health 20–21, 146–47. *See also* suicide
Mercury, F 54, 63, 65
misogyny and sexism xxi, 50, 54, 69, 75, 98, 109–10, 117–18, 144–45
Michael, G 15–16, 132–35, 143

Mitchell, J 3, 43, 79–80, 82 n.[**], 108–9, 110–11
Monroe, M 13, 47–48, 112–13, 114
Montserrat 3–4
MTV xxi n.[§], 2, 73–74, 76
Mulcahy, R 2*f*, 2, 60–61
Murray, D 3–4, 40, 128
metaphor and meaning in songs 3, 9–17, 41, 42–47, 48, 50–52, 103, 108–9, 112–13

Napier-Bell, S 133
NASA 36, 39–40
NME (*New Musical Express*) 6–7, 54, 81, 146
nepantla 25, 32, 54–55, 58–59

Olsson, N 3–4, 40, 106, 128, 142
origin mythology xvii–xviii, xx–xxi, 20, 22–33, 120–21, 135
Osborne, G 7–8, 60–61

Pet Shop Boys 41–42, 144
Philadelphia 49, 50–52, 93–94
Pinner 7, 24, 26, 50–52, 93
Pnau 34–35, 66 n.[*], 123–24, 125*f*
Presley, E xv n.[†], 26–28, 108, 115–16, 121–22, 151

Quatro, S 54, 81
Quaye, C 13 n.[*], 15, 30–31, 89
Queen (band) 19–20, 54, 91
Queen Elizabeth 30, 117, 118, 120, 121–22, 152

radio xviii–xix, 19–20, 26–28, 34–36, 53, 57–58, 90–92, 94–95, 98, 104–5, 113, 134, 137, 148
Rapp, T 39–40
rehab 4, 8–9, 14, 62, 63, 79, 129, 134, 148–49
Reid, J 12, 36, 53, 61
retirement xv, 3–4, 78, 142, 143–46, 147–48, 150–51
Rice, T 66–67, 84–85
R&B and soul music, 67–68, 69, 73, 74, 76–77, 88–91, 92, 93–96, 99*f*, 143
Richard, C 36, 130–31
Ritts, H 118, 137–38
rivalries, musician xv, 38–39, 40–41, 133–34
Robinson, T 56, 60–61
Rocket Fund 36, 64
Rocket Hour xxi, 36, 135–36
Rocket Records 3, 36, 54, 130–31
Rolling Stones xvi–xviii, 70–71, 73, 74–75, 79–80, 144, 145–46

Rolling Stone 19, 27*f*, 34–35, 54, 55–58, 58*f*, 59*f*, 60, 106, 110
Russell, L 85, 92, 96, 132–33

Sedaka, N 36, 130–31
Sex Pistols 78–79
sexism. *See* misogyny and sexism
Shatner, W 47–48
Simon and Garfunkel xviii–xix
Slade 81, 91
soundtracks 1, 3, 4, 5–6, 63, 66–68, 83–85, 106, 149
soul music. *See* R&B and soul music
Soul Train 92–93
space songs 34–46, 35*f*, 45*f*, 130*f*
Spears, B 10, 128–31
Springfield, D 88
Springsteen, B xvi–xvii, 108
Squeeze 6–7
stage persona and presence 22–26, 29–32, 42, 53, 54, 55, 57, 63, 65, 80–81, 86. *See also* costumes
Sting 108–9, 114
Stewart, R xx–xxi, 57–58, 61–62, 69–77, 72*f*, 78–79, 82–83, 91, 96–97, 120–21, 147–48
suicide 21, 142, 146–47

Summer, D 3, 32–33, 54
swansongs 41–42, 142, 143
Sweet 81, 91

tabloid press xv, 4, 23, 30, 38, 60–61, 62, 144
Tilbrook, G 6–7
Top of the Pops xxi, 5, 6, 39, 79, 88, 144
Trombley, R 90–91

Versace, G 16 n.[†], 118, 119*f*, 136
videos, music 2*f*, 2–3, 15–16, 60–61, 76–77, 85, 98, 133–34, 142, 144
Visconti, T 37–38

Walliams, D 1
Watford Football Club 60
White, B 52
White, R 62
Windsor 73–74, 78–79, 115–16, 117, 119*f*, 121
Windsors 115–18, 120–22. *See also* Margaret, Princess; Queen Elizabeth
Wonder, S 96–98, 97*f*, 114

Ziggy Stardust 22–23, 24–26, 32, 39, 42, 46, 55, 57, 91